A Vanishing West
in the Middle East

A Vanishing West in the Middle East

The Recent History of U.S.-Europe Cooperation in the Region

Charles Thépaut

I.B. TAURIS
LONDON • NEW YORK • OXFORD • NEW DELHI • SYDNEY

THE
WASHINGTON INSTITUTE
for Near East Policy

BLOOMSBURY ACADEMIC
Bloomsbury Publishing Plc
50 Bedford Square, London, WC1B 3DP, UK
1385 Broadway, New York, NY 10018, USA
29 Earlsfort Terrace, Dublin 2, Ireland

BLOOMSBURY, BLOOMSBURY ACADEMIC and the Diana logo are trademarks of
Bloomsbury Publishing Plc

First published in Great Britain 2022

Typeset by Sensical Design, Washington, DC

To find out more about our authors and books visit www.bloomsbury.com
and sign up for our newsletters

Contents

List of Illustrations

Acknowledgments

In publishing this book, I owe a tremendous debt of gratitude to Washington Institute research assistants Elise Burr, Calvin Wilder, and Lauren Morganbesser. Their remarkable research skills made it possible for me to cover a dense literature, and helped me process interviews with many experts and practitioners. While working remotely through the pandemic, their curiosity, cheerfulness, and humor enabled this project to remain fun and enjoyable.

This book is also the product of a personal reckoning after a decade of working in the Middle East and North Africa, and of following the region closely from Paris, Berlin, Brussels, and Washington. Over the years, many people served as "door openers" and "translators" for me, explaining the specifics of their societies along with broader regional realities. This book is therefore a tribute to all the friends and colleagues who have improved my understanding of Arab societies and of U.S. foreign policy. Some of them have played an invaluable role in providing feedback on parts of this book, and I am deeply grateful for their help.

This research project would not have been possible without the support of the Washington Institute for Near East Policy. The book came to fruition through the endless discussions I had with the Institute's leadership and fellows, and would not be even approaching its current shape without the outstanding support of its editorial team. The Washington Institute has accumulated an incredible amount of knowledge and experience, and I am grateful to have been part of it.

All along, this project relied on the unwavering support of Chloe, to whom I owe everything.

Note: All opinions expressed in this book are purely the author's and do not reflect the views of any of his past or present employers.

Acronyms

AWACS	airborne warning and control system
BRI	Belt and Road Initiative (China)
CBRN	chemical, biological, radiological, and nuclear
CJTF-OIR	Combined Joint Task Force–Operation Inherent Resolve
CSDP	Common Security and Defense Policy
CTF	Coalition Task Force
DCFTA	Deep and Comprehensive Free Trade Area
DRM	dispute resolution mechanism
ECFR	European Council on Foreign Relations
EMASOH	European Military Awareness in the Strait of Hormuz
ENP	European Neighbourhood Policy
FFS	Funding Facility for Stabilization
GCC	Gulf Cooperation Council
GNA	Government of National Accord (Libya)
HTS	Hayat Tahrir al-Sham
IAEA	International Atomic Energy Agency
IMSC	International Maritime Security Construct
INSTEX	Instrument in Support of Trade Exchanges
IRGC	Islamic Revolutionary Guard Corps
ISR	intelligence, surveillance, and reconnaissance
JCPOA	Joint Comprehensive Plan of Action
KRG	Kurdistan Regional Government
LNA	Libyan National Army
NSC	National Security Council
PKK	Kurdistan Workers Party (Turkey)
PMF	Popular Mobilization Forces (Iraq)
PSC	Political and Security Committee (EU)
PYD	Democratic Union Party (Syria)

SDF   Syrian Democratic Forces
SECI   U.S. Special Envoy to the Global Coalition to Counter
          Daesh/ISIS
SPRING   Support for Partnership Reform and Inclusive Growth
STANAVFORMED
          Standing Naval Force Mediterranean (NATO)
UNDP   United Nations Development Program
USAID   U.S. Agency for International Development
YPG   People's Defense Units (Syria)

Introduction

Many in the Middle East and North Africa see America and Europe as a collective "West." From Napoleon's 1798 expedition in Egypt to the Cold War and the invasion of Iraq, this perception is understandably rooted in a long history of Western countries intervening in the region. Even today, politics in the Middle East is often seen as overwhelmingly shaped by Western interference.

An extensive literature covers European and American interventions in the Middle East. Less attention, however, has been paid to the way Europeans and Americans have operationally worked together in that context. In many areas, transatlantic cooperation is well established and has kept the United States and Europe close to each other for decades—through NATO with respect to defense but also through a large network of trade and cultural relations that have created deep interdependence, especially after World War II. Yet given the Cold War legacy, transatlantic foreign policy debates have traditionally focused on NATO's eastern flank, rather than its southern one. Although the NATO framework has sometimes been used to support interventions in Arab countries, most notably Libya in 2011, most cooperation between European countries and the United States in the Middle East has happened outside NATO. Such cooperation has mostly depended on ad hoc coalitions, exemplified by the "coalition of the willing" assembled for the 2003 invasion of Iraq, and on various sets of bilateral and multilateral relationships.

In a region that has faced both European colonization and American hegemony, the absence of a clear "Western" framework for engaging countries there is not, as such, a problem. It may even limit assertions related to a supposed clash of civilizations or a clear East-West divide. The connection between the United States and Europe nevertheless deserves scrutiny, so as to better clarify how these two broad actors influence the Middle East. Imbalances between American and European military capabilities have, for instance, often allowed Washington to dominate ad hoc partnerships. U.S. administrations have tended to look for European political and financial backing rather than seeking a strategic dialogue *with* Europe on the Middle East. Many European countries have likewise been satisfied with piggybacking when it comes to security issues in the Mediterranean and Eastern Europe.

In that sense, caricatures of the relationship between the United States and European countries have been easy to come by. The Americans come from Mars and the Europeans from Venus, as the analyst Robert Kagan famously put it.[1] Europe wishes to speak with one voice but has no phone number, as Henry Kissinger once allegedly said. The history of U.S. cooperation with European countries in the Middle East since 2001, however, reveals more complex trends.

As the Biden administration tries to spare resources formerly invested in the Middle East to refocus them on competing with China, this book tries to reckon with the changes that occurred since the end of the Cold War from conceptual, institutional, and operational perspectives. It provides a recent history of Western involvement in the Middle East, based both on academic literature and on accounts and testimonies gathered in more than fifty interviews with practitioners held between 2019 and 2021. It looks at the way military and diplomatic aspects of Western cooperation have recently shaped the American and European footprints in the Arab world, and presents in-depth analyses of three sets of recent events that have profoundly reshaped Western influence in the region: the response to the Arab uprisings between

2011 and 2015; the fight against the Islamic State jihadist group, in Iraq and Syria, between 2014 and 2020; and the U.S. "maximum pressure" policy against Iran conducted between 2017 and 2020. The concluding chapter describes how American and European approaches to the Middle East have diverged, to produce a geopolitical landscape much more fragmented than in the past century.

At least since the Obama administration and the first withdrawal from Iraq in 2011, U.S. administrations have been trying to reduce the American military footprint in the Middle East and have called for more "burden sharing" from European allies, while often disregarding some of these allies' input. Most recently, the American conversation on "endless wars," along with its inward-looking tendencies, has left limited space for European allies to make the case for extended transatlantic cooperation in the Middle East. On the other side, European divisions and lack of collective hard security tools have frustrated the United States in its call for more burden sharing. If one wanted to paraphrase Kagan and Kissinger, one could say that Venus (Europe) has recently often tried to convince a tired and undecided Mars (America) to remain committed. Today's diplomatic communication also occurs in a more intense, fragmented form. One might say that while Europe now has a "phone number," the nature of today's diplomacy requires work through multiple "WhatsApp groups."

Despite intense consultations among transatlantic partners, these trends have played out in an especially messy fashion with respect to some key issues between 2011 and 2021. The case studies presented in this book show how diverging interests, institutional differences, and tactical disagreements have undermined shared strategic goals (e.g., nuclear counterproliferation, the enduring defeat of the Islamic State, containing Russian influence). While European divisions and Europe's lack of sufficient military capabilities remain key issues, the United States struggles to reconcile its desire to reduce its footprint in the Middle East with its habit of leading coalitions rather unilaterally.

In many ways, Barack Obama's "pivot to Asia" was continued by Donald Trump despite his disdain for his predecessor's legacy. The two presidents also shared the experience of being forced back to the Middle East. On the other side of the Atlantic, European countries and institutions have been working slowly but steadily toward bringing about a more geopolitically engaged Europe. The lack of an efficient foreign policy process along with tactical disagreements remain major obstacles to a unified European foreign policy, but a number of European countries have been active on both military and diplomatic fronts, and some have joined forces in several instances. The United States, seeking regional minimalism vis-à-vis the Middle East as well as a more geopolitically involved Europe, offers an opportunity to reset the transatlantic discussion.

With Joe Biden now president of the United States, Europeans and Americans can reinvent their cooperation. Both Republicans and Democrats tend to want to reduce the U.S. military footprint in the Middle East. While Republicans still favor asserting American military hegemony, Democrats want to invest more in diplomatic negotiations. In both cases, they need allies; but traditional American allies from the Middle East seem to be less engaged in strategic alignment with the United States and more invested in leveraging Washington as well as hedging their bets between Washington, Moscow, and Beijing. The increasing autonomy of the foreign policies of Washington's allies might increase the need for renewed cooperation with Europe, especially since the current focus on Great Power competition will force America to strike a balance between withdrawing assets from the Middle East and containing China and Russia in the region. On the other hand, Europe will have to deal with its neighborhood in a more autonomous way. The "arch of crisis" around Europe, once identified as somewhere between Iraq, Somalia, and Mali, now spans Ukraine to Libya through the eastern Mediterranean.

Reinventing cooperation will not be easy in the context of multiple crises. Besides, Europe will not be able to build up its military and security capabilities overnight, and many member states will still do everything they can to rely on Washington for their security. Both European sovereignty and America's Great Power competition will require a transatlantic partnership that can design a mutually beneficial process.

A reset of the transatlantic dialogue on the Middle East requires, first and foremost, acknowledging changes in the region as well as the limits of excessively militarized engagement. This reset would also need to take account of each actor's bilateral relations in the region, including their partnerships with regional allies. The United States and Europe would probably have to start by articulating more modest goals and strategies in a region whose own geopolitics seems more and more driven by local and fragmented dynamics. A reconstructed transatlantic policy toward the Middle East is likely to avoid large military engagements, but it should also incorporate a more robust policy of promoting better governance and greater socioeconomic empowerment. In that sense, reassessing transatlantic cooperation in the Middle East could be a way for the "West" to rethink its relations with the region.

Ultimately, an updated dialogue would go beyond a technical discussion on the modalities of military and diplomatic actions in the Middle East; it would likewise embrace questioning what the West actually is when it comes to Middle East politics. The international conversation on the region still relies significantly on the idea of "Western intervention." Notwithstanding the relevance of this idea to describing the past role of European countries and the United States in Middle East politics, the gaps among Western allies are today so large that the "West" almost certainly does not exist in the Middle East as a political force as it did during the colonial period and the Cold War. The question, then, is not so much whether this is a positive or negative evolution, but how this change reshapes regional and international geopolitics.

Notes

1   Ivo H. Daalder, "Americans Are from Mars, Europeans from Venus," *New York Times*, March 5, 2003, https://www.nytimes.com/2003/03/05/books/books-of-the-times-americans-are-from-mars-europeans-from-venus.html.

1

Transatlantic Asymmetry During
the U.S. Unipolar Moment, 1990–2011

Unpacking the idea of Western intervention in the Middle East requires first explaining its practical realities, including the ways by which European countries and the United States have cooperated to pursue their policies in the region. Channels between Washington and European capitals are well established: the United States has had intense bilateral relations with all European countries, and NATO has been the prime forum for discussions of transatlantic security. Yet the post–Cold War history of the transatlantic dialogue shows that the Middle East falls into a sort of gray area.

On the one hand, Middle East issues since 1990 have been among the most divisive for the transatlantic relationship.[1] Major policy differences between the United States and European nations have arisen from geography, distinct histories, a military power gap, divergences in foreign policy culture, and domestic items. On the other hand, no real framework has been set up to address these frictions beyond traditional bilateral relations. The first part of this book will thus show how each crisis in the region has triggered different possibilities for cooperation.

Imbalances, Capability Gaps, and "Burden Sharing"

Differing geographies and interests, along with the deep imbalance in the U.S.-Europe relationship, are likely reasons for the presence of so many different frameworks for cooperation with respect to the Middle East.

Diverging Interests and Geographies

Western cooperation in the Middle East requires two levels of convergence, involving not only some level of U.S.-Europe understanding but, even more importantly, some level of European unity.

A Disunited Europe in the Middle East

European unity with respect to the Middle East is traditionally hard to achieve, owing to diverging interests and levels of commitment. The number of EU member states historically involved in the Middle East is limited, and some member states are historically not interested in the Middle East at all.

Rather than there being one "European" approach, European foreign policy in the Middle East is composed of an aggregate of foreign policies shaped by the most active European member states, which are mostly those with the greatest interests at stake. Southern member states and member states with strong historical legacies in the region (related to colonialism, the Holocaust, or Soviet-era cooperation) maintained distinctive bilateral policies. Together, they have shaped a complex patchwork of European ties to the region.

Thus, France retained deep but complicated ties with former colonies and mandates, as did Britain in Egypt, Jordan, and the Gulf. Britain retains a strong footprint in the Gulf, especially relating to security, investment, and arms sales. In 1996, Britain and the United Arab Emirates signed the Defense Cooperation Act, making it one of London's most significant non-NATO defense commitments.[2] In 2018, the British opened their first permanent military base in the Middle East in more than forty years, in Bahrain.[3] And in 2019, Britain and Egypt conducted their first bilateral military exercise in thirty years.[4]

Italy kept a strong connection to Libya and considers the "enlarged Mediterranean" a strategic priority. Italy also defines the Mediterranean as its third circle of interest, after its European and transatlantic ones.[5]

Spain had specific relations with countries such as Morocco after the French protectorate (1912–56), and also entertained strong diplomatic relations with other Arab countries during the Franco period (1936–75) as a way to break isolation and leverage support at the UN regarding the status of Gibraltar.[6] Spain only established relations with Israel in 1986 because of Franco's relations with Nazi Germany.[7]

Farther from the Mediterranean, other European countries have entertained specific connections to the sea's southern shores. Germany's "raison d'état" remained attached to Israel, and the Czech Republic and Romania preserved Soviet-era relations with countries such as Syria, especially through diasporas of students who had initially come to these European countries to study in the 1960s and 1970s.[8] Others, especially Scandinavian countries, focused on mainstreaming goals like human rights promotion or gender equality in Arab countries.

In the second half of the twentieth century, each member state further developed its national foreign policy along specific lines. Germany increased its market share in trade with North Africa and the Gulf, and invested a lot in technical assistance and civil society support. France developed strong military and economic partnerships with Gulf countries, starting with Saudi Arabia in 1967, and kept invested in cultural, academic, and scientific cooperation in the Middle East while capitalizing on its UN Security Council role to maintain diplomatic sway in the region.

British ties with Egypt are stronger than its ties with other North African states. Trade and energy have also deepened the interdependence. Private investors in the Gulf and in sovereign wealth funds have invested so heavily in Britain's capital that then mayor Boris Johnson once described London as "the eighth emirate."[9] It is estimated that Britain is Qatar's single largest investment destination. Britain, for its part, is by far the largest single foreign investor in Egypt.[10] In 2016, Britain accounted for 41 percent of all foreign direct investment in Egypt.[11] Italy and Spain have also extended their trade relations with countries in the Middle East.

In this context, European nations have struggled to define strong "European" positions on Middle East matters. Only step by step, one treaty at a time, have they increased their coordination on foreign policy. Historical differences described above have shaped national positions until today.

Geography, People, and Trade: Diverging Perspectives

An understanding between the United States and Europe is also hard to reach. The traditional European focus on North Africa and the Mediterranean often seems disconnected from the broader U.S. interest in the Middle East (see figure 1.1 for maps of the U.S. vision of the "broader Middle East" and of the EU "neighborhood"). The Baghdad Pact of 1955—between Britain, Iran, Pakistan, Turkey, Iraq, and (in 1958) the United States—initially sought to replicate in the Middle East the same sort of alliance that the United States had created in Europe through NATO, but the project failed, and U.S. policy in the Middle East remained dominated by bilateral partnerships. Historic U.S. partnerships with Saudi Arabia, Israel, Turkey, and Egypt challenged the role of former colonial powers in the second half of the twentieth century and forced France and Britain to adapt their foreign policy to the growing challenge posed by American influence. The 1956 Suez crisis specifically, which saw the United States opposing the British-French operation in support of Israel against Egypt, marked a turning point in transatlantic relations in the Middle East.

Perceptions related to geography are a key aspect explaining numerous transatlantic misalignments when it comes to the Middle East. In general, the Mediterranean is understood in the United States as NATO's southern flank, strategically less important than the eastern one. But for Southern European states, the Mediterranean defines their strategic depth, and is an immediate area for power projection. Likewise, the area of priority for Spain and France in North Africa—Morocco and Algeria—is not a U.S. priority.[12]

Spain, Italy, and France have historically pushed for a more unified European policy toward the Mediterranean. The launch of the Barcelona Process in 1995 remains one of Madrid's key diplomatic successes,[13] and created a multilateral dialogue between the countries of the South and North of the Mediterranean[14] on an array of issues, from culture to security. Though Spain launched the Barcelona Process capitalizing on the positive dynamic created by the Oslo Accords, Southern European countries had a consistent Mediterranean focus before then, as reflected in the Spanish-Italian Conference for Security and Cooperation in the Mediterranean (1990); NATO's Mediterranean Dialogue in 1994; the agreement at the Valencia Euro-Mediterranean conference in 2002; the French-led Union for the Mediterranean in 2008; and the Summit of the Two Shores in 2019. Northern and Eastern European countries' interest in North Africa has been limited, but Southern European countries still managed to push the EU to add a southern component to its neighbor-hood policy. This policy was originally copied from the membership process focusing on Eastern Europe and not on the Mediterranean. Southern European member states also entertained informal diplomatic formats, like the "5+5 dialogue" with North African countries.

"But," as one study put it, "proximity goes even beyond geography."[15] In the case of Europe, the relationship to the Middle East and North Africa is also about binational communities and diasporas. While Spain is obviously geographically very close to North Africa, especially con-sidering the Ceuta and Melilla enclaves, the size of the North African diaspora in Southern Europe and even in Belgium has created deep ties. The United States also has diasporas and binational communi-ties, but they do not represent the same proportion of its population. Based on census data, the U.S. government estimates that as of 2019, roughly two million people in the United States self-reported having Arab ancestry (less than 1 percent of the U.S. population), in addition to 468,000 with Iranian heritage, 460,000 with Armenian ancestry, 144,000 with Israeli origins, and 94,000 with Assyrian/Chaldean/Syriac

Figure 1.1 U.S. Vision of the "Broader Middle East" and EU Vision of Its "Neighborhood"

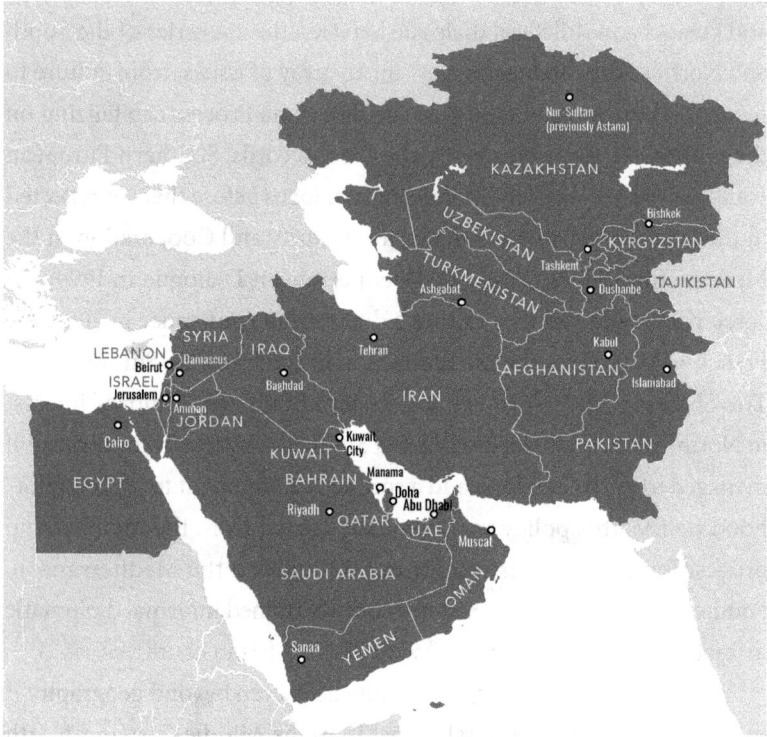

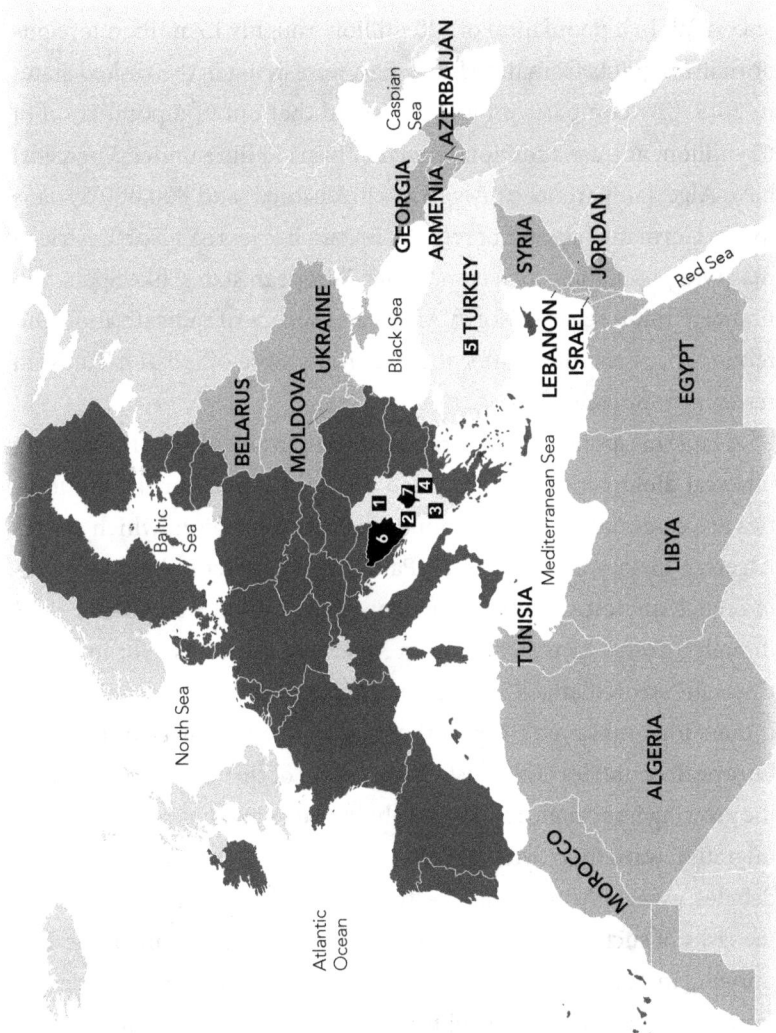

EU states

Candidate countries
1. SERBIA
2. MONTENEGRO
3. ALBANIA
4. NORTH MACEDONIA
5. TURKEY

Potential candidate countries
6. BOSNIA
7. KOSOVO

European Neighbourhood Policy countries
ALGERIA
ARMENIA
AZERBAIJAN
BELARUS
EGYPT
GEORGIA
ISRAEL
JORDAN
LEBANON
LIBYA
MOLDOVA
MOROCCO
PALESTINIAN TERRITORIES
SYRIA
TUNISIA
UKRAINE

ancestry.[16] In a population of 320 million, roughly 1.7 million foreign-born immigrants from the Middle East were living in the United States in 2018.[17] By comparison, it is estimated that out of a population of 65 million, at least 2 million French citizens (a little under 3 percent) have Algerian parents or Algerian citizenship,[18] and 800,000 Syrians live in Germany (about 1 percent).[19] Britain has less of a North African diaspora population than some other European states, like Spain and France,[20] but it regards North Africa as a source of radicalization and terrorism, particularly after thirty Britons were killed at a Tunisian resort near Sousse in 2015.

A large diaspora makes it strategically important to have functioning bilateral diplomatic channels. Arab and Jewish binational communities are essential to French connections to the region, which makes Algerian history and the Israeli-Palestinian conflict polarizing issues in French domestic politics more than in the United States. France was directly affected by the civil war in Algeria in the 1990s—for instance, through terrorist attacks in the Paris subway in 1995. These domestic dimensions make stability in the region a key security interest for European countries. The most visible aspect of this interdependence is the growing importance of debates about managing migration. The 2015 migration wave from Syria played a significant role in shaping European debates, especially in Germany—though Italy had been warning about the risks of such large-scale migration since the beginning of the 2011 uprising in Tunisia. Thus, numerous efforts have been made to design frameworks to better control migration flows coming from Turkey, Morocco, Libya, and Egypt.

Another structural aspect of the triangle formed by the Middle East, Europe, and the United States is its trade component (see figures 1.2 and 1.3). Europe is the biggest trade partner of Middle East countries:

Taken as a whole, the EU is the MENA region's most important trading partner: the value of trade between the two averaged $637 billion per year between 2014 and 2017. This represents around 21 per cent of the MENA region's global trade—far more than that with other international partners, such as China ($209 billion) and the U.S. ($137 billion). France, Germany, Italy, Spain, and the United Kingdom collectively sold weapons worth $12 billion to Middle Eastern countries between 2014 and 2017, ranking behind the U.S. ($22 billion), but ahead of Russia ($6 billion) and China ($1 billion)."[21]

North African economies therefore rely heavily on trade with the European market. Europe accounts for a third of Egypt's trade,[22] and is the primary source of tourists to Tunisia, Morocco, and Egypt. Spain has imported Libyan oil since the 1970s, and 46 percent of its gas comes from Algeria.[23] Numerous European countries rely on energy supplies transiting the Mediterranean via ships and pipelines linking Europe with North African countries.[24] The contest for prospective eastern Mediterranean gas is also a vital geopolitical issue for Greece and Cyprus.

These differences predictably create gaps vis-à-vis U.S. interests and pose obstacles to a U.S.-EU accord. The United States and Europe have similar interests when it comes to energy, like maintaining oil markets' stability, but America historically discusses oil prices with Saudi Arabia more than Algeria or Libya. Washington also focuses more clearly on maintaining security alliances, such as with Israel. The EU is more concerned about the consequences of migration and diasporas for domestic politics than about grand strategy.

In this context, arms sales are a key but neglected challenge with respect to transatlantic competition. Five of the ten biggest arms importers from 2016 to 2020 are located in the Middle East and North Africa; combined, these five countries (Saudi Arabia, Egypt, Algeria, Qatar, and the UAE) account for over a quarter of all global arms imports in that period, with Saudi Arabia alone accounting for 11 percent of all imports. Egypt accounted for 5.8 percent, Algeria for 4.3 percent, Qatar for 3.8 percent, and the UAE for 3 percent.

Figure 1.2 MENA Trade in Goods and Services, 2014–17 (billion US$)

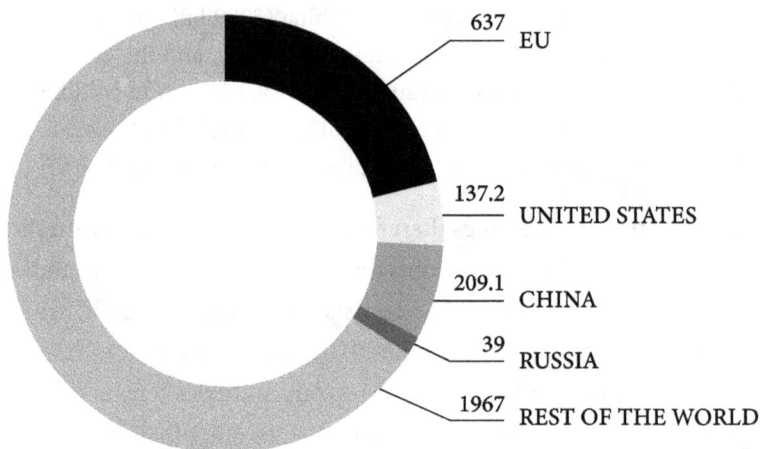

637 —— EU

137.2 —— UNITED STATES

209.1 —— CHINA

39 —— RUSSIA

1967 —— REST OF THE WORLD

Source: European Council on Foreign Relations, Mapping European Leverage in the MENA Region, *https://ecfr.eu/special/mapping_eu_leverage_mena/.*

Figure 1.3 Bilateral Aid to the MENA Region, 2014–17 (million US$)

UNITED STATES   10,944.8

EC+5*   8,261.8

RUSSIA   29.5

*European Commission, France, Germany, Italy, Spain, Britain
Source: European Council on Foreign Relations, Mapping European Leverage in the MENA Region, *https://ecfr.eu/special/mapping_eu_leverage_mena/.*

Britain is the second largest exporter of arms to Saudi Arabia, although it remains distantly behind the United States.[25] Between 2015 and 2019, meanwhile, Algeria accounted for 79 percent of North Africa's arms imports, which came mainly from Russia, followed by China and Germany. Out of all arms transfers to the Middle East between 2015 and 2019, the United States supplied 53 percent, France supplied 12 percent, and Russia supplied 11 percent.[26] The breakdowns for the top three suppliers of the world's top ten arms importers are displayed in figure 1.4. (Major arms exporters are detailed in figure 1.5; see figure 1.6 for arms sales to the region.)

Beyond the numbers, these arms sales have multiple implications. First, they reflect the depth of certain strategic partnerships, like the U.S.-Saudi partnership and the French-Emirati one. These relationships are never only about selling hardware but also imply providing training and maintenance, as well as strategically determined compromises balancing the freedom the buyer wants regarding the final use of the weapons over and against the seller's need to track how their equipment will ultimately be used. Each relationship is different in this respect, and related European or transatlantic cooperation is difficult—because Western countries are competitors with each other, and they also fear losing market share to Russia and China if they reduce sales to the Gulf.

European Security Policies: America First

Another element of transatlantic relations in the Middle East derives from the relationship European nations have with the United States itself. As Jeremy Shapiro, an expert at the European Council on Foreign Relations, put it: "Europe's dependence on the U.S. for its own security places a firm limit on the degree of opposition it will muster to American policies."[27] Some European countries will prioritize their partnership with Washington before considering specific actions other European countries might take in the Middle East, especially when they do not have vital national interests at stake. The American position

Figure 1.4 The Forty Largest Importers of Major Arms and Their Main Suppliers, 2016–20

Importer	Share of arms imports (%)		Percent change from 2011–15 to 2016–20	Main suppliers (share of importer's total imports, %), 2016–20		
	2016–20	2011–15		1st	2nd	3rd
1. Saudi Arabia	11	7.1	61	USA (79)	UK (9.3)	France (4.0)
2. India	9.5	14	-33	Russia (49)	France (18)	Israel (13)
3. Egypt	5.8	2.4	136	Russia (41)	France (28)	USA (8.7)
4. Australia	5.1	3.6	41	USA (69)	Spain (21)	Switzerland (3.4)
5. China	4.7	4.4	5.5	Russia (77)	France (28)	Ukraine (6.3)
6. Algeria	4.3	2.6	64	Russia (69)	Germany (12)	China (9.9)
7. South Korea	4.3	2.7	57	USA (58)	Germany (31)	Spain (6.5)
8. Qatar	3.8	0.8	361	USA (47)	France (38)	Germany (7.5)
9. UAE	3.0	4.7	-37	USA (64)	France (10)	Russia (4.7)
10. Pakistan	2.7	3.4	-23	China (74)	Russia (6.6)	Italy (5.9)

Note: Percentages below 10 are rounded to one decimal place, percentages over 10 are rounded to whole numbers.
Source: Pieter Wezeman et al., SIPRI, March 2021, https://sipri.org/sites/default/files/2021-03/fs_2103_at_2020.pdf.

Figure 1.5 The Twenty-Five Largest Exporters of Major Arms and Their Main Recipients, 2016–20

Importer	Share of arms exports (%)		Percent change from 2011–15 to 2016–20	Main recipients (share of exporter's total exports, %), 2016–20		
	2016–20	2011–15		1st	2nd	3rd
1. United States	37	32	15	Saudi Arabia (24)	Australia (9.4)	South Korea (6.7)
2. Russia	20	26	-22	India (23)	China (18)	Algeria (15)
3. France	8.2	5.6	44	India (21)	Egypt (20)	Qatar (18)
4. Germany	5.5	4.5	21	South Korea (24)	Algeria (10)	Egypt (8.7)
5. China	5.2	5.6	-7.8	Pakistan (38)	Bangladesh (17)	Algeria (8.2)
6. United Kingdom	3.3	4.6	-27	Saudi Arabia (32)	Oman (17)	USA (14)
7. Spain	3.2	3.5	-8.4	Australia (33)	Singapore (13)	Turkey (9.7)
8. Israel	3.0	1.9	59	India (43)	Azerbaijan (17)	Vietnam (12)
9. South Korea	2.7	0.9	210	UK (14)	Philippines (12)	Thailand (11)
10. Italy	2.2	2.8	-22	Turkey (18)	Egypt (17)	Pakistan (7.2)

Note: Percentages below 10 are rounded to one decimal place, percentages over 10 are rounded to whole numbers.
Source: Pieter Wezeman et al., SIPRI, March 2021, https://sipri.org/sites/default/files/2021-03/fs_2103_at_2020.pdf.

Figure 1.6 Arms Sales to the MENA Region, 2014–17 (billion US$)

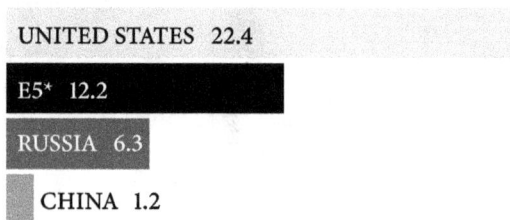

| UNITED STATES 22.4 |
| E5* 12.2 |
| RUSSIA 6.3 |
| CHINA 1.2 |

France, Germany, Italy, Spain, Britain
Source: *European Council on Foreign Relations,* Mapping European Leverage
in the MENA Region, *https://ecfr.eu/special/mapping_eu_leverage_mena/.*

tends to be the main point of reference for these European capitals when
it comes to the situation in the Middle East.[28] As a diplomat from an EU
member state put it, "When there is a crisis, we tend to ask first, 'What
does Washington think?' and second, 'What do we think ourselves?'"[29]

For countries like Germany or Italy, the presence of U.S. or NATO
military bases and the relationship of their armies with the United
States are structural dimensions of their foreign policy, which can
take precedence over the considerations raised by any particular issue.
Denmark has opted out of EU defense and engages only with NATO;
it has historically engaged militarily only when the United States was
involved. Tensions with Turkey are central to Greek's foreign policy and
force Washington into recurring balancing acts between two NATO
members with advanced naval forces.

Asset and Capability Gaps

Because its relations with the Middle East differ from those of the
United States, Europe can influence these countries and enhance its
diplomacy through a perceived neutrality.[30] EU diplomacy benefits
from France and Britain having seats in the United Nations Security

Council, as well as from a set of bilateral agreements ranging from trade to technical assistance and university cooperation. The EU also has a convening power that can complement diplomatic processes led by the U.S. and by Arab governments. The positive image of European societies has also, despite ups and downs, provided real soft power to Europe, especially since many cities—London, Paris, and more recently Berlin—have been Arab intellectual hubs. Individually and collectively, the Europeans have the ability to engage with societies and governments in the Middle East and North Africa on multiple issues.

Soft power, however, is often regarded as insufficient to wield decisive influence in a region dominated by hard power and realpolitik. The U.S. military footprint has therefore often been considered the main element underlying American leadership in the region between 1990 and 2011. Indeed, the United States sent 500,000 troops to the Gulf in 1991,[31] and had around 285,000 troops in Iraq and in the region as a whole in 2003,[32] 120,000 in the Middle East in 2009,[33] and around 30,000 in the Gulf in 2020.

But although Europe's military assets are not comparable to those of the United States, the picture of an EU without military might is more complex than it seems. There are three layers to this issue: a military one, a legal one, and political one.

So, notwithstanding the military disparity between Europe and the United States, Europe does have deployable firepower. Some member states, particularly Britain and France, have a specific military tradition that includes close cooperation with the United States. France has conducted more than thirty foreign operations since the 1980s, including participation in several coalitions with the United States (the 1991 Gulf War) and with NATO (the Balkans).[34]

Collectively, Europeans have been slowly responding to U.S. pressure and have established goals to increase deployability. The European Council, meeting in Helsinki in 1999, set "Headline Goals" for the EU to increase its military deployment and expand its crisis

management operations by 2003. While these goals were theoretically reached and updated in 2010, the 60,000 forces supposed to be
simultaneously deployable have not been used by the EU. However,
the EU launched smaller military and civilian missions through the
Common Security and Defense Policy (CSDP) to train local forces,
to initiate and maintain peacekeeping operations, and to launch
surveillance operations. The CSDP is dependent on cooperation
among and collective action on the part of EU member states, as each
must contribute based on its capabilities.

In 2003, European countries collectively had around 90,000 troops
deployed in more than twenty countries, including in the Gulf, in the
framework of a UN, NATO, EU, or national mandate.[35] These numbers
decreased between 2003 and 2017, but the EU still initiated numerous
military missions and deployed its forces across Central Asia, Europe,
and Africa, with a total of 23,490 employed personnel and troops in
2017, at a total cost of €5 billion.[36] Since then, to take one example, in
2019 there were thirty-four Italian missions abroad, involving a total
of around 5,700 soldiers.[37]

The issue regarding deploying European troops in the Middle
East and North Africa is therefore not so much about the numbers
themselves. One more crucial element relates to European military
capabilities, which are not always relevant with respect to intervention
in the Middle East. Though France and Britain have military bases in
the region along with specific military traditions, not all EU countries
have experience with autonomous foreign military missions. The
United States has increasingly drawn from its 70,000 available Special
Forces, rather than regular combat units, in the Middle East since 9/11,
whereas the total number of European special forces is comparatively
small: fewer than 15,000 soldiers. European armies also lack specific
capabilities, such as intelligence, surveillance, and reconnaissance
(ISR) systems, and hence are limited with respect to counterterrorist
operations without some U.S. support.

Legally, European military capabilities are more difficult to wield in the Middle East, as many EU member states favor contributing to UN-mandated peacekeeping missions rather than to ad hoc combat missions. Austria has, for instance, regularly sent troops to the Middle East within a UN framework to monitor the ceasefire in the Golan Heights.

The primary consideration governing the European military footprint in the Middle East, however, is a political one: most European countries are unwilling to commit to combat missions. In that respect, it has been less difficult for the EU to pool resources for peacekeeping operations in Africa than in the Middle East. Thus, demand for EU military missions in the latter region increased significantly since the 2000s, but only a small number of member states have contributed to meet those demands. According to the Stockholm International Peace Research Institute, "the eight top contributors are currently providing 69 per cent of all seconded mission staff."[38]

Applied to the Middle East, then, the debate over burden sharing is not so much about NATO commitments vis-à-vis specific thresholds (e.g., 2 percent of GDP devoted to defense spending) but about respective national political alignments dealing with crises and preparing relevant capabilities for foreign deployment and counterterrorism operations.

Addressing the Military Gap: Burden Sharing Within NATO

The United States is well aware of Europe's collective assets, and Washington often tries to benefit from three of them: money, troops, and legitimacy.[39] But the question of "sharing the burden" between allies is both a very tangible issue pertaining to financial and military contributions on the ground, and a highly symbolic one that says a lot about the deep imbalances between Europe and the United States.

Burden sharing has always been a point of contention within the transatlantic alliance. During the Cold War, the United States had more than 300,000 troops in Europe and accounted for about 50 percent of total allied defense spending. With the end of the Cold War, the U.S. share of NATO spending increased to 68 percent.[40] This frustrated U.S. administrations, and they sought ways to share the burden. Defense spending targets for European countries were eventually established: 3 percent of GDP in 1997, later changed to 2 percent in 2006.

Though the burden sharing debate has mostly taken place within NATO, operations in the Middle East have not been immune to it. Cooperation between the United States and Europe during Operation Desert Storm was strong, but participation remained lopsided and American-controlled. In two major demonstrations of cooperation, France agreed to send troops under U.S. operational control, and Germany covered roughly 10 percent of the coalition's cost.[41] But overall, the contribution from European countries to Operation Desert Storm remained modest: U.S. troops still made up three-quarters of coalition forces. Direct cooperation on Iraq diminished throughout the 1990s as European countries began questioning the sanctions regime and no-fly zones. France ended its enforcement of the no-fly zone in northern Iraq in 1996 on the basis that it no longer constituted a humanitarian operation but rather served as a military operation lacking UN authorization.[42]

Following the September 11 attacks, the U.S. administration exerted pressure on the EU to increase its financial and military contribution toward the war on terror.[43] The impact of the terrorist attack forced European nations to comply with American pressure for support in the campaign in Afghanistan. Yet the United States expressed frustration that European nations had not devoted sufficient military capacity in the years after 9/11, and this frustration has continued up to recent years. The Trump administration expressed this frustration even more bluntly, describing NATO as "obsolete."[44]

In January 2019, Secretary of State Mike Pompeo reaffirmed this idea in a speech to the American University in Cairo when he said, "Our aim is to partner with our friends and vigorously oppose our enemies, because a strong, secure, and economically vibrant Middle East is in our national interest, and it's in yours as well… But as President Trump has said, we're looking to our partners to do more, and in this effort we will do so going forward together."[45] On January 8, 2020, after Iranian ballistic missile attacks on a U.S. base in Iraq, Trump restated this point in a White House speech: "Today, I am going to ask NATO to become much more involved in the Middle East process."[46]

Trump's criticisms regarding burden sharing within NATO were not unprecedented and seemed to echo those of previous administrations, but his focus on NATO's role in the Middle East specifically was new. But the role of NATO in the region will most likely continue to center around military assistance and training, as there is little interest on the part of Europeans in sending troops into places like Iraq or Syria after U.S. forces leave.[47] Furthermore, NATO lacks the resources, manpower, training, and equipment necessary to take over for the United States,[48] and members are unlikely to devote the extensive resources that this would require. NATO member states, especially the Europeans, have other conflicts and issues that are more pressing, including both domestic concerns and the expanding reach of Russia. Expansion of NATO to the Middle East would also require unity with respect to methods, which does not exist among member states. For example, when it comes to counterterrorism missions, some countries want to limit it to raising awareness, others want a focus on capacity building, and some want NATO engagement but are not sure what that should look like. NATO was not created to deal with today's conflicts, and given the limited interest among member states in increasing their spending or other contributions, it seems unlikely that NATO will greatly expand its operations in the Middle East.

In other words, the only organization wherein the United States and European countries could theoretically have agreed on a trajectory for balancing their military cooperation in the Middle East and their strategic goals in the region was in reality not in a position to accommodate this process. NATO's focus remains on Europe and not the power projection capacity of the United States and Europe together.

Lack of Institutional Space for Transatlantic Cooperation

Looking at the practicalities of European-American cooperation in the Middle East also requires diving into an analysis of foreign policy making. The complex foreign policy making process of each side in the U.S.-EU relationship provides limited space for deep cooperation on issues related to a third region. The U.S. system is complex on account of the interagency process and the dynamics of budgetary oversight in Congress; the European system is worse, because the relevant authorities and capabilities are split between the national level and the EU.

The Making of U.S. Foreign Policy

The key question underlying a discussion on transatlantic cooperation is whether the U.S. foreign policy making process leaves space and time for real consultation and smart cooperation with European partners.

Although constitutionally the right to declare war resides with Congress, power in the United States has shifted so that it now lies largely with the president, who has been able to deploy armed forces without congressional approval thanks to the Authorization for Use of Military Force. This joint congressional resolution, which became law on September 18, 2001, authorized the use of the U.S. military against those responsible for the September 11 attacks, but was also used in a broader sense to authorize a vast array of counterterrorism activities.[49]

Congress retains the "power of the purse," as it controls government spending and taxation, and follows a two-step legislative process that includes authorization and appropriation for foreign assistance.[50] The

House and Senate Appropriations Committees have been primarily responsible for foreign aid programs, and for coordinating foreign assistance through continuing resolutions or omnibus appropriations bills.[51] But the authorizing committee (the House Foreign Affairs Committee) has become somewhat less relevant over the years, as it has not passed an authorization bill since 2003,[52] and is now used primarily for oversight.

In recent years, the Senate Foreign Relations Committee has also not passed foreign assistance authorization bills, but it does approve treaties and State Department nominations, which allows Congress to block individuals whose past foreign policy experience or pronouncements are deemed to depart too far from the bipartisan consensus. Congress can also conduct investigations into foreign policy or national security concerns, such as after the 9/11 attacks or the 2012 attack on U.S. diplomatic facilities in Libya.[53] And Congress can create, eliminate, or restructure executive branch agencies, as when it created the Department of Homeland Security after 9/11. Some senators are key, like the chairs of the Committee on Foreign Relations and the Armed Forces Committee, as well as the majority and minority leaders. Other powerful congressional political tools include legislative resolutions and calling hearings involving administration officials.

In order to implement the foreign policy decisions made by these two branches of government, various machinery is in place, beginning with the Department of State, with the secretary of state at its helm.[54] Another agency that implements foreign policy is the Department of Defense; it was created in 1949 through a consolidation of the Department of the Navy, the War Department, and the U.S. Air Force. The security apparatus also plays a role in foreign policy: The Central Intelligence Agency, for example, is responsible for information relating to the national security of the United States, and is famous for conducting covert operations abroad. Other intelligence arms include the National Security Agency, the Defense Intelligence Agency, and the intelligence branches in the armed services and in executive departments.[55]

Atop the interagency process stands the National Security Council (NSC), created in 1947. This cabinet-level agency includes the president, the vice president, the secretaries of state and defense, the chairman of the Joint Chiefs of Staff, and the director of the CIA. The staff of the NSC consists of specialists in various geographic and functional areas, and helps the president on foreign policy issues. The way each president has decided to use the NSC has had implications for the possibility and possible scope of cooperation with European allies, especially in the Middle East. According to a former NSC official under George W. Bush, coordinating with the "Europeans" on the Middle East meant "the British, the French, sometimes the Germans and on some specific issues the Italians, and that was it."[56]

On the one hand, it seems logical that a system the size of America's, with its military firepower, has multiple layers of internal governance to process information and decisions all the way to the head of the executive branch; a superpower is expected to have a sophisticated system of decisionmaking. On the other hand, U.S. partners have to adapt to that system if they want to coordinate with Washington. Depending on the context and the nature of any given crisis, it can be challenging to find enough time to articulate multinational capabilities in a smart way. Some perceive this interagency foreign policy making as a process weakening the possibility of cooperation more than enabling it. As one U.S. diplomat put it: "the interagency process does not give space for strategic cooperation."[57] It is difficult to share options with partners before the interagency process has produced a decision. But by the time U.S. agencies have defined a position or gotten approval from the White House of a given option, it may no longer be possible for the U.S. government to take constraints articulated by American partners into consideration. The temptation is thus strong for a superpower to make a decision and present it to partners as a "take it or leave it" situation.

Other former officials have a more balanced viewpoint. Regular contacts and a history of cooperation help agencies prepare and plan with relevant partners to be ready to react together to a crisis. According to Dennis Ross,[58] who has served in several administrations, the degree to which the decisionmaking process at the White House involves allies, including Europeans, has a lot to do with the "sociology" of the particular administration or president. In an interview, he described the George H. W. Bush administration as working extensively with its European counterparts, both as a departure from the bureaucratic infighting of the Reagan administration and owing to the experience of advisors such as James Baker and Brent Scowcroft. According to Ross, the involvement of embassies in Washington was critical to keeping the Europeans abreast of what the administration was doing. To the contrary, the Clinton administration, according to Ross, got off to a difficult start with the Europeans because of disagreements over the war in the Balkans and especially Bosnia, the most salient European issue at the time and one on which the administration lacked bureaucratic consensus. George W. Bush's first term did not involve extensive coordination, but by the second term it had expanded.

Dennis Ross noted that in the Obama administration, there was an extensive process of discussion with Europeans. Ben Fishman,[59] another former member of the National Security Council staff, described how Tom Donilon, Obama's national security advisor from 2010 to 2013, established a regular channel to talk to Britain, France, and Germany; they would send an agenda in advance, according to Fishman, and try to meet regularly. There were significant barriers to these conversations, however, such as how some of Donilon's counterparts in the administration thought it was the State Department's job to talk to Europeans.

Ross believes that the NSC under the Trump administration did not continue this close cooperation and discussion. State Department officials in the Trump administration kept in regular contact with their British and French counterparts, but dialogue at the NSC level was less frequent.[60] Ross emphasized that having agreement on a basic approach to issues makes coordination easier, but process can only help to a certain point when disagreements inside the administration and with European partners are too significant.

Beyond high-level diplomatic contacts between allies, another factor influencing the possibilities of American-European cooperation is the nature of civilian-military relations within the American system. Stefano Recchia, for instance, argues that military officials are multilateral-minded, while civilian leaders are unilateral-minded. When the military leadership is less vocally involved in planning an intervention (e.g., Iraq in 2003), the intervention tends to be more unilateral. Military officials are known to have strong concerns about mission creep and other problems, and when they express these concerns vigorously, the result is often a more multilateral engagement.[61]

European Foreign Policy Decisionmaking: A Work in Progress

If in transatlantic cooperation the possibilities are hampered by the U.S. interagency policy process, European foreign policy making is problematic because the relevant actors, levels of governance, and instruments available to shape external actions are too widely dispersed. No single actor has authority with respect to all the tools of foreign policy making—and Europe as a whole does not have as many tools available as the United States, because it lacks many hard security capabilities. Understanding how the European side of the transatlantic community decides Middle East policy, therefore, requires breaking down processes taking place in various capitals and institutions.

In theory, the European Union has been building a common foreign and security policy since the 1992 Maastricht Treaty, creating processes for coordination and pooling resources to gain leverage. European countries developed diplomatic tracks, like the earlier-noted Barcelona Process (1995), that gathered countries from the southern and northern shores of the Mediterranean to advance their political dialogue. Through the EU, European countries pooled resources and designed instruments, like the European Neighbourhood Policy (ENP) (2004), to provide financial and technical assistance to countries neighboring Europe to the south and east. The 2008 Lisbon Treaty upgraded the EU, and ENP reforms provided a mandate and instruments to enhance coherence in the relations of Europe with North African states.

The EU's foreign and security policymaking process remains controlled by European nations, not by the institutions of the European Union. The participation of the European Commission (the EU's executive branch) and the European Parliament (the EU's legislative branch) in decisionmaking is limited, mostly to budgetary and treaty-making procedures. Strategic guidelines for the EU as a whole are defined by the European Council (consisting of the heads of states, or heads of governments, of EU countries), and implemented both by the European External Action Service and by national diplomatic services. The president of the European Council and the high representative of the European Union for Foreign Affairs and Security Policy represent the EU in matters of common foreign and security policy.[62]

Accordingly, member states' institutions are driving European foreign policy in the Middle East more than EU institutions. The European Union is not a federation, and that becomes very clear in matters of foreign and security policy. Although EU treaties insist that national and European foreign policies should not contradict each other, in practice this system has allowed member states to maintain their respective individual foreign policies while pursuing bilateral cooperation parallel to EU outreach. And not all member states have had the same level of capabilities, interest, and involvement with respect to discussing and shaping EU policies in North Africa and the Middle East.[63]

The reality is that European involvement in Middle East countries is therefore very fragmented: national policymaking can shape the

European process and vice versa. National decisionmaking continues parallel to EU processes. Depending on the constellation of member states' interests, European meetings can be limited to a loose exchange of positions, may allow for more substantial coordination, or can even determine compulsory steps to be taken by individual nations.

Some national foreign policies have had an increasingly strong European component, as when member states who have taken strong stances against the Syrian regime pushed for European sanctions in 2011. Some member states, like Spain and Germany, have a more Europeanized foreign policy than others. The most Europeanized foreign policies have in some cases abandoned national instruments altogether and chosen to consider only European ones. Thus, the German government's position is to push only for European sanctions and not impose its own national sanctions anymore.

Some policy tools are available at either the national level or the EU level or both. Sanctions, as well as humanitarian and stabilization support, are available both at the national level and through EU entities like the Directorate General for European Civil Protection and Humanitarian Aid Operations for humanitarian assistance, whose financial power makes it a central piece of European soft power within the NGO community and multilateral institutions and on the ground. Hard security tools like intelligence and military instruments, on the other hand, remain at the national level, even if the EU has coordination and expertise resources like the EU military staff and the Joint Situation Centre.

Pooling resources is a goal of EU foreign policy, and the EU has conducted a large number of joint civilian and military missions overseas, including six in the Middle East (Iraq and Palestinian territories) and one in North Africa (Libya).[64] The process of negotiating the mandate of these missions is often a difficult and long one, however, which limits the EU's reactiveness and its ability to launch large operations, as the EU as such has no troops it can directly commit and relies on contributions from member states. In most cases, rapid actions were taken at the national level and through other frameworks (like NATO, in the case of the Libya intervention in 2011), and the EU added its component at a later stage.

The flexibility as well as the complexity of this institutional context are amplified by striking national differences in terms of foreign policy competencies. Thus, the French president has the constitutional power to personally run French foreign policy, whereas the German chancellor may intervene only as a last resort, when the foreign minister, who often comes from a different party within the ruling coalition, has a conflict with another minister. Moreover, though the French parliament only has to be kept regularly informed of foreign policy matters, the German Bundestag has extensive budgetary and thematic oversight with respect to most foreign policy actions. The clearest consequence of these differences is evident in the timing of deployments of troops abroad. So France can deploy troops instantly with a presidential decision (and the parliament just must be informed), while Germany needs first to negotiate a detailed mandate with the Bundestag.

Because of this combination of national and Europe-wide decision-making, combined with various sets of instruments depending on the issue, the European foreign policy process is mostly about building a coalition of countries and launching an institutional response. A key phenomenon in that context has been the growing relevance of the EU-3 (Britain, France, and Germany). The group's role became central after 2003, with the European rift on whether to support the U.S. invasion of Iraq, when foreign ministries and heads of state of the three countries worked together to enable negotiation on the Iranian nuclear issue. The EU-3 eventually became a formal part of the JCPOA but also turned more broadly into an informal driver of European foreign policy, issuing statements on such issues as Syria and Libya.[65] The group closely coordinated with the high representative of the EU, a new position created through and for Javier Solana in 1999 as a first step toward establishing a more coordinated voice. This connection with the high representative survived Solana and became instrumental to connecting the foreign policy positions of Britain, France, and Germany to those of Europe in general, while making sure that other member states would support endeavors like the nuclear deal. Member states like Italy, Poland, and Spain became unhappy with the EU-3 role, however, and this explains why the group remained mostly an informal setting for dialogue and not an official part of EU diplomacy beyond the JCPOA.

In a way, while the U.S. foreign policy decisionmaking process is driven by checks and balances as well as interagency intricacies, European foreign policy is more a matter of which member state leads which foreign policy and which EU instrument it thinks it needs in order to do so. Another defining difference is that the U.S. process is stable but potentially adjusted every four years as a new administration reconsiders the decisions of the previous one, whereas European countries gradually strengthen EU foreign policy when a crisis forces them to.

In this context, the evolution of European foreign policy is often influenced by the U.S decisionmaking process. The lack of European influence on coalition operations during the first Gulf War, for instance, created an additional incentive to forge a European Common Foreign and Security Policy in 1992 under the Maastricht Treaty.[66] The St. Malo declaration of 1998 between Britain and France to develop greater military cooperation in Europe was also an indirect consequence of the frustration of European armies, deployed in the Balkans under U.S. command, who felt they had no control over their operations. These examples shed light on the reflexive nature of transatlantic cooperation in defense and security issues. The EU foreign policy making process is a dynamic one, which has been updated continually based on European reactions to American leadership.

One of the conventional references in the debate regarding transatlantic cooperation is a question attributed to the former U.S. secretary of state Henry Kissinger: "Who do I call if I want to call Europe?" Today, the EU has a phone number, and the U.S. secretary of state can call the EU high representative. But diplomacy today is less like a landline and more like a messaging app through which one connects both with individuals and with diverse groups. As frustrating as this might be, the EU is better described as being a set of WhatsApp groups than anything else.

A Messy Toolkit

A third way to understand the progression of transatlantic cooperation in the Middle East is to analyze the chronology of U.S.-Europe intervention in the Middle East since the end of the Cold War, and the different forms of cooperation evident in these interventions. One can argue from the history of Europeans and Americans acting together that transatlantic cooperation in the region does not always take on the same form or pattern; rather, instruments are combined differently to address each crisis. This section highlights some specific models of transatlantic cooperation: ad hoc military coalitions of the willing, ad hoc multilateralism, bilateral tracks leading to UN Security Council negotiations, and institutional cooperation through NATO or with the EU.

Ad Hoc Coalitions of the Willing: The 1991 Gulf War, the 2003 Iraq War, and the Global War on Terror

Saddam Hussein's invasion of Kuwait sparked the first Middle East crisis that American and European allies had to react to since the end of the Cold War. The United States forged a coalition of thirty-nine countries, which benefited from meaningful buy-in from partner countries and concrete military contributions from European allies, ranging from access to ports and airports to frigates, fighter squadrons, and armored divisions.[67] It was relatively easy for many European countries to rally behind a response to Saddam Hussein's clear violation of international law.

In that sense, Operation Desert Storm was consistent with a model used by the United States beyond the Middle East, in accordance with which Washington has used multilateral rather than unilateral force in eight out of its ten post–Cold War conflicts, despite overwhelming U.S. military superiority.[68] In this model, coalitions provide two key benefits: they confer legitimacy, and they allow for burden sharing. The United States only forgoes these benefits when it perceives that it must act too quickly to form a coalition.

Operation Desert Storm introduced post–Cold War cooperation between the United States and Europe in the Middle East, even if America was leading the international coalition, committing the most troops, and controlling operations. The U.S. Department of Defense estimated that the war cost approximately $61 billion, out of which allies provided $54 billion: the biggest donors included the Arab Gulf states, which contributed roughly $36 billion in total. Germany and Japan covered $16 billion.[69] Though European countries had limited influence over the U.S. agenda in the Gulf and could not shape operational decisions made in Washington, they still had some degree of influence. Some argue, for example, that President Bush's decision not to remove Saddam Hussein from power in 1991 was influenced by a desire to keep the international coalition intact, in part to build momentum for the Madrid Conference in 1991.[70]

The 9/11 attacks pushed the United States to replicate the ad hoc coalition model, and led to a major increase in U.S.-Europe cooperation. Like most European leaders, German chancellor Gerhard Schröder pledged Germany's "unrestricted solidarity to United States President George Bush" following the attacks.[71] In an expression of serious European solidarity, on September 13, 2001, NATO for the first time in its history invoked Article 5 of the founding Washington Treaty, which stipulates that "an armed attack" on one of NATO's European or North American members "shall be considered an attack against them all."[72]

But although transatlantic counterterrorism cooperation increased significantly after 9/11, it was hindered by diverging conceptions of terrorism. Initial counterterrorism cooperation with the United States led to the United States and the EU signing agreements on mutual legal assistance and money laundering.[73] But the United States tended to view terrorism as an external threat that should be dealt with militarily, as exemplified by the "war on terror," while European states tended to conceptualize terrorism primarily as a domestic threat, to be addressed by law enforcement and courts.[74] This position was influenced, in part, by many European countries' long history with domestic terrorism, such as the IRA, Basque separatists, and the ramifications of the Algerian civil war in France. And it may also have been informed by a European understanding that terrorism is a tactic attached to different roots and political goals, not a finite issue that can be stamped out in totality.[75]

European countries quickly grew uncomfortable with an American war on terror conducted as a geopolitical campaign against a number of regimes, rather than regarded as constituting a security issue in itself. French foreign minister Hubert Védrine argued after Bush's "axis of evil" speech that "we are threatened by a simplistic quality in United States policy that reduces all the problems of the world to the struggle against terrorism."[76] The Obama administration did transform the war on terror and was interested in increasing European participation in counterterrorism efforts: President Obama's National Strategy for Counterterrorism stated in June 2011 that, in addition to bilateral cooperation with European allies, "the United States will continue to partner with the European Parliament and European Union to maintain and advance [counterterrorism] efforts that provide mutual security and protection to citizens of all nations while also upholding individual rights."[77]

Beyond counterterrorism cooperation, however, the period of transatlantic cohesion following the September 11 attacks and the Afghan campaign had begun falling apart long before the Obama administration, in the wake of the American invasion of Iraq in 2003. After unanimously supporting the United States in Afghanistan, Europe split into two broad camps on Iraq, led by Britain on one side and Germany and France on the other.

France could not block a U.S. military operation and was reluctant to openly and fully oppose the United States, but it could prevent it from getting a UN mandate, and it used the threat of a Security Council veto to call for a more gradual approach. In trying to keep the United States within the UN framework, and to prevent it from attacking unilaterally, France signaled a willingness to bolster the UN position on Iraq and potentially even support military action if Saddam Hussein continued violating UN resolutions.[78] France and the United States initially overcame their differences and agreed on UN Security Council Resolution 1441 in November 2002, giving Iraq a "final opportunity" to disarm. Disagreements between Paris and Washington reemerged a few months later, however, and France led Security Council efforts to block the U.S.-initiated resolution to clearly authorize the use of force against Iraq.[79] France claimed that there was not sufficient justification for the use of force, as Iraq had fully complied with the UN Monitoring, Verification, and Inspection Commission in charge of disassembling its weapons of mass destruction.[80]

Germany also opposed the American invasion early on. In September 2001, U.S. deputy secretary of defense Paul Wolfowitz warned German foreign minister Joschka Fischer that the Bush administration would eventually shift its focus from Afghanistan to Iraq.[81] Germany consistently voiced its opposition. In May 2002 during a trip to Berlin, President Bush, in part as a response to Germany's participation in the war in Afghanistan, pledged to consult Germany on any decision made on Iraq.[82] The United States did not fulfill this commitment, however. Germany's fears were validated when Vice President Dick Cheney openly called for regime change without reference to the UN, on August 26, 2002.[83] Coinciding with a German election, Gerhard Schröder unilaterally escalated opposition to United States policy with the goal of appealing to the German population, as opposed to rallying support against U.S. policy.[84]

The United States then made an appeal to Central and Eastern European governments to undermine Germany's and France's claims to represent all of Europe.[85] And many Eastern and Central European countries subsequently aligned with the United States in order to bolster their security vis-à-vis a potentially aggressive Russia.[86] The Spanish government was also more focused on strengthening cooperation with Washington than on toppling Saddam Hussein.[87]

The international coalition formed by the United States was therefore less robust than the one assembled for the first Gulf War,[88] and from a legal perspective, it had no UN mandate. The United States and Britain excluded France from the traditional "P-3" policy deliberations at the UN Security Council and accelerated military deployments to the region in preparation for the Iraq invasion.[89] When the United States did invade Iraq, it justified its actions under Security Council Resolution 1441, though Germany and France considered this to be shaky legal ground.[90]

From a coordination perspective, the coalition appeared to be even more unilaterally driven by the United States than the first Gulf War coalition. Washington treated its remaining European allies mostly as rubber stamps. The British government substantively supported the invasion of Iraq but still remained wary of U.S. hegemony, and British officials complained that they were not consulted about the various policy choices made by the United States. British prime minister Tony Blair was chided for finding "it easier to resist the public opinion of Britain than the request of the United States president,"[91] but he maintained that he was not a blind follower of United States policy: He believed that by remaining close to the United States, Britain would be able to influence American policy. Defense Secretary Donald Rumsfeld's comments on March 11, 2003, demonstrated that Blair overestimated both Britain's ability to influence Washington and the importance of Britain's participation.[92] Rumsfeld said, "What will ultimately be decided is unclear as to [Britain's] role in the event that a decision is made to use force,"[93] implying that Britain's participation in the invasion was superfluous.

From a burden-sharing perspective, the 2003 coalition was also weaker than that assembled for the first Gulf War. With many traditional U.S. allies opposing the 2003 invasion of Iraq, the United States looked elsewhere for partners, many of them merely nominal. The United States cobbled together an ad hoc coalition of forty-six countries willing to support the mission, but only three allies—Britain, Australia, and Poland—contributed combat troops. Defense Secretary Donald Rumsfeld insisted that the invasion of Iraq "is not a unilateral action, as is being characterized in the media. Indeed, the coalition in this activity is larger than the coalition that existed during the Gulf War in 1991."[94] But America's coalition of the willing included many countries, such as Micronesia and Palau, that lacked standing armies. The government of the Solomon Islands announced soon after the unveiling of the coalition that they were not aware they were a part of it.[95] The United States could offer development aid, free trade agreements, and support for NATO membership bids in exchange for participation in the coalition, which some dubbed the "coalition of the billing."[96]

As the study of the anti–Islamic State coalition formed in 2014 will later confirm, Washington seemed to favor the "coalition of the willing" model for military interventions. The United States built different forms of coalitions depending on its objectives, but left limited space for European partners to influence policy decisions. According to former senior European officials, American officials mostly built coalitions to secure European support, without giving them a political say extending beyond small gestures. The diplomatic skills of national security advisors like the late Brent Scowcroft allowed him to "politely" manage potential disagreements among partners, but decisions were mostly made by the United States without in-depth consultation with European partners[97]—and actions not fully in line with U.S. options would be severely criticized. From 1991 to 2003 and 2014, this model displays a consistent pattern: the

United States provides most of the hard power, keeps full political and operational control, uses different multilateral institutions (e.g., NATO, the UN) pragmatically to project its own decisions, and favors having a UN mandate but is willing to work without it.

Ad Hoc Multilateralism: Dealing with the Middle East Conflict and the Iran Nuclear Program

The 1990s paved the way for both the U.S. and European roles in the Middle East peace process. These roles were largely complementary, with the United States using its status as a superpower to organize the Madrid process and enforce the Oslo agreements. The Europeans focused on multilateralism to get relevant parties to work together— gradually transforming Yasser Arafat, for example, into a legitimate interlocutor for the West. The United States was seen by all stakeholders as the only real broker, however, and the United States and European countries did not entirely share the same vision for the resolution of the conflict.

The United States focused on creating mutual confidence and strengthening the relationship between the two sides, believing that this would increase the likelihood of an agreement.[98] A key endeavor was to convince the Israeli side that its security interests would not be harmed in the negotiation process—and this was more logically a role for the United States, because it had been more directly and operationally engaged vis-à-vis the security of Israel than had been Europe. Israel has been the largest cumulative recipient of U.S. foreign assistance: Since its founding, the United States has provided Israel with $142.3 billion in bilateral assistance and missile defense funding, a significant part of which has been security assistance.[99] So when it comes to America's policy toward Israel, security cooperation is at the forefront of the discussion. Although bilateral security cooperation between Israel and EU member states exists, Israel's lack of trust prevents Europe from playing as significant a role as the United States in Israeli security affairs.

Europeans have tended to be more focused on the peace process and on the Palestinian issue as the priority in addressing what it sees as the roots of the security threats targeting Israel. Europe focused its efforts on the outcome of the dispute, pushing for a permanent solution, and grew frustrated by the lack of a clear vision for the future in the Oslo Accords.[100] Europeans later developed their own collective corpus of positions on the Middle East peace process: With the 1999 Berlin Council declaration and the 2002 Seville declaration, Europe articulated its belief in a two states solution, based on the end of occupation and the establishment of a Palestinian state on the basis of the 1967 borders.[101] These positions were fueled both by Europe's proximity to Arab countries and by its deepening economic engagement in Middle East peacemaking, as Europe became a key donor to the Palestinian Authority.[102] From 1994 to 2002, the EU's and EU member states' funding to Palestinians reached $5 billion, including grants, loans, and UNRWA support.[103] Ultimately, the EU played a critical role in setting up Palestinian administrations and local authorities, which created frustration on the Israeli side despite the significant deepening of EU-Israel ties in terms of trade or science cooperation. The primacy of national security in Israeli policy led Israel to put more trust in the Americans.

Notwithstanding the different perspectives they had on the resolution of the conflict, Europeans and Americans together designed an ad hoc multilateral format: the Middle East Quartet, comprising the UN secretary-general, the EU, the United States, and Russia, which helped address economic and humanitarian problems. This format helped create a common language for discussion among the Europeans, the United States, and Russia. The peace process is therefore a good example of transatlantic cooperation designed around the dominant role played by the United States, as the European position has in this case not been aligned with that of the United States. Europe could not be decisive in solving the conflict, but the European contribution was nevertheless indispensable in supporting the Palestinian side.

Until the Trump administration, transatlantic cooperation on the peace process had been premised on the parameters defined by the UN Security Council, referred to as the "land for peace" formula and described primarily in Security Council Resolutions 242 (1967) and 338 (1973).[104] The United States had to use its veto right on fourteen occasions[105] between 1990 and 2016 to block Security Council resolutions considered detrimental to Israel. Despite this, Europeans and Americans have still managed to work together on numerous issues since the end of the Cold War to protect the idea of two states—for example, through Security Council Resolution 1397 (2002), and via affirmation of the Quartet's 2003 Roadmap peace initiative (endorsed in UNSC Resolution 1515).[106]

The cooperation between the United States and Europe to contain the Iranian nuclear program provides another good example of a semi-multilateral process built on complementarity. A high point in transatlantic relations was indeed the signing of the Joint Comprehensive Plan of Action (JCPOA) in 2015. Creating the agreement took years of proposals and negotiations; the various steps to agreement provide an example of a different dynamic, wherein transatlantic partners agreed on the strategic counterproliferation goal but diverged in method and tactic.

The discussions started as a European initiative, with the Europeans aware that the United States and Iran ultimately had to be seated at the same table. So in this case, the United States was not leading in devising a format or creating a coalition, but rather reacting to European initiatives. Europe was both a mediator with economic leverage and, on account of France and Britain, a smaller but still important player with respect to nuclear military technology and counterproliferation. London and Paris could therefore rely on deep technical and legal knowledge and could also join forces with

Germany to create economic incentives. These elements were key to creating a negotiating space.

Starting in 2003, Iran agreed to a deal with European foreign ministers to suspend its uranium enrichment activities after an International Atomic Energy Agency resolution calling for this. Iran did not cooperate with IAEA inspectors; but in 2004, it agreed to suspend the program for the duration of talks with France, Germany, and Britain. But these negotiations were stopped in 2005, when Iran began producing uranium hexafluoride.

In February 2006, the IAEA referred Iran to the UN Security Council. In April, Iran announced it had started enriching uranium for the first time. Two months later, the P5+1 (China, France, Russia, Britain, and the United States, plus Germany) proposed a framework agreement to Iran that included incentives to halt its enrichment program.[107]

The United States and the EU-3 started with divergent tactics: Washington favored isolating the Tehran regime, while the EU-3 preferred starting with negotiations and carrots, such as the incentive of closer bilateral ties.[108] Many in the Bush administration were also interested in regime change, but several conditions made the military option unattractive: The United States was already bogged down in Iraq and Afghanistan; Iran was much bigger than Iraq; America had fewer allies willing to strike Iran than they would Iraq; and Iranian nuclear sites were well dispersed and concealed.[109]

In the second Bush administration, Secretary of State Condoleezza Rice began wielding more power: she tilted U.S. foreign policy toward alliance building and increased pragmatism. The United States looked for ways to heal the rift from the Iraq invasion and realized that involving the United Nations Security Council could be effective in pressuring Iran to reveal details of its nuclear program, policies, and intentions, especially since the IAEA Board of Governors had also referred the issue to the UN Security Council. Additionally, if Iran refused U.S. incentives, U.S. sanctions might gain more international support. Under these conditions, the Bush administration broke with nearly three decades of policy and joined talks between Europe and Iran in early 2006.

The United States offered proposals to incentivize Iran to take the negotiations seriously. Washington controlled virtually all the incentives Tehran cared about and possessed a more credible threat of the use of force than Europe did. Yet U.S. participation in the talks moved America toward the European position. For its part, the EU-3 continued to rely on the goodwill of the United States and Iran simultaneously; but U.S.-Iran divergence left little room for the Europeans to mediate. From 2006 onward, Europe has acted as more of a party to the nuclear conflict than as an arbiter between Washington and Tehran.[110]

The convergence of U.S. and European strategy on Iran in 2006 involved a European shift as much as it did an American one: Europe called for Iran to give up uranium enrichment as a precursor to the talks. In addition, the EU-3 agreed that, if Iran refused that precondition, it would impose sanctions. Tehran did refuse the ultimatum to halt enrichment within a month, and the EU agreed to UN sanctions on Iran.[111]

This resulted in the UN Security Council adopting Resolution 1696, legally requiring that Iran halt its uranium enrichment. Iran responded that the resolution had "elements which may be useful for a constructive approach,"[112] but objected to the limits on enrichment. The UN Security Council then adopted Resolutions 1737, 1747, and 1803, levying sanctions against Iran. From 2010 to 2012, Europe and the United States sanctioned Iran more and more, but starting in 2012, talks began for what would become the JCPOA. Through a secret channel in Oman, the United States and Iran negotiated for months in 2013 the first draft of a deal to halt the Iranian nuclear program in exchange for sanctions relief.

The final agreement was negotiated with the P5+1. It built on the Geneva agreement that went into effect in January 2014, wherein Iran agreed to limit its nuclear program in exchange for relief from sanctions.

The JCPOA went further, including setting limits on uranium enrichment and agreeing to inspections from the IAEA in return for the lifting of many of the sanctions imposed by the UN, the United States, and the EU. Despite the frustration created by the secret negotiations organized in Oman, the entire endeavor was a moment of collaboration between Europe and the United States, as they worked together to create a deal to address the proliferation crisis.

Both the Middle East peace process and the nuclear negotiations relied on the same cocktail: U.S. hard power to pressure and negotiate; European soft power to provide expertise, mediate, and offer economic incentives; and transatlantic dialogue to design UN resolutions. Both also relied on the creation of an ad hoc multilateral format (EU3+3 and the Quartet) working on the basis of UN Security Council resolutions (242, 338) or providing the substance for new ones (1397, 1515, 1737, 1747, 1803).

Expelling Syria from Lebanon: From a Bilateral Track to the UN Security Council

U.S.-France cooperation in Lebanon in the early 2000s serves as a clear example of a bilateral dialogue becoming effective cooperation at the multilateral level, with major geopolitical significance. In this case, transatlantic cooperation led to UN Security Council Resolution 1559 and the withdrawal of Syrian forces from Lebanon.

Syrian interference in Lebanon provided the United States and France with an opportunity to repair their relationship vis-à-vis the Middle East after tensions surrounding the invasion of Iraq in 2003. Increased U.S.-France cooperation in Lebanon began as their positions converged over the Israeli withdrawal from southern Lebanon in 2000. Though Israel withdrew to the UN-demarcated line, Lebanon held that the withdrawal was incomplete, as Israel continued to occupy Shebaa Farms.[113] Both France and the United States grew frustrated by Lebanon's insistence and believed that Syrian hegemony was to blame for their position. By 2003–4, this frustration led the two countries to reexamine their previous acquiescence to Syrian influence in Lebanon.[114]

Though both the United States and France favored a Lebanon free from Syrian influence, France was initially more conciliatory toward Damascus until 2004. French president Jacques Chirac had tried to engage Bashar al-Assad when he came to power in 2000. Assad's insistence on extending Lebanese president Emile Lahoud's term, however, and his harassment of Rafiq Hariri, a personal friend of Chirac, drove France to change its policy and take a harder line against Syria in Lebanon. This hardening aligned France with the United States.

In January 2004, the White House senior director for Near East and North African Affairs asked the French government to send Damascus "a strongly worded United States message regarding Syrian presence in Lebanon" after meeting with the French chargé d'affaires in Washington.[115] Chirac and Bush discussed Syrian hegemony in Lebanon during the commemoration in summer 2004 of the sixtieth anniversary of the Allied landing at Normandy,[116] and by the end of that year, France and America had converged on goals and strategies.

In a 2005 interview published in *Le Figaro*, President Bush said that France and the United States "have an important opportunity to work for democracy in the greater Middle East and in Lebanon. This is a region where we have shared concerns. President Chirac raised the idea of a resolution in the Security Council to tell the Syrians that they have to leave Lebanon. And resolution 1559 became a reality."[117] At France's suggestion, the United States and France jointly introduced Resolution 1559 at the Security Council, where it was additionally supported by Britain and Germany.[118] Other European countries may have supported the resolution to capitalize on a moment of transatlantic cooperation, rather than in support of its content. One German legislator commented, "It was important that the French and the Americans were at least working through the Security Council, so why shouldn't we support it?"[119]

The resolution called for the withdrawal of foreign troops, the disbanding of militias, and respect for Lebanese sovereignty.[120] Rafiq Hariri distanced himself from Syria and was assassinated on February 14, 2005. The resolution, along with suspicion that the Syrian regime was behind the assassination and international support for a large anti-Syrian protest in Lebanon, forced Syria to begin withdrawing troops from the country. The United States and France continued to cooperate after the passage of the resolution to support anti-Syrian political movements within Lebanon,[121] and French-American cooperation persisted after the assassination of Hariri. On February 22, 2005, Chirac and Bush issued a joint statement declaring that France and the United States "have the same approach to Lebanon, especially following the murder of former Prime Minister Hariri, who enshrined the ideals of democracy, independence, and liberty of that country."[122] France and the United States then passed a series of UN Security Council resolutions aimed at creating a framework to investigate Hariri's assassination.[123]

Other forms of cooperation have also relied on bilateral relationships, but this example displays an extensive level of coordination between the United States and one specific European country, based on that country's special legacy in the Middle East (and in Lebanon in particular). While the positions of the two countries were initially different, the evolution of the situation on the ground along with intensive work at different levels (locally, between capitals, and between heads of state themselves) created a powerful dynamic to shape UN resolutions and ultimately support a local mobilization and bring about significant change.

Institutional Cooperation: NATO in the Middle East

The role that NATO should play in the Middle East, and whether it should play any role at all, has always been a topic of debate. After the end of the Cold War, NATO's future was uncertain, as it was unclear whether it had a purpose beyond combatting the Soviet Union. Given

Arab public opinion's hostility to "American imperialism," NATO was also perceived in Europe as the wrong political vehicle for action despite its operational assets and mechanisms. NATO's membership continued to grow, however, including new democracies that emerged from the Soviet Union.

Southern European countries such as Italy, Spain, Greece, and Portugal also had an interest in strengthening the "southern flank" of the Alliance, and pushed at the NATO Joint Force Command in Naples for the launch of several initiatives for cooperation or dialogue with the southern shore of the Mediterranean.[124] A limited Mediterranean dialogue was initiated in 1994 to offer training and know-how. NATO developed a stable presence in the Mediterranean through its Standing Naval Force Mediterranean (STANAVFORMED), with destroyers and frigates provided by Germany, Greece, Italy, the Netherlands, Spain, Turkey, Britain, and the United States; joint air and naval exercises are carried out regularly. It remained clear, however, that the eastern flank remained the primary focus of the alliance.[125]

NATO's role expanded in part because many European countries wanted a security partnership with the United States. The comparatively smaller defense budgets of many European nations, along with fears on the part of smaller European states of being dominated by larger ones in an EU defense force, also contributed to European support for NATO. For its part and especially after the Iraq war, the United States realized that allies fostered legitimacy and mitigated the military burden, and so had an interest in NATO as well.[126] As NATO grew, the role that it played in the Middle East grew as well, although the nature of that role varied greatly. NATO's missions have ranged from deploying troops to Afghanistan to creating a chemical, biological, radiological, and nuclear (CBRN) response team to prepare for weapons of mass destruction.

Despite NATO's limited footprint in the Middle East, divisions among allies regarding Middle East issues have impacted the organization. The transatlantic rift over Iraq in 2003, for instance, hurt NATO. In

2002, the United States requested NATO to consider a preventative plan to defend Turkey in the case of an Iraqi retaliation; France, Germany, and Belgium resisted, arguing that accepting this plan would confirm the inevitability of war with Iraq. The dispute was eventually resolved, but only after a three-month standoff and resort to a committee in which France was not represented because of its decision to leave the NATO military command in the 1960s.[127] Overall, the Iraq war caused deep rifts in both transatlantic and intra-European relations. Europe learned from the war that most member states were ready to break unity if their bilateral relationship with the United States was at stake. Meanwhile, the war reinforced Washington's notion that ad hoc coalitions might be the best mechanism to use in future crises.[128]

One example of the way that NATO has been used in the Middle East is its military training mission in Iraq. In the early 2000s, the Bush administration clashed with the Europeans over his approach in Iraq. But in June 2004, NATO allies agreed to help train Iraqi military forces, creating the framework for the NATO Training Mission and Joint Staff College near Baghdad. The training mission was established at the Iraqi interim government's request, and in response, many countries agreed to send forces to contribute to the mission. In fact, at a NATO meeting on February 22, 2005, all twenty-six NATO members agreed to contribute financing, troops, or equipment to the mission. But six members (France, Greece, Spain, Belgium, Luxembourg, and Germany) refused to pledge forces, much to the frustration of the United States.[129] At a news conference, Secretary of State Colin Powell remarked, "When it comes time to perform a mission, it seems to us to be quite awkward for suddenly members in that international staff to say, 'I'm unable to go because of this national caveat or national exception.'"[130]

Those six countries refused to send troops over concerns that the training mission could turn into a combat mission, which they were especially wary of after the invasion of Iraq. The reluctance of Germany to send troops was especially problematic, as Germany at the time accounted for a significant portion of the officers in NATO's international command staff.[131] But the Germans held fast to their position. This highlights one of the major shortcomings of NATO, as the reluctance of individual member states to participate in a mission owing to domestic opposition or other concerns limits the organization's effectiveness and reach. NATO's first deployment to Iraq—a small contingent of well under a hundred advisors—ended in 2011 when U.S. forces withdrew. During that period, the mission trained over five thousand Iraqi military personnel and several thousand police.

Transatlantic cooperation in the Middle East since the Cold War reveals a pattern of pragmatic use of institutions depending on foreign policy goals largely set by the United States. This cooperation has thus not been developed through a well-established U.S.-Europe framework devised to address the region; it is more about groping than relying on tools specifically intended for the Middle East. This pattern is consistent with a broader tendency in international relations since the Cold War, according to which Western actors have "cannibalized" existing frameworks to achieve goals not fully consistent with the frameworks' initial aims.[132]

Western reactions to the Arab Spring demonstrate that, over time, the tools available for transatlantic collaboration have evolved depending on America's fatigue in the region, as well as on the trauma among European allies and in the region regarding external military intervention. This legacy will appear clearly in the case studies highlighted in the next chapter of this book.

Notes

1   Daniel Möckli and Victor Mauer, *European-American Relations and the Middle East: From Suez to Iraq*, CSS Studies in Security and International Relations (London: Routledge, 2011), 1–2.

2   Antoine Vagneur-Jones, *Global Britain in the Gulf: Brexit and Relations with the GCC* (Paris: Fondation pour la Recherche Strategique, 2017), https://www.frstrategie.org/sites/default/files/documents/publications/notes/2017/201713.pdf.

3   Malak Harb, "UK Opens Persian Gulf Military Base in Bahrain," Associated Press, April 5, 2018, https://apnews.com/article/403eea90b7054edaa978c0e51fd182c4.

4   "British Armed Forces Minister Bolsters UK-Egypt Defence Ties," gov.uk, June 13, 2019, https://www.gov.uk/government/news/british-armed-forces-minister-bolsters-uk-egypt-defence-ties.

5   "This expression refers not only to the region washed by the historic Mare Nostrum, but also the Maghreb and Sahel, the Horn of Africa and the Middle East between the Persian Gulf, the Black Sea and the Caspian Sea." Alessandro Marrone, *Security Policy in the Southern Neighbourhood* (Rome: Friedrich Ebert Stiftung, 2020), 2, available at http://library.fes.de/pdf-files/bueros/rom/16768-20200421.pdf.

6   Eduard Soler i Lecha and Pol Morillas, *Middle Power with Maghreb Focus: A Spanish Perspective on Security Policy in the Southern Neighborhood* (Berlin: Friedrich Ebert Stiftung, 2020), available at http://library.fes.de/pdf-files/id/ipa/16307-20200722.pdf.

7   Maria Algora and Dolores Weber, "España en el Mediterráneo: Entre las Relaciones Hispano-Arabes y el Reconocimiento del Estado de Israel," *Revista CIDOB d'Afers Internacionals* (2017), 15–34, available at https://www.raco.cat/index.php/RevistaCIDOB/article/view/86661/111675.

8   Eastern European diplomat, interview by author, Washington DC, September 2020.

9   Vagneur-Jones, *Global Britain in the Gulf*.

10 "Egypt: Foreign Investment," Santander Trade, https://santandertrade.com/en/portal/establish-overseas/egypt/foreign-investment.

11 "Jeffrey Donaldson, UK Trade Envoy to Egypt: Interview," Oxford Business Group, https://oxfordbusinessgroup.com/interview/ strengthening-ties-jeffrey-donaldson-uk-trade-envoy-egypt-uk-egypt-trade-relations-and-building.

12 Eduard Soler i Lecha, senior research fellow at Barcelona Centre for International Affairs, interview by author, August 10, 2020.

13 Soler i Lecha and Morillas, *Middle Power with Maghreb Focus*, 7, available at http://library.fes.de/pdf-files/id/ipa/16307-20200722.pdf.

14 At the initial meeting in 1995, the following members were present and agreed to the Barcelona Declaration:
    • The fifteen EU member states at the time: Austria, Belgium, Denmark, Germany, Finland, France, Greece, Ireland, Italy, Luxembourg, Netherlands, Portugal, the United Kingdom, Spain, and Sweden;
    • Five non-EU member states at the time: Croatia, Cyprus, Macedonia, Malta, and Turkey;
    • Nine governments from the wider Mediterranean region: Algeria, Egypt, Israel, Jordan, Lebanon, Morocco, Syria, Tunisia, and the Palestinian Authority; and
    • Representatives from two European institutions: the Council of the European Union and the European Commission.

15 Soler i Lecha and Morillas, *Middle Power with Maghreb Focus*, http:// library.fes.de/pdf-files/id/ipa/16307-20200722.pdf.

16 "2019: ACS 1-Year Estimates Detailed Tables for People Reporting Ancestry," American Community Survey, retrieved June 3, 2021, https://data.census.gov/cedsci/table?q=%22TOTAL%20 ANCESTRY%20REPORTED%22&tid=ACSDT1Y2019.B04006.

17 Abby Budiman et al., "Facts on U.S. Immigrants, 2018," Pew Research Center, August 20, 2020, https://www.pewresearch.org/ hispanic/2020/08/20/facts-on-u-s-immigrants-current-data/.

18 "L'essentiel sur…les Immigrés et les Étrangers," *Insee*; "Descendants d'Immigrés par Pays d'Origine," Institut National d'Études Démographiques, https://www.insee.fr/fr/statistiques/3633212.

19 "How Syrians Are Reshaping German Society," *Der Spiegel*, July 23, 2020, https://www.spiegel.de/international/germany/

how-syrians-are-reshaping-german-society-a-cc336157-d244-493e-abeb-6f51db4d6a0f.

20   Henry Peck and Alex Walsh, "The Future of the UK's Relationship with the Maghreb," Middle East Institute, January 6, 2020, https://www.mei.edu/publications/future-uks-relationship-maghreb.

21   "Strengthening European Autonomy Across MENA," in *Mapping European Leverage in the MENA Region*, European Council on Foreign Relations, November 2019, https://www.ecfr.eu/special/mapping_eu_leverage_mena/.

22   "Egypt," European Commission Directorate-General for Trade, April 23, 2020, https://ec.europa.eu/trade/policy/countries-and-regions/countries/egypt/.

23   Soler i Lecha and Morillas, *Middle Power with Maghreb Focus*, 9, available at http://library.fes.de/pdf-files/id/ipa/16307-20200722.pdf.

24   Marrone, *Security Policy*, 4, available at http://library.fes.de/pdf-files/bueros/rom/16768-20200421.pdf.

25   Pieter D. Wezeman, Alexander Kuimova, and Siemon T. Wezeman, *Trends in International Arms Transfers, 2020* (Solna: Stockholm International Peace Research Institute, 2021), 6, https://sipri.org/sites/default/files/2021-03/fs_2103_at_2020.pdf.

26   Ibid., 11.

27   Jeremy Shapiro, "United States," in *Mapping European Leverage in MENA*, European Council on Foreign Relations, December 2019, https://www.ecfr.eu/specials/mapping_eu_leverage_mena/united_states.

28   Marrone, *Security Policy*, 7, available at http://library.fes.de/pdf-files/bueros/rom/16768-20200421.pdf.

29   European diplomat, private discussion with author, 2016.

30   "Strengthening European Autonomy," https://www.ecfr.eu/specials/mapping_eu_leverage_mena/.

31   "Conduct of the Persian Gulf War," final report to Congress, April 1992, 136, available at https://www.globalsecurity.org/military/library/report/1992/cpgw.pdf.

32   Amy Belasco, *Troop Levels in the Afghan and Iraq Wars, FY2001–FY2012: Cost and Other Potential Issues* (Congressional Research

Service, July 2009), 36, 64, https://fas.org/sgp/crs/natsec/R40682.pdf.

33 Army Posture Statement, 2009, https://www.army.mil/e2/downloads/
rv7/aps/aps_2009.pdf; some 30,000 U.S. troops are stationed in the
Gulf as of 2020. For an updated map of U.S. troop levels, see Tom
O'Connor, "Where Are U.S. Troops near Iran?" *Newsweek*, January 6,
2020, https://www.newsweek.com/where-us-troops-near-iran-1480617.

34 Justin Vaïsse, "Le Passé d'un Oxymore: Le Débat
Français de Politique Étrangère," *Esprit Presse*, November
2017, https://esprit.presse.fr/article/justin-vaisse/
le-passe-d-un-oxymore-le-debat-francais-de-politique-etrangere-39714.

35 Bastian Giegerich and William Wallace, "Not Such a Soft Power: The
External Deployment of European Forces," *Survival* 46, no. 2 (Summer
2004): 163–82.

36 Danilo di Mauro, Ulrich Krotz, and Katerina Wright, principal
investigators, "EU's Global Engagement: A Database of CSDP Military
Operations and Civilian Missions; Worldwide Version 2.0," Ann Arbor,
Mich., Inter-university Consortium for Political and Social Research,
2017, https://doi.org/10.3886/E100218V3.

37 Marrone, *Security Policy*, 4, available at http://library.fes.de/pdf-files/
bueros/rom/16768-20200421.pdf.

38 See Renata Dwan and Zdzislaw Lachowski, "The Military and
Security Dimensions of the European Union," in *SIPRI Yearbook 2003:
Armaments, Disarmament and International Security* (Oxford: Oxford
University Press, 2003), 9.

39 Shapiro, "United States," https://www.ecfr.eu/specials/
mapping_eu_leverage_mena/united_states.

40 Fabrice Pothier and Alexander Vershbow, *NATO and Trump: The Case
for a New Transatlantic Bargain* (Washington DC: Atlantic Council,
2017), https://espas.secure.europarl.europa.eu/orbis/sites/default/files/
generated/document/en/NATO_and_Trump_web_0623.pdf.

41 Gerd Nonneman, "Iran and the Bomb: Washington, the EU, and
Iranian Nuclear Ambitions," in *European-American Relations and the
Middle East: From Suez to Iraq*, ed. Daniel Möckli and Victor Mauer
(London: Routledge, 2011), pp. 203–20, esp. 208.

42 Ibid., 209.

43   Dwan and Lachowski, "The Military and Security Dimensions," 9, https://www.sipri.org/ sites/default/files/213-236%20Chapter6.pdf.

44   Jenna Johnson, "Trump on NATO: 'I Said It Was Obsolete. It's No Longer Obsolete,'" *Washington Post*, April 12, 2017, https:// www.washingtonpost.com/news/post-politics/wp/2017/04/12/ trump-on-nato-i-said-it-was-obsolete-its-no-longer-obsolete/.

45   Mike Pompeo, "A Force for Good: America Reinvigorated in the Middle East," U.S. Department of State, January 10, 2019, https://www. state.gov/a-force-for-good-america-reinvigorated-in-the-middle-east/.

46   Aaron Mehta and Joe Gould, "Trump Wants NATO to Be More Involved in the Middle East. That May Take Some Convincing," *Defense News*, January 8, 2020, https://www.defensenews.com/smr/ nato-2020-defined/2020/01/08/trump-wants-nato-to-be-more-involved-in-the-middle-east-that-may-take-some-convincing/.

47   See response from Erik Brattberg in Judy Dempsey, "Judy Asks: Should NATO Stay Away from the Middle East?" Carnegie Europe, January 2020, https://carnegieeurope.eu/strategiceurope/80815.

48   Ibid.

49   U.S. Congress, "Public Law 107–40," September 18, 2001, https://www. congress.gov/107/plaws/publ40/PLAW-107publ40.pdf.

50   Cory Gill, Marian Lawson, and Emily Morgenstern, *Department of State, Foreign Operations, and Related Programs: FY2020 Budget and Appropriations* (Congressional Research Service, updated March 2020), https://fas.org/sgp/crs/row/R45763.pdf.

51   "Foreign Assistance Legislation: The Authorization and Appropriation Process," Arab Center Washington DC, http://arabcenterdc.org/ congressional_corner/foreign-assistance-legislation-the-authorization-and-appropriation-process/.

52   "Foreign Relations Reauthorization: Background and Issues," Congressional Research Service, June 27, 2019, https://crsreports. congress.gov/product/pdf/IF/IF10293.

53   Jonathan Masters, "U.S. Foreign Policy Powers: Congress and the President," Council on Foreign Relations, March 2, 2017, https://www.cfr. org/backgrounder/us-foreign-policy-powers-congress-and-president.

54   "How U.S. Foreign Policy Is Made," Foreign Policy Association, https://www.fpa.org/features/index.cfm?act=feature.

55   Bolko Skorupski and Nina Serafino, *DOD Security Cooperation: An Overview of Authorities and Issues* (Congressional Research Service, August 2016), https://fas.org/sgp/crs/natsec/R44602.pdf.

56   Former U.S. official, interview by author, March 2020.

57   U.S. diplomat, interview by author, August 2020.

58   Dennis Ross, interview by author, on June 10, 2020. Among other roles, Ross served as the director of policy planning in the State Department under President George H. W. Bush, the special Middle East coordinator under President Bill Clinton, and a special advisor for the Persian Gulf and Southwest Asia for Secretary of State Hillary Clinton.

59   Ben Fishman, interview by author, April 27, 2020. From 2009 to 2013, Fishman served on the National Security Council, where he held several posts, including executive assistant to Ambassador Dennis Ross; director for Libya, wherein he coordinated U.S. support for Libya's revolution; and later director for North Africa and Jordan.

60   Former U.S. official, interview by author, June 2021.

61   Stefano Recchia, *Reassuring the Reluctant Warriors: U.S. Civil-Military Relations and Multilateral Intervention* (Ithaca, NY: Cornell University Press, 2015).

62   "Division of Competences Within the European Union," EUR-Lex, January 26, 2016, https://eur-lex.europa.eu/legal-content/EN/TXT/?uri=LEGISSUM%3Aai0020.

63   Tom Delreux and Stephan Keukeleire, "Informal Division of Labour in EU Foreign Policy-Making," *Journal of European Public Policy* 24, no. 10 (2017): 1471–90.

64   "Military and Civilian Missions and Operations," European Union External Action Service, March 5, 2019, https://eeas.europa.eu/headquarters/headquarters-homepage/430/military-and-civilian-missions-and-operations_en.

65   Erik Brattberg, "The E3, the EU, and the Post-Brexit Diplomatic Landscape," Carnegie Endowment for International Peace, June 18, 2020, https://carnegieendowment.org/2020/06/18/e3-eu-and-post-brexit-diplomatic-landscape-pub-82095.

66   Nonneman, "Iran and the Bomb," 208.

67   "Conduct of the Persian Gulf War," available at https://www.
     globalsecurity.org/military/library/report/1992/cpgw.pdf.

68   Sarah E. Kreps, *Coalitions of Convenience: United States Military
     Interventions After the Cold War*, 1st ed. (New York: Oxford University
     Press, 2001).

69   "Gulf War Fast Facts," CNN, July 29, 2020, https://www.cnn.
     com/2013/09/15/world/meast/gulf-war-fast-facts/index.html.

70   Möckli and Mauer, *European-American Relations and the Middle East*, 29.

71   Ibid., 34.

72   Suzanne Daley, "For First Time, NATO Invokes Joint Defense Pact
     with U.S.," *New York Times*, September 13, 2001, https://www.nytimes.
     com/2001/09/13/us/after-attacks-alliance-for-first-time-nato-invokes-
     joint-defense-pact-with-us.html. The NATO treaty text is available at
     https://www.nato.int/cps/en/natohq/official_texts_17120.htm.

73   Stefan Fröhlich, *The New Geopolitics of Transatlantic Relations:
     Coordinated Responses to Common Dangers* (Washington DC:
     Woodrow Wilson Center Press, 2012), 22.

74   Marc Smyrl, "European Anti-Terrorism Policy: A Trans-Atlantic
     Perspective," *Politique Européenne* 23, no. 3 (2007): 115–32, https://doi.
     org/10.3917/poeu.023.0115.

75   Ibid.

76   "Analysis: Iran and the 'Axis of Evil,'" BBC, February 11, 2002, http://
     news.bbc.co.uk/2/hi/middle_east/1814659.stm.

77   Kristin Archick, *U.S.-EU Cooperation Against Terrorism* (Congressional
     Research Service, December 2014), 6, https://fas.org/sgp/crs/row/
     RS22030.pdf.

78   Möckli and Mauer, *European-American Relations and the Middle East*, 35.

79   Sami E. Baroudi and Imad Salamey, "U.S.-French Collaboration
     on Lebanon: How Syria's Role in Lebanon and the Middle East
     Contributed to a U.S.-French Convergence," *Middle East Journal* 65, no.
     3 (2011): 398–425, esp. 400, https://doi.org/10.3751/65.3.13.

80   Ibid., 400.

81   Möckli and Mauer, *European-American Relations and the Middle East*, 34.

82   Ibid.

83 Ibid., 35.

84 Ibid.

85 Ibid., 33.

86 Ibid., 34.

87 Soler i Lecha and Morillas, *Middle Power with Maghreb Focus*, 10, available at http://library.fes.de/pdf-files/id/ipa/16307-20200722.pdf.

88 Baroudi and Salamey, "U.S.-French Collaboration on Lebanon," 401.

89 Möckli and Mauer, *European-American Relations and the Middle East*, 35.

90 Baroudi and Salamey, "U.S.-French Collaboration on Lebanon," 401.

91 Möckli and Mauer, *European-American Relations and the Middle East*, 32.

92 Ibid., 33.

93 Paul Waugh and Mary Dejevsky, "Rumsfeld: U.S. May Have to Launch War Without Britain," *Independent*, December 12, 2003, https://www.independent.co.uk/news/world/politics/rumsfeld-us-may-have-to-launch-war-without-britain-122420.html.

94 Ivo Daalder, "The Coalition That Isn't," Brookings Institution, March 24, 2003, https://www.brookings.edu/opinions/the-coalition-that-isnt/.

95 Alan Perrott, "Coalition of the Willing? Not Us, Say Solomon Islanders," *New Zealand Herald*, March 27, 2003, https://www.nzherald.co.nz/world/coalition-of-the-willing-not-us-say-solomon-islanders/MV6BQNXTQHY2UXEKTAY5VLVJQ4/.

96 Laura McClure, "Coalition of the Billing—or Unwilling?" *Salon*, March 13, 2003, https://www.salon.com/2003/03/12/foreign_aid/.

97 Former European senior official, interview by author, March 2020.

98 Patrick Clawson, "U.S. and European Priorities in the Middle East," in *Shift or Rift: Assessing U.S.-EU Relations After Iraq*, ed. Gustav Lindstrom (Paris: EU Institute for Security Studies, 2003), 127–45, https://www.iss.europa.eu/sites/default/files/EUISSFiles/bk2003_01.pdf.

99 Jeremy Sharp, *U.S. Foreign Aid to Israel* (Congressional Research Service, November 2020), https://fas.org/sgp/crs/mideast/RL33222.pdf.

100 Clawson, "U.S. and European Priorities," https://www.iss.europa.eu/sites/default/files/EUISSFiles/bk2003_01.pdf.

101 Stephan Keukeleire and Jennifer G. MacNaughtan, *Foreign Policy of the European Union* (Basingstoke: Palgrave Macmillan, 2018), 283.

102 Möckli and Mauer, *European-American Relations and the Middle East*, 108.

103 Keukeleire and MacNaughtan, *Foreign Policy of the European Union*, 283. UNRWA refers to the UN Relief and Works Agency for Palestine Refugees in the Near East.

104 UN Security Council Resolution 242 is available here, http://undocs.org/S/RES/242(1967)

105 "Security Council—Veto List," United Nations, https://research.un.org/en/docs/sc/quick.

106 "The Question of Palestine and the Security Council," United Nations, accessed November 18, 2020, https://www.un.org/unispal/data-collection/security-council/.

107 "Timeline of Nuclear Diplomacy with Iran," Arms Control Association, September 2020, https://www.armscontrol.org/factsheets/Timeline-of-Nuclear-Diplomacy-With-Iran.

108 Harsh V. Pant, "Conclusion: Major Trends in European-American Relations and the Middle East," in *European-American Relations and the Middle East*, ed. Möckli and Mauer, 220–35, esp. 224.

109 Ibid., 229.

110 Ibid., 226.

111 Ibid., 230.

112 "Timeline of Nuclear Diplomacy," https://www.armscontrol.org/factsheets/Timeline-of-Nuclear-Diplomacy-With-Iran.

113 Baroudi and Salamey, "U.S.-French Collaboration on Lebanon," 402.

114 Ibid.

115 Ibid., 404.

116 Baroudi and Salamey, "U.S.-French Collaboration on Lebanon," 404.

117 Lara Marlowe, "Syria High on Agenda for Chirac Talks," *Irish Times*, February 21, 2005, https://www.irishtimes.com/news/syria-high-on-agenda-for-chirac-talks-1.416903.

118 Manuela Paraipan, "UN Resolution 1559 in Perspective," World Security Network, July 25, 2005, http://www.worldsecuritynetwork.com/Broader-Middle-East/manuela-paraipan/UN-Resolution-1559-in-Perspective.

119 Philip H. Gordon et al., "Syria and Lebanon: A U.S. Perspective," in *Crescent of Crisis: U.S.-European Strategy for the Greater Middle East* (Washington DC: Brookings Institution Press, 2005), 86.

120 Baroudi and Salamey, "U.S.-French Collaboration on Lebanon," 404.

121 Ibid., 407.

122 Ibid.

123 Ibid., 408.

124 Marrone, *Security Policy*, 7, available at http://library.fes.de/pdf-files/bueros/rom/16768-20200421.pdf.

125 Constantinos Filis, *Troubled Waters in the Eastern Mediterranean? A Greek Perspective on Security Policy in the Southern Neighbourhood* (Berlin: Friedrich Ebert Stiftung, 2020), 4, available at http://library.fes.de/pdf-files/id/ipa/16306.pdf.

126 Philip Gordon, "NATO's Growing Role in the Greater Middle East," lecture, Emirates Center for Strategic Studies and Research, 2006, https://www.brookings.edu/wp-content/uploads/2016/06/emirates20060530.pdf.

127 Philip H. Gordon, "The Crisis in the Alliance," Brookings Institution, February 24, 2003. https://www.brookings.edu/research/the-crisis-in-the-alliance/.

128 Möckli and Mauer, *European-American Relations and the Middle East*, 237.

129 Jeremy Sharp, *Post-War Iraq: Foreign Contributions to Training, Peacekeeping, and Reconstruction* (Congressional Research Service, September 2007), https://fas.org/sgp/crs/mideast/RL32105.pdf.

130 Joel Brinkley, "NATO Agrees to Expansion of Forces Training Soldiers in Iraq," *New York Times*, December 10, 2004, https://www.nytimes.com/2004/12/10/world/europe/nato-agrees-to-expansion-of-forces-training-soldiers-in-iraq.html.

131 Ibid.

132 Olivier Schmitt, interview by author, August 27, 2020.

2

The Arab Uprisings, U.S. Fatigue, and the Vanishing West, 2011–21

The Arab uprisings have reshaped local and regional politics until today (see figure 2.1 for a depiction of the protests). The year 2011 also opened a new phase in the three-way relationship between the Arab world, Europe, and the United States. That year marked the official withdrawal of U.S. troops from Iraq, eight years after the military campaign that came to be regarded as the paradigm of America's "unipolar" overreach in the region. Additionally, 2011 was the year the European Union was supposed to renew its Neighbourhood Policy, a toolkit for assistance and cooperation projects in the Mediterranean and the Caucasus. Following major changes in the European foreign policy framework with the Lisbon Treaty in 2009, the goal was now to make the ENP less technocratic and more values-based.

The Western response since 2011 provides examples of inadequate anticipation during the initial phase of the so-called Arab Spring; a "reverse" coalition of the willing in Libya; and a reluctance to intervene militarily in Syria until the rise of the Islamic State—shortcomings that have allowed other actors to reshape the Middle East. The Joint Comprehensive Plan of Action, or Iran nuclear deal, was a remarkable diplomatic success story under President Obama, but its discarding by the Trump administration illustrated a pattern of transatlantic misalignments, along with the inability to devise a smarter transcontinental division of labor. Taken together, these different foreign policy challenges connected to the 2011 uprisings amounted to a significant

Figure 2.1 Protests by Country Since the Arab Spring, 2011–20

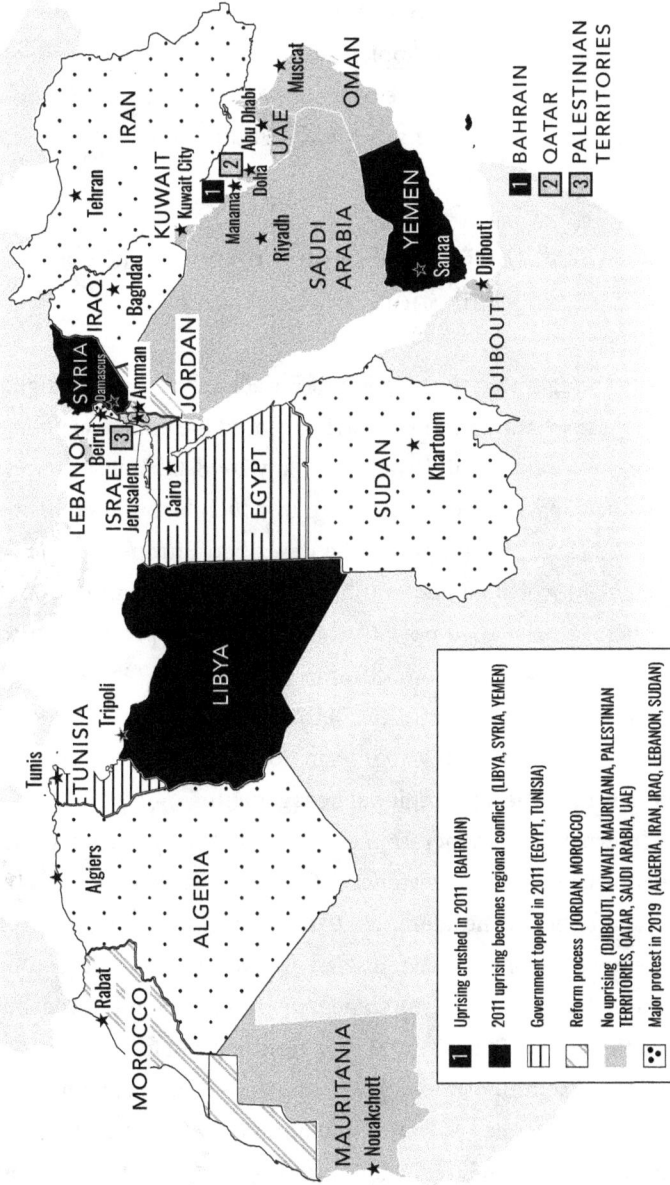

MOROCCO
Rabat

MAURITANIA
Nouakchott

ALGERIA
Algiers

TUNISIA
Tunis
Tripoli

LIBYA

EGYPT
Cairo

SUDAN
Khartoum

ISRAEL
Jerusalem
LEBANON
Beirut [3]

SYRIA
Damascus
Amman
JORDAN

IRAQ
Baghdad

IRAN
Tehran

KUWAIT
Kuwait City

SAUDI ARABIA
Riyadh

Manama [1]
Doha [2]
Abu Dhabi
UAE

Muscat
OMAN

Sanaa
YEMEN

DJIBOUTI
Djibouti

[1] BAHRAIN
[2] QATAR
[3] PALESTINIAN TERRITORIES

1 — Uprising crushed in 2011 (BAHRAIN)

— 2011 uprising becomes regional conflict (LIBYA, SYRIA, YEMEN)

— Government toppled in 2011 (EGYPT, TUNISIA)

— Reform process (JORDAN, MOROCCO)

— No uprising (DJIBOUTI, KUWAIT, MAURITANIA, PALESTINIAN TERRITORIES, QATAR, SAUDI ARABIA, UAE)

— Major protest in 2019 (ALGERIA, IRAN, IRAQ, LEBANON, SUDAN) transformation of the cooperation model for Western countries. The validity of the "West" as an analytical concept by which to understand international influence on Middle East politics was already debatable during the American unipolar moment, but the Arab Spring induced changes that have made the concept even less relevant for understanding external interventions in Middle East politics.

Both the "Long Game" and the "Old Game" Fall Short on the Arab Spring

Many thought that the election of Barack Obama would signal a new era in transatlantic relations, leaving behind the unilateral policies of the George W. Bush administration. In July 2008, Obama, as a presidential candidate, gave a speech in Berlin in which he outlined his priorities for American foreign policy: he described Europe as America's best partner in world affairs, emphasizing international partnership and cooperation as "the one way, the only way, to protect our common security and advance our common humanity."[1] Obama's statements stood in stark contrast to the actions of Bush, and seemed to signal a candidate ready to revive international cooperation and change the models for American regional engagement.[2]

International cooperation did not necessarily deepen transatlantic relations, however. A key tenet of Obama's foreign policy was his "pivot to Asia," whereby he attempted to rebalance the role America played in different parts of the world. Instead of devoting so many resources to the Middle East and investing so heavily in security in Europe, he argued that the United States would gain from instead focusing resources on the Asia-Pacific. Former deputy secretary of state William Burns noted that Obama wanted to avoid "the morass of a region that remorselessly drained...[the] political capital [of his predecessors] and consumed their attention."[3] Obama's goal was to induce gradual changes in the U.S.

approach to the Arab world and play the "long game" corresponding to this "pivot"—and he started revealing several principles intended to transform U.S.-Arab relations in his Cairo speech of 2009.

These changes were soon discarded, however, as the Arab uprisings forced Obama to adjust rather than reshape U.S. engagement in the Middle East. According to Burns, the administration's "long game," predicated on "gradually addressing the region's decades-long psychological, military, diplomatic, and political hold on American foreign policy," was "held hostage" by the pressing reality of the Arab Spring uprisings.[4] Others, like Emile Hokayem, a senior fellow at the International Institute for Strategic Studies, regard Obama's policy toward the Middle East as always having been ambivalent. Hokayem describes Obama's Middle East policy as oscillating between a principled approach aimed at bringing regional actors together to design a regional architecture and a more "cynical" approach aimed at preserving bilateral ties without designing multilateral mechanisms for the region. The Arab uprisings pushed the administration to mostly engage in the latter.[5]

The Arab Spring brought many structural governance challenges to the surface in the Middle East. The United States and Europe were both mostly caught by surprise and pursued a generally pragmatic policy influenced by a number of old assumptions about the Arab world. In general, while both sides of the Atlantic wanted to support democracy, they also had other concerns—such as the risk that instability would end up strengthening the position of Islamist actors. Western governments viewed their close relations with many of the challenged authoritarians as being important to the regional order but wanted to appear on the "right side of history." Europe and the United States alike were unprepared for authoritarians to actually step down so quickly in response to protests, and processed the first days of the Tunisian uprising according to the "old game" playbook. On January 4, 2011, reporters requested a comment from the State Department about unrest in Tunisia, weeks after Muhammad Bouazizi self-immolated. The State Department officials replied that they had not recently been briefed on Tunisia.

Just ten days later, Zine al-Abidine Ben Ali fled Tunisia after twenty-three years of rule.[6] That same day, President Obama called for "free and fair elections"[7] in Tunisia. Meanwhile, representatives of EU member states in Brussels were still drafting a joint statement calling for restraint in Ben Ali's response to the uprising when they learned that he had fled the country. The response then split Western governments into a more cautious camp and a camp favoring support for democratic movements.[8] After the Tahrir demonstrations in Egypt less than a month later, the Obama administration's initial caution was undergirded by the need to preserve the peace agreement between Egypt and Israel as well as by vested economic, security, and military interests in Egypt. But after violent pro-Mubarak protests broke out on February 2, the administration's rhetoric shifted.[9] Obama now urged Hosni Mubarak to make "the right decision" about a week before Mubarak stepped down, despite a longstanding partnership between the two countries.[10]

A Pragmatic Response to the First Uprisings

Once Mubarak and Ben Ali were ousted, the EU and the United States voiced stronger and clearer support for the democratic transition process. Britain's public reaction was tentatively positive, generally seeing Mubarak's downfall as an important milestone on Egypt's road to democracy. About a week after Mubarak's ouster, David Cameron remarked that this uprising was about "people who want to have the sort of basic freedoms that we take for granted."[11] Western leaders generally did some soul-searching after their initial surprise. On April 16, the then French foreign minister Alain Juppé delivered a speech acknowledging Western complacency with authoritarian regimes.[12] On May 19, 2011, President Obama argued that the United States should no longer support the "unsustainable" status quo.[13] With the support of countries like Spain,[14] the EU used an already planned review of its European Neighbourhood Policy to take the uprisings into consideration. But the EU mostly just reshuffled priorities, while neither changing its instruments nor defining a clearer, value-based conditionality.[15]

To facilitate the transition in Tunisia, the EU increased its bilateral aid to Tunisia by €390 million for 2011–12, up from the originally planned €240 million for 2011–13.[16] In addition to this aid, the EU established several new funds, including the €350 million SPRING (Support for Partnership Reform and Inclusive Growth) fund that would provide fledgling Arab democracies more aid in exchange for continued reforms, of which Tunisia received €100 million.[17] The EU also approved a new €80.5 million aid package for the region, along with €26.4 million EUR for strengthening civil society.[18] This all fit within a two-pronged approach advocated by the EU, intended to both "build 'deep democracy'" and "ensure inclusive and sustainable economic development."[19] Although the U.S. aid package was smaller, it sought, like the EU's, to both reinforce democratic institutions and alleviate economic woes. Within a year, the United States had provided more than $32 million in aid to Tunisia, including $19 million through the U.S. Agency for International Development, specifically intended to support a democratic transition.[20] By 2012, USAID's mission had grown to disburse $130.8 million in aid, though it shrank considerably back to $32.4 million in 2013.[21]

In retrospect, it is doubtful that these amounts were actually sufficient to meet the enormous needs of North African economies. In addition, these figures masked severe operational limitations. The political conditionality of the EU was still ill defined, and the Union's rushed short-term update in May 2011 did not really address the lack of incentives for North African countries like Tunisia.[22] Political conditionality ended up being stricter for the governments emerging from the revolution than for the previous authoritarian ones. For its part, the

USAID had had no in-country presence for twenty years prior to the uprising, and employees working in the country after the Arab Spring reported challenges to getting started without existing in-country contacts and operations.[23]

In addition to these financial contributions, the EU and the United States worked to foster stronger diplomatic ties to Tunisia. Obama announced his intention to designate Tunisia a leading non-NATO ally of the United States, while the EU announced a joint EU-Tunisia task force, among a range of other initiatives.[24]

Following Mubarak's ousting, the United States and EU adopted a similar approach with respect to Egypt, providing economic support while at the same time seeking to strengthen not just the country's democratic institutions, but also the broader civil society that had been suppressed under Mubarak. In 2011 the EU allocated €2 million to support the country's electoral commission and another €20 million for civil society, in addition to €132 million for infrastructure development and poverty alleviation.[25] Along with this direct assistance, the EU worked to sign longer-term trade agreements with both Egypt and Tunisia (as well as with Morocco and Jordan) to integrate their economies with the European single market.[26] These Deep and Comprehensive Free Trade Area (DCFTA) agreements were intended both to boost these countries economically and to bring them more closely into Europe's orbit. Yet though these agreements were marketed by the EU, that they were advanced not just to Tunisia and Egypt but also to other Arab countries whose nondemocratic leadership remained in power casts doubt on whether they were truly intended to help budding democracies, or merely to replicate a Eurocentric system of trade relations.

Whatever the EU's motives, its approach in Egypt was again closely mirrored by the United States. Although the United States never explicitly endorsed the EU's two-tracked approach to foster both "deep democracy" and economic growth, its own methods amounted to the same thing. Within a month of the revolution, USAID had allocated $165 million to "support the country's transition to democracy." The money went not only to bolstering the electoral process, but also to projects to promote human rights, support nonviolent protestors who had been imprisoned, and otherwise create the "deep democracy" the EU advocated.[27] At the same time, USAID redoubled its efforts "to support economic growth…including job creation, economic development, and poverty alleviation."[28]

Implementing an entirely pro-democracy agenda proved difficult depending on each national situation, however. For example, EU special representative Bernardino León supported the Moroccan government, labeling the domestic situation an "evolution, not revolution,"[29] but supported the protestors in Tunisia. Britain offered a somewhat tepid condemnation of the crushing of the Bahrain uprising by Bahraini authorities supported by Saudi Arabia, with the foreign secretary saying he was "seriously concerned" about police brutality against protestors in March 2011, but declining to voice support for the protestors or call for anyone's resignation.[30] Both sides of the Atlantic ended up with a pragmatic approach, whereby successful uprisings were met with endorsements once they had gained momentum, while less fruitful ones were tacitly ignored so as to facilitate business as usual.

In summer 2013, Egypt's Gen. Abdul Fattah al-Sisi seized power, arresting President Mohamed Morsi. Despite joint mediation efforts on the part of the United States and the EU, a large number of members of the Muslim Brotherhood were detained and a thousand people were killed in Rabaa al-Adawiyya Square. In order to prevent the suspension of all American aid, Washington refused to label the events a coup; but the Obama administration did refuse to ship multiple weapons systems to Egypt in summer 2013, thereby conveying its condemnation of recent events.[31] Thereafter, the White House expressed a more limited view of what the United States could achieve in the region when it came to democracy.

By default, then, in the initial stage of the Arab uprisings there was similar transatlantic surprise and a common pragmatism, but not a substantial reconsideration of how to approach the region. The EU accepted regime change in Tunisia and Egypt while supporting regime continuity in Morocco, Jordan, and Algeria. Responses proved to be more complicated where the uprisings developed into civil conflicts, as in Libya and Syria.

In Libya, a Coalition Not So Willing

In Libya, the United States and Europe were aligned in their opposition to Muammar Qadhafi's human rights abuses but divided on how to proceed in light of them. The decision to ultimately intervene displayed a reverse dynamic compared with previous coalitions of the willing in Iraq, with France and Britain pushing the United States to intervene over objections from Italy and Germany. The Iraqi legacy made Washington a reluctant partner in this mission, and pushback in Libya against a large international footprint as well as domestic politics in Western countries caused international commitment to Libya to be insufficiently coordinated, opening up space for regional competition—and for spoilers among Libyan representatives to block any sustainable political resolution.

Compared with 1991 and 2003, transatlantic roles appeared reversed in the decision to intervene in Libya. The key impetus came from the European side, with French president Nicolas Sarkozy and British prime minister David Cameron pushing to support the uprising that had begun in February 2011 in Benghazi, both in an attempt to show support for the broader "Arab Spring" movement after reacting late to the Tunisia uprising and in order to prevent a potential bloodbath in case of a repression by Qadhafi in eastern Libya. This push was not unanimously endorsed in Europe, as both Germany and Italy feared the consequences of the fall of Qadhafi.[32] On the U.S. side, instead of being at the forefront of action, the United States adopted a cautious approach. At the time, President Obama had already accepted a surge in Afghanistan and was therefore wary of additional foreign intervention.

Both the United States and Europe initially expressed support for the uprising and sanctioned Qadhafi. The French authorities pressed for accelerated international decisionmaking by officially recognizing the Libyan opposition on February 20. While Britain and France were in favor of a military operation, Germany opposed it. Angela Merkel explained the German position in March 2011 at an EU summit: "What is our plan if we create a no-fly zone and it doesn't work? Do we send in ground troops? We have to think this through."[33] Merkel's opposition was not merely rhetorical: when the UN Security Council ultimately voted to impose a no-fly zone, Germany abstained.

As for the United States, senior officials in the White House split into two camps, with one side skeptical of military intervention while the other supported humanitarian intervention.[34] The eventual decision to engage militarily in Libya was described by Obama as a "51–49" call,[35] and President Obama later said that if he "did not feel Sarkozy or Cameron were far enough out there to follow through," that "might have changed [his] decision."[36]

Both the British prime minister and the French president were integral to the passage, in record time, of UN Security Council Resolutions 1970 and 1973 on February 26 and March 17. The U.S. delegation in New York played a central role in negotiating with the Russian delegation to avoid a veto not only from Moscow, but also from China.[37] This UN mandate gave political and legal backing to the intervention but did not create a coalition as such. The EU could theoretically have played a strong role in the Libya crisis, but it was short of quick military coordination capability and was not united, as Germany was opposed to intervention. This divergence among Europeans led France, Britain, and the United States to resort to NATO to coordinate national contributions on an ad hoc basis, and to include contributions from

Arab countries. While Operation Odyssey Dawn was mainly run by the United States to prepare the ground for NATO, Operation Unified Protector was launched with a wave of French strikes against Libyan regime troops on March 19.

One of the particular features of this operation, then, was the disconnect between the military mechanism used to coordinate actions (NATO) and the political oversight of the intervention, accomplished via an ad hoc political coalition involving both European and Arab nations (the "friends of Libya" group). Politically, NATO was divided, and indeed it could not have been used as a source of political oversight because of German opposition, which extended to abstention in the vote on the intervention at the UN Security Council. Other means of control existed, like the one that coordinated nations conducting airstrikes—operationally supported by NATO even though some participants, like Qatar, were not NATO members.

Although these problems of coordination existed from the outset, they grew far worse once Qadhafi was ousted. The coalition lacked a cohesive political agenda, while the Libyan actors themselves pushed back against a major international footprint for a variety of reasons. That pushback, combined with the lack of a strong preexisting diplomatic framework, was reflected in a limited UN mandate to support the political transition. This triggered a vicious circle through which the UN mandate limited the coordination of bilateral cooperation and assistance, and also created a deeper problem: weakly supported by international actors, the UN action was not perceived as transparent, and different Libyan actors feared that some factions would be empowered against others.[38] The United States, the EU, and the European bilateral missions were funding the same limited number of organizations, which were largely elite and professionalized and based in Tripoli.[39] This led to different pushbacks, with local NGOs complaining to the EU, for instance in Darnah in fall 2011, because funding did not seem to be coordinated. Aware of this coordination issue, NGOs would play donors off against each other.

This weak diplomatic framework ultimately created one of Libya's most intractable (and ongoing) problems: the rise of spoiler groups that had more to gain from a stalled political "transition" than from a successful one and that could play international actors off against each other. One of the peculiarities of the Libyan conflict is indeed that all parties continue to be funded through public finances and share the oil revenues distributed by the central bank. In this system, where "everybody is a civil servant,"[40] political figures have an incentive to hold on to their interim positions and block any change in the institutional configuration that could reduce their access to public revenues.

A notable exception to this limited coordination was the 2012 elections. The UN managed to hold weekly meetings with all embassies, and the implementing partners present agreed on a division of labor, including organizing joint demarches to the electoral commission to help monitoring the transparency of the vote. Technical expertise and resourcing were backed diplomatically, and the organization of the elections "was a true success."[41] This more efficient coordination process did not survive the elections, however, and was not replicated to support the new parliament. Western missions in Libya seemed to take for granted that the UN would lead this effort and did not exert pressure on it to do so, leading to another cycle of insufficient coordination of bilateral programs of support.[42]

Although these elections were a rare bright point in the Libyan intervention, the failure to replicate this success highlighted another challenge the coalition never fully surmounted: the difficulty of effectively providing technical assistance to Libya to assist the new institutions, but without creating rents for domestic actors who had limited individual interests in the success of the UN process. Where transatlantic interests converged, as with respect to the extraction by the United States and Denmark of Libya's chemical weapons supply, the coalition was sometimes able to score quick wins. But numerous well-intentioned international initiatives—regarding election monitoring, military training, reform of the security sector, and the development of Libya's infrastructure—failed to take off, owing to governance problems within the new institutions but also to insufficient coordination between coalition countries, even when they agreed about the desired outcome. The UN framework never had enough support to facilitate these initiatives, and the ad hoc coordination that arose outside of it also proved insufficient.

In terms of security, in 2013, Italy, Turkey, Britain, and the United States offered training programs through partnering agreements with Libya's national security forces.[43] Some training programs, like one funded by the British government, ended up as embarrassing disasters because of trainee misconduct.[44] In 2013 and 2014, the European Union Border Assistance Mission helped the Libyan authorities control the country's borders, ports, and other points of entry; but its staff faced difficulty even with respect to traveling outside Tripoli, and their freedom of movement was even more limited after the EU evacuated Libya in July 2014.

Domestic constraints also limited the contributions of European countries to the intervention. Italy was reluctant to participate from the outset, fearing that the fall of Qadhafi, an important partner for Italy, would increase migration flows. In the United States, meanwhile, the 2012 killing of Ambassador Chris Stevens in Benghazi turned major U.S. involvement in the Libyan peace process into a political nonstarter. François Hollande's 2012 victory against Nicolas Sarkozy in the French presidential race similarly led to a shift in policy, as the Sarkozy-backed 2011 intervention came under scrutiny by the new government and also because the progress of jihadist groups in Mali led to a French intervention there in January 2013.

In Britain, views on Libya also shifted decisively after the September 2012 Benghazi attack. In January 2013, the British Foreign Office urged all citizens to leave Benghazi immediately because of a "specific and imminent threat," which prompted harsh criticism from Libyan politicians.[45] UK officials had an increasingly pessimistic outlook on Libya, and talked about the country more in the context of security issues than as a budding democracy. The 2016 Brexit campaign and the consequences of the "yes" vote absorbed a lot of domestic political attention and limited the Foreign Office's ability to maintain the same level of engagement in Libya.

And although Libya was not related to the 2015 migration wave into Germany from Syria, the political consequences for German politics, especially with the rise of the far-right party AfD, influenced the way the German government looked at the Libyan crisis. Similarly, Italian politics subsequently also played a role in shaping the international discussion on Libya, when politicians like Matteo Salvini used the issue of migration from Libya to put pressure on other political parties. The fragile consensus that led to Obama's "51–49" decision to intervene fell apart under these varied domestic considerations, greatly exacerbating the international community's inability to solve Libya's more intractable political questions.

As international interest in Libya declined, the security and political situation in the country continued to deteriorate. A turning point on the political scene was a bill in 2013 excluding all former Qadhafi officials from office. Political assassinations increased and polarization between Islamist militias and their adversaries grew, derailing the political process. Election turnout dropped from 62 percent in 2012 to 18 percent in 2014, leading to a contested result and the separation of Libyan institutions into two rival governments based in Tripoli, the capital, and in eastern Tobruk, where the legally elected chamber, the House of Representatives, fled after being expelled from Tripoli by Islamist militias. As Islamist forces increased their influence in Tripoli, the anti-Islamist coalition of Khalifa Haftar controlled the east.[46] In this context, most foreign missions were evacuated from Tripoli. Ad hoc cooperation and dialogue have still been possible from Tunis, where most missions resettled, but the remote nature of the Western diplomatic presence impaired efficiency. Different diplomatic efforts tried to avoid escalation: Spain, for example, organized a regional conference, involving all of Libya's neighbors, in an attempt to avoid a failed transition. But it did not succeed.[47]

The expansion of jihadist groups in Libya was one of the notable consequences of the degraded security situation. In 2014, the Islamic State (IS) and other groups had particularly increased their influence in cities like Benghazi, Sirte, and Darnah. Both the so-called Libyan National Army led by Haftar and militias in the west received support from regional and international actors to fight against terrorist cells. Darnah was mostly cleared of the Islamic State fighters by local groups, some of them close to al-Qaeda, after IS assassinated several local figures. In Benghazi, the United States, France, and Britain coordinated to provide support to the Libyan National Army[48] against the Benghazi Revolutionaries Shura Council led by Ansar al-Sharia. In Sirte, Western countries supported forces close to the Tripoli authorities to fight foreign fighters and former Ansar al-Sharia members leading the local IS franchise.

The United States carried out a series of targeted strikes aimed at IS leaders and Tunisian terrorist figures from August 2016 until the end of 2017, especially in Sirte, where 495 strikes were carried out that killed around 900 IS fighters between August and December 2016.[49] According to the French press, some of these operations were coordinated with France—for example, the strikes of November 2015 in Darnah that killed Abu Nabil al-Anbari, an Iraqi who led the Islamic State's arm in Libya.[50] Another joint strike was coordinated between France, the United States, and Britain to hit an IS facility in Sabratha in February 2016, killing Noureddine Chouchane, who had been involved in the Sousse and Bardo attacks in Tunisia in May and June 2015.[51] Cooperation with the Tripoli authorities also included the extradition of Hashem Abedi, the brother of Salman Abedi, the Manchester Arena bomber.[52]

While this Western cooperation with local factions proved effective from a counterterrorism perspective, it evolved in the context of a complex and unstable institutional landscape. When different Libyan groups signed the Libyan Political Agreement, or Skhirat Agreement, in December 2015 to reunite Libyan institutions, international recognition shifted from one executive to a new one. After several rounds of peace talks, representatives from Tripoli's General National Congress and Tobruk's House of Representatives signed the Agreement, backed by the UN, to form a unity government called the Government of National Accord (GNA). This agreement required strong but uneasy international coordination and "an enormous amount of work, and the outcome could have been derailed by any of the actors."[53] But the GNA did not manage to exert authority beyond the Libyan capital, and the eastern members of the GNA soon withdrew from it. The GNA, in turn, de facto replaced the Tripoli-based authorities—the executives appointed by the National General Congress, dominated by Islamist actors, some of whom were suspected to be using national resources to support jihadist groups—but it failed to be endorsed by the eastern House of Representatives based in Tobruk, which kept its own executive.

Divisions and tensions on each side further increased the confusion. While diplomats supported the GNA and were trying to keep the Skhirat Agreement alive, this institutional instability pushed Western countries active on the counterterrorism or migration fronts to maintain contacts in and cooperation with both the east and the west. The United States maintained cooperation on both sides. France maintained its cooperation with the Libyan National Army (LNA) and its contacts with actors close to the GNA, launching a training program for the presidential guard in Tripoli in 2017 as well as assisting forces led by Osama Juwaili, a senior commander from Zintan loyal to the GNA. Britain and Italy kept close ties to the Misratah militias, where Italian forces ran a military hospital, but also had contacts with Khalifa Haftar on specific occasions, as when Italian fishermen were captured by Haftar's forces.

In this context, one of the key issues behind the deadlocked status of the Skhirat Agreement was the role of Khalifa Haftar. Though he was not formally included in the UN process, his Libyan National Army was the strongest militia in the east, supporting the institutions that had been internationally recognized until the creation of the GNA under the Skhirat Agreement. Haftar was one of the "spoilers" blocking the implementation of this agreement, opposing the control Islamist militias had in Tripoli but also using his control over a large part of the territories to influence the political process without being accountable to it.

Western partners differed on whether it was possible for Haftar to accept civilian oversight. Countries like Italy and Germany doubted it was possible and thought Haftar should be isolated as much as possible, with other actors being empowered to reconcile eastern and western Libya. France, however, thought that Haftar would do "less damage inside than outside" of the UN process, where eastern Libya was not well represented anymore. The U.S. government was divided on the issue, but the White House seemed to have been willing to try to include Haftar in the political process. The United States led several rounds of negotiations throughout 2016 but could not reach an agreement with Haftar before the American election.[54]

For its part, Italy hosted talks between Aguila Saleh (head of Tobruk's House of Representatives) and Abdulrahman al-Swehli (head of Tripoli's High State Council) in April 2017. After the election of Emmanuel Macron in May 2017, France pushed East-West talks as well and invited Haftar and Fayez al-Sarraj, prime minister of the internationally recognized GNA, to France in May 2017 in order to prevent further escalation after new fighting between Haftar's forces and militias from Misratah. The French president hosted Haftar and the main Libyan representatives again in 2018 to press them to come up with an agreement to reunify the two sets of institutions, draft a constitution, and plan elections. Italy organized the Palermo Conference in November 2018 with similar goals and participants, without being more successful. A French-American-Emirati push with the UN led to a draft agreement between Haftar and Sarraj in Abu Dhabi at the beginning of 2019, but they ultimately did not sign it, despite a last French effort with the visit of its foreign minister to Haftar on March 19. Each time, Sarraj and Haftar would agree on a number of steps during the meeting, without delivering an agreement.

One factor behind this diplomatic deadlock was probably Haftar's impression that his military power and the support he received from the UAE and Egypt allowed him to put the burden of proof on Sarraj to demonstrate his ability to assert the authority of the GNA over the militias controlling Tripoli. The GNA was by design too weak to force the militias to agree to the terms demanded by Haftar, an actor the militias deemed illegitimate and who could challenge their control over the city. There was a consensus among Western diplomats on the need to press Libyan actors to compromise throughout this series of international meetings, but tactical divergence and short-term imperatives on the counterterrorism and migration fronts limited their ability to leverage their technical assistance.

In April 2019, Haftar launched an offensive against Tripoli, which interrupted the ongoing efforts after the Abu Dhabi talks between Sarraj and Haftar as well as UN preparation of a National Conference scheduled for April 14–16, for which UN secretary-general António Guterres had arrived in Libya on April 3, 2019. The reasons behind Haftar's attack were intensely debated within the diplomatic and expert community, but the decisive factor seemed to have been a green light from then U.S. national security advisor John Bolton, during a phone call before the attack.[55] On April 15, 2019, the U.S. National Security Council again expressed a position contrary to the stance held by the State Department when President Trump announced he had had a phone call with Khalifa Haftar. Trump "recognized Field Marshal

Haftar's significant role in fighting terrorism and securing Libya's oil resources, and the two discussed a shared vision for Libya's transition to a stable, democratic political system," according to a White House press statement released several days later.[56]

This dispute between the White House and the State Department created several months of confusion among Western partners and also amplified mutual distrust between the United States, France, Germany, and Italy, each complaining about the others' not putting pressure on the Libyan actors and their regional backers. France was accused of supporting the attack on Tripoli by Haftar; Italy of strengthening Islamist factions in Tripoli; Germany of putting the blame on French-Italian divisions while not itself being engaged enough. In practice, Western countries maintained channels of dialogue with all Libyan parties but had little leverage to stop the conflict they had not been able to prevent.

Building on earlier debates within the German system and bilateral talks with West African leaders who complained about the consequences of the Libyan conflict, Angela Merkel launched in mid-2019 the "Berlin process" to bring together regional and international players at a sufficiently high level to broker a deal. This initiative was the product of Germany's relative neutrality ever since its abstention at the UN Security Council in 2011, along with the chancellor's personal stature after fifteen years in power. From a diplomatic point of view, the process led to the Berlin conference on Libya in January 2020 and created space for three tracks of negotiations among Libyan actors, at the political, military, and economic levels. While the U.S. position was still unclear, Germany, France, and Italy developed more effective coordination to support the UN in this new framework.

Europeans also tried to develop more leverage over the crisis. Europeans launched Operation Irini in 2020 with the primary goal of impartially implementing the UN arms embargo. Drawing on maritime, aerial, and satellite assets mainly provided by Italy, France, Greece, and Germany, this operation has benefited from a robust mandate, allowing it to inspect vessels that may be carrying prohibited materiel; it uncovered Turkish and Emirati breaches of the embargo. These actions were bolstered by new European sanctions issued in September 2020, targeting companies that supply factions in eastern and western Libya. The Trump administration regarded these moves with skepticism, however, after the State Department and the U.S. Africa Command had refocused American attention on Russian influence in Libya and concluded that Irini was primarily targeting Turkey without containing Russia.

The Berlin process, however, was largely a function of military dynamics on the ground. The escalation of the conflict, and the military support received by Haftar from the UAE and Egypt, had helped bring Haftar very close to the center of Tripoli in spring 2019. The GNA thereupon requested foreign military assistance, which Turkey initially provided through drones in May 2019; this support helped stop Haftar's advance. For his part, Haftar began receiving Russian support in August 2019, which led to an additional Turkish buildup, including six thousand Syrian mercenaries and more military equipment. The Turkish drones and air defense systems sent by Ankara enabled GNA forces to establish local air superiority and ease pressure on the capital.[57] Turkish support of the GNA was later formalized in a defense agreement whose content remained secret, as well as a memorandum in November 2019 redrawing maritime boundaries in the Mediterranean in order to strengthen Turkey's argument in its old conflict with Greece and Cyprus in the eastern Mediterranean.

The Berlin process indirectly benefited from the new balance of power between Turkey and Russia, marked by a truce around the line between al-Jufrah and Sirte. While this helped the diplomatic track exert pressure on Haftar, it also challenged Western influence even more. Moscow and Ankara entertained a separate diplomatic track and pushed, unsuccessfully, for a deal between Haftar and Sarraj on January 8, 2020, days before the Berlin conference. Their goal was to leverage military escalation to a point that would strengthen their influence outside and inside the UN process. While providing military support to Haftar, Moscow was also connected to Tripoli. For its part, Turkey used its support of the GNA to expand both militarily and economically.

The new Libyan landscape still provided opportunities for European countries to support the UN process. Germany, France, and Italy worked more closely together in 2020 to support the UN, and to prepare and organize the vote in February 2021 that led to the creation of a new executive intended to unify Libyan institutions. The Libyan landscape is more fragmented than ever, however, and Western countries have not really improved the coordination of their different national assets to the point where they can together decisively pressure local and regional actors in the conflict. The initial asymmetry between European divisions and cautious American involvement remains. Since 2011, Washington has believed that Europeans should play the leading role, while a number of European governments expect the United States to play a bigger role.

An Overwhelmed Coalition in Syria

American and European interventions in Syria were initially diplomatic and aimed at tipping the balance in favor of the opposition without entering directly into the conflict. At the end of June 2011, the United States and the EU decided on a first series of sanctions against Bashar al-Assad. In August, Barack Obama called on Assad to leave power. EU High Representative Catherine Ashton spoke of "the complete loss of Bashar al-Assad's legitimacy in the eyes of the Syrian people and the need for him to step aside."[58] The EU utilized almost every sanctions tool it possessed against Syria, starting with the suspension of bilateral cooperation and of the unsigned 2008 EU–Syrian Association Agreement.[59]

Alongside that economic pressure, different diplomatic structures were assembled in search of a solution to the crisis. The first of these, the informal "Friends of Syria" group, was formed in early 2012, after China and Russia vetoed a Security Council resolution condemning Assad's violent crackdown on protestors.[60] The group, which included delegates from France, the United States, and a range of like-minded European and Arab countries, hosted delegations from the Syrian opposition and issued strongly worded statements calling for Assad's resignation. A few months after the group's first meeting, the "Action Group on Syria" was formed, this time attempting to include Russia and China in the process. The result was a watered-down call for a democratic transition that applied no particular pressure on the Assad regime.[61] This so-called Geneva I communiqué was followed by Geneva II (2014),[62] the 2015 Vienna communiqué[63] and Security Council Resolution 2254, and Geneva III (2016),[64] among other efforts, all of which involved considerable international cooperation but ultimately fell short over the Russian position on the question of allowing Assad to stay, as well as other intractable issues.

In addition to these formal processes, a near-constant backchannel was open between Russian foreign minister Sergei Lavrov and his U.S. counterpart (first Hillary Clinton, then John Kerry from 2013 onward) in order to discuss humanitarian and security issues in Syria. In 2016, frustrated over the lack of progress on these matters, Kerry "suspended" the backchannel, only to reopen it forty-eight hours later.[65] These bilateral talks proved capable of resolving some issues, mostly when the regime felt in real danger, as when, after the August 2013 chemical attack in Ghouta, Kerry and Lavrov agreed to attempt to dismantle Assad's chemical weapons stockpile.[66] But Russia always managed to use these tactical arrangements to shield Assad from more strategic consequences, such as losing his rights as representative of the Syrian people at the United Nations in New York.

After an initial phase of providing mostly diplomatic support, the issue of military support for the Syrian opposition became the central question among Western and Arab allies. There was no international appetite to form a no-fly zone, as there was with respect to Libya. Despite heated internal deliberations in 2012 regarding a more extensive train and equip program for opposition forces, the United States initially held back.[67] And in addition to Syria's enjoying Russia's diplomatic support at the UN, the structure of the regime, along with military support from Hezbollah and Iran, made it much more resilient than Egypt and Tunisia, and the regime was able to retake key cities in 2012 and 2013.

Intense debates occurred within the U.S. government as well as in Paris and London with regard to the provision of military support to armed opposition groups. Turkey, Saudi Arabia, Qatar, the United States, France, and Britain increased their support for the Syrian opposition in 2013 and provided armed opposition groups with different kinds of assistance, including weapons.[68] This support was loosely coordinated, however, and Western countries feared the equipment could be seized by more radical groups, while Gulf countries used their own channels. United States military assistance was ultimately provided through two main programs: the CIA's Operation Timber Sycamore and the Department of Defense's Syria Train and Equip Program. Both were curtailed from the outset by a risk-averse White House and Congress, which set sharp limits on both the types of weaponry that could be distributed and the groups it could be distributed to.

Timber Sycamore, most likely launched in 2013, was a joint CIA effort with the Saudi government, in which the Saudis provided most of the material support to opposition groups while the U.S. government helped train them.[69] The program achieved some early successes, but it was never allowed to distribute anti-air weapons or other much-needed heavy weaponry. When Russia entered the conflict directly in 2015, most of the CIA-backed groups were outgunned and decisively routed. By 2016, when Assad retook the rebel stronghold of Aleppo, it was clear that the regime was in no danger of succumbing to the diplomatic, economic, or military pressure that had been applied up to that point. Unwilling to supply the heavier weapons necessary to keep the rebels it worked with in the fight, the United States instead canceled the Timber Sycamore program in 2017.[70]

The Syria Train and Equip Program was launched in mid-2014 and was quietly cancelled in 2015 when it failed to produce more than a handful of the promised five thousand fighters.[71] From the outset, concerns about weapons falling into the wrong hands resulted in stringent vetting regulations, requiring that all the fighters be handpicked and be trained outside Syria, on bases in Qatar, Saudi Arabia, Turkey, and elsewhere.[72]

Although the amount of money involved—in the case of Syria Train and Equip, $500 million to train "four or five"[73] fighters—suggests abysmal mismanagement, the reality is that there was probably no way for these programs to succeed without resolving major coordination issues between the United States and its partners. Turkey protested vociferously regarding any aid that might end up in the hands of Kurdish opposition groups, which meant that some of the most effective fighting forces in northwest Syria were effectively off-limits for military aid. When the Syria Train and Equip mission was relaunched in 2016 it was allowed to work with Kurdish-aligned groups, and the program ultimately provided major support to the Syrian Arab coalition during the battle for Raqqa in 2017—at the cost of a dramatic diplomatic fallout with Turkey.[74]

Another example of the hesitant Western approach was the American response to the use of chemical weapons by the Assad regime in August 2013. Despite President Obama's "redline" of August 2012,[75] the United States finally decided not to respond militarily to the regime's use of chemical weapons in Ghouta and accepted the Russian offer to work on dismantling the regime's chemicals stocks. Though Britain's parliament had voted against a military strike against Syria,[76] the French government was deeply frustrated by this episode: Paris perceived the decision as a strategic mistake. Former U.S. ambassador to the UN Samantha Power said in 2019 that David Cameron's insistence on seeking, and then failing to obtain, parliamentary approval for airstrikes following a chemical weapons attack on the outskirts of Damascus on August 21, 2013, led the Obama administration to abandon plans to retaliate militarily against the Assad regime. According to one account:

> [A] decision was made really to give the prime minister his time so we have the biggest possible most legitimate coalition we can have. When that did not go through, the vulnerability of having a smaller coalition, the vulnerability of what happened to Cameron, made Obama feel he needed thicker ballast…To pursue that Congressional authorisation without knowing whether you have the votes, I don't think anyone can look back on that and think it is our best moment.[77]

Until today, many observers believe this was a missed opportunity to send a strong signal to the regime that might have helped the then mostly moderate armed opposition take a decisive advantage in its struggle. They also see the subsequent series of events in Crimea and Syria as the result of the United States showing Russia that it was not committed enough to risk a military confrontation with Moscow.

On multiple other fronts, Western cooperation proved effective. An impressive amount of ad hoc coordination facilitated both the anti-regime sanctions and the various initiatives to train and fund rebel groups. Throughout the crisis, the United States and Europe provided around 90 percent of the annual $3–$5 billion humanitarian response to Syrians coordinated by the United Nations. Western diplomatic coordination enabled passage of the 2014 UN Security Council Resolution 2165 allowing cross-border assistance from Turkey, Iraq, and Jordan without having to ask permission from the Syrian regime, which had been refusing or ignoring 70 percent of the requests from humanitarian actors to ship assistance "cross line," from Damascus to opposition-held areas. Western cooperation was also effective in the area of accountability, through the gathering of evidence to prosecute war criminals who had fled to Europe.

But without an actual military coalition, Western tools were eventually insufficient to launch a political transition or to challenge Assad's grip on power, especially given the number of pro-Iran mercenaries— probably up to 60,000 soldiers since 2012—but also in the context of uncoordinated interventions from Gulf countries. Russian intervention on the ground in 2015, for example, with five thousand troops and air defense, contributed to "close" the military space while affording considerable leverage to Moscow.

In truth, U.S. Syria policy has been more a by-product of U.S.-Iraq policy, U.S.-Iran policy, and U.S.-Russia policy than one based on an assessment of the situation in Syria itself.[78] Along with European risk aversion, these contradictions resulted in the like-minded diplomatic coalition formed to pressure Assad in 2011 being overwhelmed by multiple local and regional military dynamics, which ultimately shaped the conflict more than Western allies had anticipated. Ultimately, Russia, Iran, and the Syrian regime won a war the West had refused to wage.

***

In retrospect, a defining feature of transatlantic cooperation in the Arab Spring context was a clear American hesitancy that leading Europeans tried to challenge. While Western partners achieved different kinds of compromises throughout the associated crises and cooperated tactically at numerous levels, they could not agree on strategic goals beyond their short-term reactions to the uprisings and what followed. Indeed, the years after the 2011 uprisings confounded European expectations of a U.S. role comparable to what it had been in previous decades. And the urgency of crisis management did not provide time to adjust transatlantic cooperation in a more effective way.

In Libya as well as in Syria, it is difficult to say to what extent more or better alignment among allies would have changed the outcome on the ground. Local power dynamics and other foreign interventions shaped these conflicts to a large degree. One can argue in any case that the depth of the challenges posed by these conflicts, such as the institutional vacuum left by Qadhafi, suggested that real solutions were out of reach for Western actors. Nevertheless, the chronology of these crises suggests that Western actors had more influence and leverage on the ground in the early stages of these civil wars than they do in 2021. Their inability or reluctance to interfere more in local politics, to support the UN more strongly, or to shape military outcomes has created opportunities that Russia and Turkey have ultimately seized.

The Partial Defeat of the Islamic State, 2014–21

While the Western reaction to the Arab Spring uprisings has been mired in contradictions and hesitancy, the Global Coalition to Counter ISIS/Daesh provides an interesting, and somewhat more balanced, case study of European-American cooperation.

The Islamic State, which pulled off a string of high-profile attacks in Europe in 2014 and 2016 and executed American hostages, posed a direct and pressing security threat to the United States and its European allies—and its brutality and graphic propaganda shocked Western societies. Defeating IS therefore topped the agenda for the United States and Europe alike, and so can give a sense of what each partner could contribute to a mission that both prioritized. This is also an example involving a large spectrum of capabilities, from military assets to humanitarian aid and intelligence.

The coalition was created in September 2014 in response to the Islamic State's conquest of large swaths of Syrian and Iraqi territory (see figure 2.2 for maps of the two countries during the anti-IS campaign). It has been the primary framework through which eighty-one countries, among them many European ones, have coordinated their military and civilian support to local partners in Syria and Iraq to address the threat and liberate nearly 110,000 square kilometers (42,471 square miles) and some 7.7 million people from IS.

The initial construction of the anti–Islamic State coalition appeared very similar to the 1990s coalition of the willing, with the United States providing the largest political, financial, and military contribution and leading the combined efforts. The anti-IS coalition mission, however, involved much greater U.S.-Europe cooperation than did actions taken in Iraq between 2003 and 2011, which saw mostly "token European participation"; aside from British efforts, U.S.-Europe cooperation during that period was "basically nonexistent."[79] The anti-IS coalition, on the other hand, relied on more significant political alignment between the U.S. and European partners. In 2014, European partners also brought to the operation capabilities the United States might have lacked: thus, Italy's Carabinieri, or gendarmerie police, found a niche training Iraqi law enforcement in advanced policing strategies, a critical task that America's counterinsurgency-focused forces have generally not emphasized. Another example is France's contribution through an artillery component.

A second major difference compared with coalitions in 1990 and 2003 was that coordination efforts against IS required domestic actions from member states: by design, partners were required to take action not only in Syria and Iraq, but also within their home countries. For example, in addition to UN and EU measures, Italy established an autonomous national instrument to freeze assets related to IS activities and passed tougher legislation to counter terrorist financing, providing judicial authorities with stronger, more effective tools to go after the Islamic State's revenue streams. Spain was also a member of the coalition's working group to counter Islamic State financing: it adopted legal measures to cut off terrorists' cash flows and helped other countries stop terrorism financing.[80]

A third major difference compared with previous coalitions was the intensity of coordination, and the degree of division of labor between the United States and its European partners. Parallel to the military operations run by U.S. Central Command—through the Combined Joint Task Force–Operation Inherent Resolve (CJTF-OIR)—different working groups were set up with the relevant military and/or civilian departments of coalition members. Extending years of bilateral cooperation between intelligence services against al-Qaeda and its affiliates, the coalition's working groups helped intensify multilateral exchanges, mainly between "Five Eyes" countries (the United States, Britain, Canada, Australia, and New Zealand), mainland European countries, and Gulf countries in order to work on stabilizing liberated areas, countering Islamic State propaganda, preventing the movement of foreign terrorist fighters, and tackling IS financing and funding. A working group dedicated to political and military consultations between the political directors of the defense ministries of the most active countries in the coalition played a key role throughout the campaign. In that respect, the anti-IS coalition has been much more structured and better organized than previous coalitions—though the root causes of the rise of IS were ultimately not addressed.

The growing importance of burden sharing was also notable in the anti-IS coalition as compared with previous ones. As it has been discussed, the issue of burden sharing has been a recurring one between the United States and Europe, especially within NATO; it became more acute under the Trump administration in its dialogue with European counterparts, when U.S. officials made it clear that they needed to be able to give their president sufficient proof of burden sharing in order to convince him not to withdraw U.S. troops. Burden sharing was therefore primarily important for U.S. domestic purposes: though the coalition was meant to remain primarily an American vehicle, other nations, especially European and Gulf ones, were more forcefully asked to contribute. The coalition has therefore been an example of the ability of transatlantic partners, albeit with occasional difficulty, to adapt themselves to a new context and invest resources

Figure 2.2 Syria and Iraq During the Fight Against the Islamic State

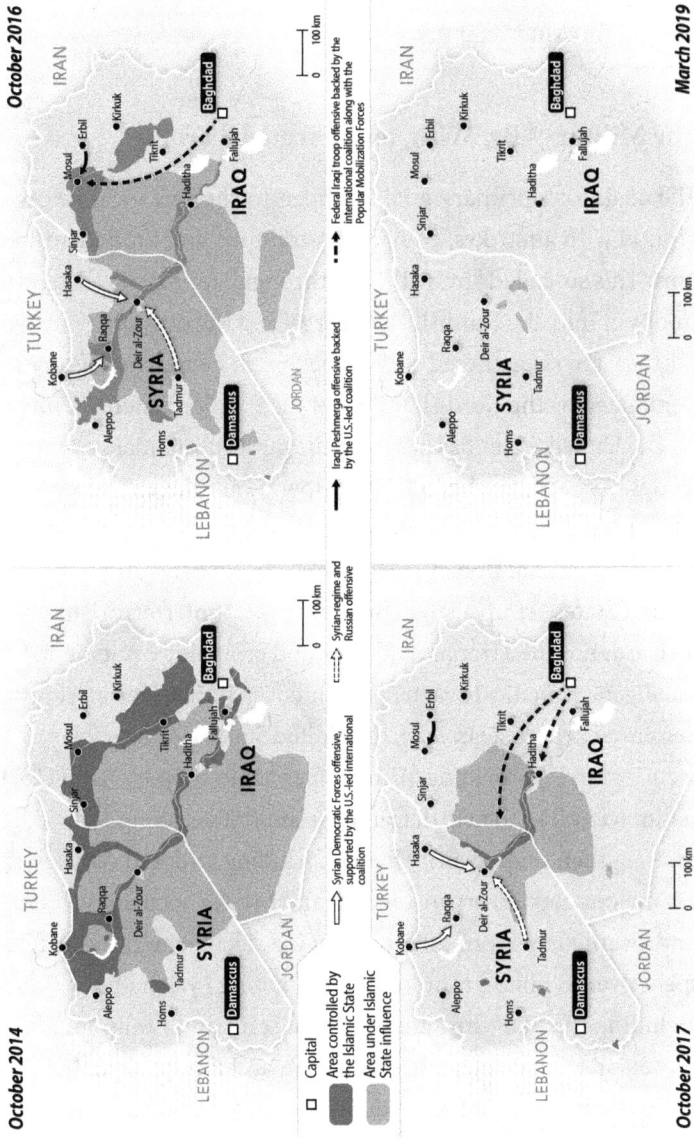

October 2014

October 2016

October 2017

March 2019

Capital

Area controlled by the Islamic State

Area under Islamic State influence

⟹ Syrian Democratic Forces offensive, supported by the U.S.-led international coalition

⟹ Syrian-regime and Russian offensive

→ Iraqi Peshmerga offensive backed by the U.S.-led coalition

┅▶ Federal Iraqi troop offensive backed by the international coalition along with the Popular Mobilization Forces

0   100 km

TURKEY · IRAN · SYRIA · IRAQ · LEBANON · JORDAN

Kobane · Aleppo · Raqqa · Hasaka · Sinjar · Mosul · Erbil · Kirkuk · Deir al-Zour · Homs · Tadmur · Damascus · Tikrit · Haditha · Fallujah · Baghdad in an operation. And as with the coalition to intervene in Libya—but as opposed to the two Iraq wars—the anti–Islamic State coalition displayed another version of a reverse dynamic whereby Europeans pushed for American involvement.

The Military "By, With, and Through" Front

The coalition's primary goal has been to support local forces on the ground with airstrikes, equipment, training, and limited ground support. This so-called "by, with, and through" approach relied on federal troops in Iraq, the Kurdish Peshmerga, and Kurdish and Arab troops in northeast Syria gathered within the Syrian Democratic Forces (SDF), dominated by the Kurdish militia of the People's Defense Units (YPG).

The United States has provided the most substantial support to these troops. As of September 30, 2019, Operation Inherent Resolve had cost $40.5 billion,[81] and the United States conducted more than 90 percent of the 25,000 coalition airstrikes between 2014 and 2017.[82] In Syria, the United States set up a small but effective counterterrorism operation, with around 2,000 troops on the ground providing equipment, training, intelligence, medical evacuation, air cover, humanitarian support, and demining expertise. In Iraq, the United States led the efforts to rebuild security forces, providing $15 billion a year to support 5,200 U.S. troops stationed in Iraq to help defeat the Islamic State, along with $5.4 billion to strengthen Iraqi security forces, including armored vehicles, support for the counterterrorism service, and border security infrastructure improvement.[83] From 2015 on, the U.S. Department of Defense also spent over $1 billion training and equipping Syrian opposition forces, including the SDF through the Syria Train and Equip Fund[84] and its successor, the Counterterrorism Train and Equip Fund.[85]

For their part, European countries—Britain, France, Germany, Italy, the Netherlands, Spain, Portugal, Slovenia, Romania, and the Czech Republic—complemented U.S. actions at various levels, contributing via intelligence collection, airstrikes, equipment provision, and military training. The French army deployed four CAESAR howitzers and 150 to 200 soldiers at al-Qayyara Airfield West, who conducted 2,100 artillery missions,[86] including during the battle of Mosul. An additional 150 soldiers were in Erbil,[87] east of Mosul; a total of 800 French troops were involved in the battle of Mosul in 2016. The French military also trained 9,000 Iraqi troops between 2014 and 2018. In terms of aircraft, France was the third largest contributor to the campaign after the United States: thirty-six Rafale jets were deployed in the mission, with twenty-four on the *Charles de Gaulle* aircraft carrier and twelve operating out of French air force bases in Jordan and the United Arab Emirates.[88] France carried out a total of more than 10,600 flights and 1,550 strikes, which destroyed nearly 2,390 targets in Iraq and Syria. One French soldier died in action in Syria.[89] The French military operation against the Islamic State cost $430 million a year,[90] probably around $2 billion in total.

Britain carried out 1,700 airstrikes in Iraq and Syria, second most after the United States. Britain also contributed five times as many troops as France, according to British defense secretary Michael Fallon.[91] The British operation against the Islamic State cost between $1 and $2.3 billion.[92]

Although Germany refused to be involved in combat operations, it contributed in several ways to the coalition's support of partner forces in Iraq. German aircraft carried out reconnaissance and air refueling flights, and participated in NATO-AWACS surveillance flights.[93] Berlin delivered €100 million worth of vehicles, arms, and ammunition up until 2016, along with military equipment to Erbil via Baghdad, as well as nonlethal military equipment to the central authority security forces in Baghdad. In addition, from January 2015 until April 2018, about 17,600 Peshmerga (Kurds, Kakai, and Yazidis) received military training from German instructors in Iraqi Kurdistan, and 314 Peshmerga received training in Germany.[94] Overall, almost 1,600 German soldiers were involved in this training mission.

Italy trained 58,000 members of the Iraqi security and police forces and Iraqi Kurdish forces, and deployed some 1,497 soldiers, 390 land vehicles, and 17 aircraft.[95] In Erbil, Italy and Germany led the Kurdistan Training Coordination Center and coordinated trainers[96] from nine nations (Italy, Germany, the Netherlands, Finland, Sweden, Britain, Hungary, Slovenia, and Turkey).

The Netherlands contributed four F-16 planes to the coalition air campaign over Iraq and eastern Syria, which were used to provide close air support and conduct armed overwatch. Dutch soldiers also trained Iraqi forces on the ground in northern Iraq, and have trained over 100,000 federal and Peshmerga Iraqi forces through the Capacity Building Mission Iraq.[97]

Spain has contributed 480 Spanish military personnel who have helped thousands of Iraqi security forces with training and capacity building and helped stabilize liberated IS territories. They have also provided training on demining, and helped improve the capacity of the Iraqi Border Guard to protect the border with Syria.

The fragmentation of the European military contribution made it harder to assess its overall value to the United States. Several examples do help illustrate the contribution, however. One example related to fighting activities is the frontline between the Kurdistan region of Iraq and the territory controlled by the Islamic State, in 2015–16. There were "about five different nationalities of special forces along that frontline, including Canadians, Americans, Norwegians, Swedes, and French,"[98] based in the Kurdistan Region of Iraq (KRI) and fighting into IS-held federal Iraq. The European contribution in this case implied a fighting component, and is an example of what could theoretically have been achieved in Syria, with its patchwork of sectors, each held by a different nationality.

European and Australian trainers also carried out a significant number of training missions, and the United States supported specific units of the Iraqi security forces as well as of the Iraqi Peshmerga, such as the Counter Terrorism Service and the *quwat khasah* (special forces).[99] There was a division of labor among Western trainers that proved effective in covering a larger spectrum of trainings than what the United States alone could have provided.[100]

Another example of successful cooperation was the Mosul Dam stabilization project. The potential collapse of the Mosul Dam posed a massive threat to Iraq: the dam was built in the 1980s on a bed of soluble rock and therefore requires a constant influx of fresh concrete to prevent a collapse, which would unleash a wave up to a hundred feet high down the Tigris, flooding not only Mosul but also all the towns and cities downstream, including Baghdad. Such a catastrophe could potentially kill up to 1.5 million people and leave an eighth of the Iraqi population homeless.[101] The Islamic State gained control of the dam for less than two weeks in 2014, destroying equipment and preventing essential maintenance operations. The day after IS took control, Vice President Biden called Masoud Barzani, president of the Kurdistan Regional Government (KRG), and urged him to make retaking the dam a top priority for the Peshmerga forces under KRG control. The dam's structural deficiencies, and the massive humanitarian implications of a collapse, caused the U.S. Army Corps of Engineers to dub it "the most dangerous dam in the world."[102] For that reason, the Corps, along with Italian engineers and with protection provided by Italian troops,[103] undertook a joint effort to protect the surrounding area, and Iraq signed a $300 million deal with the Italian company Trevi to shore up the dam permanently.[104]

The anti-IS coalition, therefore, displayed a high level of burden sharing, but as has been noted, the debate over burden sharing became more acute after the election of Donald Trump, at which point the Mosul campaign was over and the most distinctive portion of military burden sharing had already worked. At that point, military burden sharing made sense for Syria. But the U.S. operation in Syria was led entirely by U.S. Special Forces (Combined Joint Task Force–Operation

Inherent Resolve), whereas the operations in Iraq, for both legal and political reasons, had been led by conventional U.S. forces. And while Iraq's government was internationally recognized, the Syrian regime was no longer recognized by most coalition members, and the unstable situation on the ground made the legal justification for intervention in Syria more complex. In addition, a number of European countries were reluctant to be too visible in northeast Syria so as not to damage their bilateral relations with Turkey. Several countries used the right to self-defense to justify participating in operations in Syria. The use of special forces in Syria did not afford much discretion, however (since it is difficult to "hide" two thousand troops), and some of the tasks required on the ground were not specifically related to special forces competencies. But the use of U.S. Special Forces in northeast Syria did give the operation a lighter footprint—not only in a military sense but also legally and politically.

The difference between special and conventional forces seems to be more limited on the American side than on the European one.[105] In the United States, both conventional forces and special forces typically fall under Title 10 authority, which provides the legal basis for armed forces under the control of the Department of Defense, and are overseen by Congress; using special forces does not "confer some special hidden nature."[106] For increased secrecy, the United States has Title 50 authority, which is the legal basis for the CIA's intelligence missions and covert operations such as working with opposition groups in northwest Syria. Employing special forces does, however, enable more flexibility and a smaller force size; and using special forces is ideal for keeping a small staff, as they require less logistical support than conventional forces. This is especially useful when there are manning limits, such as the ones imposed in Syria under the Obama administration. A smaller force posture can also cut through red tape.

One consequence of the American choice to use special forces, however, was that operational cooperation was possible only with

European countries that had their own special forces deployable abroad. Countries like Germany were therefore unable to respond to U.S. calls to share the military burden on the ground, even in noncombat missions.

Even for countries using special forces abroad, the size of these units made it in most cases impossible to really compensate for a U.S. withdrawal. The increased use of U.S. Special Forces, especially since 9/11, meant that there were in total around 70,000 U.S. Special Forces,[107] compared with approximately 3,000 French Special Forces and around 3,500 British Special Forces (before the latter were decreased to 1,700 in 2014).[108] Thus, a "small" special forces operation like the U.S. one in Syria, which at its peak involved at least 2,000 troops,[109] would already have been enough to stretch European special forces to their limit.

The theoretical possibility that U.S. troops could have been replaced by European troops in northeast Syria was therefore difficult to entertain. Yet it is striking that U.S. leadership continued to demand a level of burden sharing from Europe that Europeans could barely satisfy. Aware of the risk of a withdrawal, France and Britain increased their deployments in 2019.[110] The British prime minister at the time, Theresa May, apparently even considered a joint endeavor whereby Britain and France would each provide a thousand troops and replace U.S. troops.[111] But this would have required around a third of existing French and British Special Forces, even assuming that France could have deployed this number of troops while sustaining their existing operations in West Africa. And beyond just troops on the ground, a precondition to a French-British deployment would have still been that the United States keep providing key logistical support on the ground in northeast Syria, as well as air protection.[112] Though military officials assumed that an arrangement would have been possible,[113] lawyers questioned the ability of the U.S. military to maintain air support if American soldiers were not directly on the ground.[114]

The example of military burden sharing in northeast Syria highlights a key aspect of transatlantic cooperation in the Middle East: outside the European territory, operational cooperation is limited to a handful of countries. And the number of potential partners for the United States on the ground was even more limited by the legal uncertainties with respect to northeast Syria.

The Civilian Front

Although only a limited number of countries have participated militarily, the anti-IS coalition has been an effective mechanism for all eighty-one members to cooperate on other crucial efforts, such as stabilization assistance, countering jihadist ideology and terrorist financing, stabilizing former Islamic State territories, impeding the flow of IS fighters, and prosecuting returnees. Thus, coalition working groups helped coordinate efforts to address the issue of jihadist propaganda on the Internet, engaging tech companies and designing projects to develop counternarratives. Information sharing on terrorist financing and foreign fighters has been improved as well within the framework of the coalition.

Humanitarian and stabilization support has probably been the most active component of transatlantic cooperation within the coalition. These programs have contributed to clearing land mines left by IS,[115] alleviating humanitarian crises in refugee camps, repairing basic infrastructure, providing primary health care, and relaunching local economies. The coalition has also promoted bilateral and multilateral support to Iraq—for example, to rebuild the University of Mosul.[116] Such efforts were crucial to restoring decent living conditions for populations who suffered during IS rule and the war against it.

European countries—Germany, France, the Netherlands, Italy—have provided specific capabilities to coalition efforts in close coordination with the United States. Chairing the stabilization working group of the coalition, and building on its then newly created Stabilization

Department,[117] Germany's Foreign Ministry has influenced the way the coalition has conceptualized and coordinated its different members' programs, especially in Iraq.

The Civilian Front: Iraq

In Iraq, the United States has provided more than $2.6 billion in assistance since 2014, including for food, water, medicine, and shelters, making it Iraq's largest humanitarian donor.[118] The United States has been the largest donor to demining operations, clearing over 86 million square meters of land since 2015. Germany alone has also provided up to €1.3 billion of humanitarian assistance in Iraq.

Because the central government in Bagdad was internationally recognized, humanitarian and stabilization efforts in Iraq have been easier to coordinate. They have been led mostly by the UN, in partnership with the Iraqi government and in constant coordination with the coalition. Beyond emergency relief, the UN Development Program (UNDP) ran projects in all IS-liberated provinces of Iraq, rebuilding basic infrastructure, creating short-term employment, building up the capacity of local institutions, and supporting local reconciliation. Three multilateral instruments were set up.

The Funding Facility for Stabilization (FFS), created in 2015 at the request of the Iraqi government and extended until 2020, was managed by the UNDP to work on both immediate stabilization—urgent provision of means of subsistence, particularly for displaced populations, which still numbered 1.6 million people in 2019; rehabilitation of light infrastructure; capacity building for local organizations; social cohesion—and stabilization in the medium term, meaning rehabilitation of more substantial infrastructure. Since 2015, this fund has received $1 billion from twenty-seven donors. More than two thousand projects have been carried out by the FFS.

A second instrument was the Iraq Recovery and Resilience Trust Fund, set up following the International Conference for Reconstruction of Iraq, co-organized by the EU and Kuwait in February 2018 and implemented by the UNDP for a period of two years (2018–20) to support the social dimension of reconstruction. Donor countries pledged around $30 billion to help Iraq rebuild, around €400 million of which came from EU grants.[119]

And the third instrument was a Multi-Donor Trust Fund for Iraq, set up by the World Bank around three components: economic recovery and reconstruction, advisory support and reform assistance, and coordination and effectiveness of the reconstruction process.

European contributions to all three of these vehicles have been extensive. Germany has contributed €340 million to stabilization efforts in Iraq since 2014 and provided a credit line of €500 million to the Iraqi government to support the return of internally displaced persons to areas liberated from IS and to facilitate the transition from stabilization to development cooperation. France has provided humanitarian and stabilization assistance of €90 million in Iraq since 2014, a loan of €430 million to the Iraqi government, and support for various United Nations agencies (UNDP, the World Food Program, the UN High Commissioner for Refugees) and French NGOs operating in the field.[120]

Other European countries have contributed financially to humanitarian aid as well. The Netherlands provided about €86.7 million in humanitarian relief between 2014 and 2018 and have sent surgical teams to Baghdad in light of the limited medical capacity there.[121] Spain has contributed nearly €48 million in humanitarian aid since 2012, which has gone to helping refugees, supplying water and basic sanitation, and helping the people of Mosul.[122] Italy provided $430 million in grants and soft loans for Iraq.

In total, since 2014, the EU has provided more than €1 billion in support to Iraq, including €435 million in humanitarian aid, €320 million in development funding, and €6.5 million in European Instrument for Democracy and Human Rights funding for civil society organizations.[123]

The Civilian Front: Syria

Reckoning international contributions in Syria in the anti-IS framework is more difficult. Methodologically, this study assumes that all funding directed to northeast Syria contributed to the fight against the Islamic State, but the geographical breakdown of humanitarian funding in Syria is not always clear. UN data is often not area-specific, and in northeast Syria most NGOs worked outside the UN framework through direct bilateral funding, out of fear that the Syrian regime's influence on the UN in Syria would endanger their activities (see figure 2.3 for coalition pledge drive figures).

The United States and Europe have in any case provided by far the largest contribution, amounting to around 90 percent of UN funding, to humanitarian support for Syrians. The U.S. government has provided more than $10 billion in assistance to Syrians in Syria and neighboring countries since 2012;[124] the EU and its member states have given over $20 billion since the crisis in Syria began in 2011.[125] Between 2014 and 2018, Germany alone provided some €1.23 billion in Syria.[126] Italy provided $400 million in support to Syria and the region as part of a comprehensive aid package for the years 2016–18. The Netherlands has provided €458 million in mostly unearmarked humanitarian assistance in response to the Iraq and Syria crises since 2012.

The breakdown of stabilization funding is easier to track geographically. Since the United States and European countries refused to fund stabilization activities in regime areas—and the majority of stabilization activities in northwest Syria stopped because of fears of aid diversion by jihadist groups like Hayat Tahrir al-Sham (HTS)—stabilization funding has mostly been allocated to northeast Syria. Including bilateral contributions to NGOs working in the area, the author estimates that European stabilization contributions under the coalition framework totaled more than $400 million between 2017 and 2019 in northeast Syria.[127] Other means of U.S. and European funding included €116 million in stabilization measures, like the rehabilitation of basic services through the multidonor Syria Recovery Trust Fund (€38.7 million since 2013), created by the United States, Germany, and the UAE, and the clearance of explosive hazards in areas liberated from the Islamic State in Raqqa province (€12 million).

European countries have resorted to different stabilization funding strategies. While Berlin was hesitant in 2017 and 2018 to fund stabilization activities in areas controlled by the Syrian Democratic Forces (SDF) and the Democratic Union Party (PYD), Germany ended up providing $20 million directly to the U.S. Syria Transition Assistance Response Team programs run by the U.S. State Department in 2019. Britain also provided $2 million in that framework. An additional $100 million from Saudi Arabia and $50 million from the UAE supported U.S.-led activities. These contributions were very valuable at the time, considering that President Trump told an Ohio rally in March 2018 that U.S. troops would be leaving Syria "very soon," and then unilaterally froze $200 million of stabilization assistance intended for Syria, combined with a call for Gulf Arab states "to take over and pay for stabilizing and reconstructing areas liberated from the Islamic State."[128] The president's emphasis on burden sharing led the U.S. Special Envoy to the Global Coalition to Counter Daesh/ISIS (SECI) to step up his efforts to solicit monetary contributions from U.S. coalition partners for stabilization programs—and European and Gulf partners did fund U.S. stabilization operations between March 2018 and November 2019.

France has used a different approach, taking advantage of its more reactive internal process to disburse funding to NGOs at times when the humanitarian response in northeast Syria was insufficient—such as right after the liberation of Raqqa in October 2017, and during the military operation in the border area with Iraq in July 2018. Since these operations, French funding has supported NGOs in activities like water-trucking to reach zones close to the front line, but outside the area where the U.S. military would deliver emergency humanitarian support.

Figure 2.3 National Contributions to the "International Coalition Against ISIS," June 30, 2019

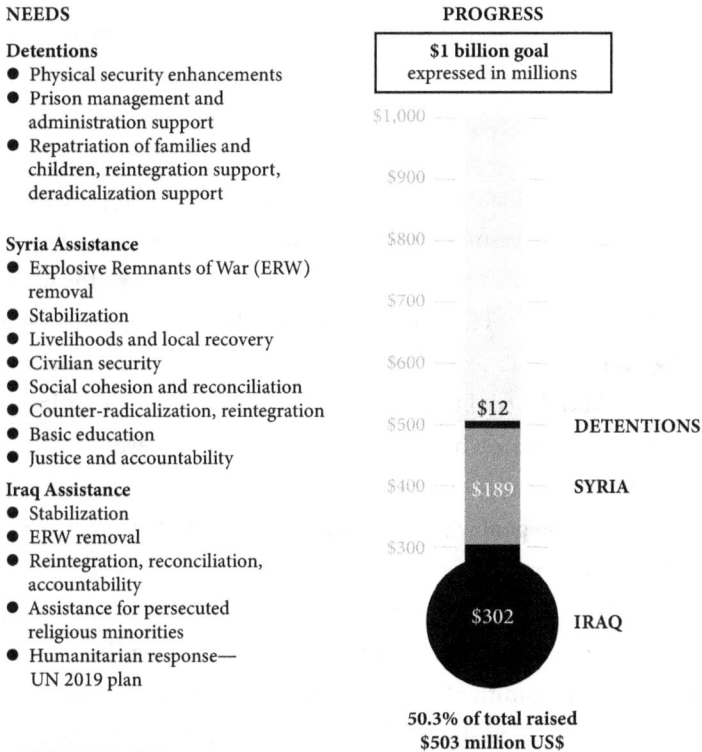

NEEDS

PROGRESS

Detentions
- Physical security enhancements
- Prison management and administration support
- Repatriation of families and children, reintegration support, deradicalization support

Syria Assistance
- Explosive Remnants of War (ERW) removal
- Stabilization
- Livelihoods and local recovery
- Civilian security
- Social cohesion and reconciliation
- Counter-radicalization, reintegration
- Basic education
- Justice and accountability

Iraq Assistance
- Stabilization
- ERW removal
- Reintegration, reconciliation, accountability
- Assistance for persecuted religious minorities
- Humanitarian response—UN 2019 plan

$1 billion goal
expressed in millions

$1,000

$900

$800

$700

$600

$500 $12 DETENTIONS

$400 $189 SYRIA

$300

$302 IRAQ

50.3% of total raised
$503 million US$

CONTRIBUTORS

Norway
UK
Sweden
Estonia
Denmark
EU
France
Germany
Netherlands
Italy
USA
Iraq
Australia
New Zealand

Office of the Inspector General, Operation Inherent Resolve: Lead IG Report to the U.S. Congress, April 1, 2019–June 30, 2019, 36, https://www.stateoig.gov/system/files/q3fy2019_leadig_oir_report.pdf.

These examples of European and American contributions to humanitarian aid and stabilization in former Islamic State territories show how complex the architecture of the funding, both bilateral and multilateral, has been, comprising a very large number of actors: governments, UN agencies, local actors, NGOs, and implementing companies.

A Missing Political Track

The coalition has been militarily effective in defeating the Islamic State: in the short term, its process and architecture have played an integral role in the liberation of all territories controlled by the terrorist organization. It has not fully accomplished its long-term goals, however, having failed to stabilize former IS territories, both materially and politically. And the coalition was not able to address the political root causes of the rise of IS, which ended up curtailing whatever stabilization it could achieve.

A key coalition goal was helping to create a legitimate alternative to IS in Sunni Arab areas in Iraq and in northeast Syria. But the political agenda in Iraq has been dominated by post-2003 politics, especially the sectarian nature of the political system—making the Shia bloc, even if divided, dominant. To some extent, the modalities of the fight against IS exacerbated this problem. The coalition, often strapped for boots on the ground, had to work, or at least deal, with the Iran-backed Popular Mobilization Forces (PMF, aka *al-Hashd al-Shabi*) to retake IS territory. The various plans to rein in Shia militias after the war ended never came to fruition, and these sectarian groups are now stronger than ever, creating a new obstacle for an Iraqi state seeking to cultivate its legitimacy in Sunni territory.

In Syria, meanwhile, both the Obama and Trump administrations were opposed to involving the coalition in the political issues, preferring to focus primarily on counterterrorism operations. Especially toward the end of these operations, however, a key problem was that the absence of a political process to stabilize these areas in the long term threatened to unravel the gains of counterterrorism itself.

Iraqi Politics Undermines the Anti-IS Fight

In Iraq, intra-Shia dynamics in Baghdad and the Kurdish independence referendum in September 2017 created tensions that ended the national front launched in 2014 against the Islamic State. Spurred on by the Shia cleric Ali al-Sistani's 2014 fatwa against IS, the mostly Shia paramilitary Popular Mobilization Forces (PMF) mobilized to fight alongside the Iraqi security forces and in coordination with Iraqi Kurdish troops to retake the territory that had fallen under the terrorist group's control. In that context, the counter-IS mission has relied on solid cooperation between federal Iraqi authorities, Shia militias loosely connected to the federal state, and the Kurdistan Region of Iraq. To effectively defeat IS, there needs to be a right of hot pursuit and close intelligence coordination; the Islamic State remains most stubborn in areas where there is a lack of coordination. The biggest missed opportunity of the anti-IS mission was likely the inability to build peace between Erbil and Baghdad, and to reduce the influence of Shia militias. The United States and Europe would have needed to create joint security mechanisms between Baghdad and Erbil.

It is not clear whether this issue was discussed within the anti-IS coalition, or if it received much attention before the Battle of Mosul in 2016–17. In the first week of the battle, there was solid cooperation between the two sides. Federal Iraqi troops were transported through Kurdish areas successfully, and cooperation between federal Iraqi troops and Kurdish Peshmerga conveyed the impression that every element of Iraqi society was ready to defeat IS. This camaraderie began to wane after the first week of the battle, however, when Kurdish troops stopped advancing and federal Iraqi troops proceeded. The discrepancy created ill feelings, and separated the Kurdish struggle from the Iraqi struggle.

The key issue for our analysis of U.S.-Europe cooperation is whether the United States and the Europeans would have had the power and the opportunity to prevent the Kurdish referendum and subsequent skirmish in Kirkuk in October 2017 if they had focused on Baghdad-Erbil peace building earlier. Washington missed cues indicating the potential for Kirkuk, and did not focus on the Baghdad-Erbil rift until it was too late.[129] In general, its European partners tended to wait for the United States to take the lead on this issue; perhaps a more aggressive European actor could have taken a proactive stance on Baghdad-Erbil peace building and left the counter-IS mission in a stronger position. Senior European officials interviewed believe that Europe was not in a position to influence the Kurdish leadership or the federal government; European countries such as Germany played an advising role on issues related to economic reform, but had little political leverage over Bagdad or Erbil. When the referendum project became clear, U.S. and European officials warned KRG leadership against the idea, but their advice was not heard in Erbil.[130] Officials who were in Washington at that time acknowledged that the United States may not have conveyed the message to the Barzani family at a high enough level.[131]

Another way in which Iraqi politics affected the anti-IS fight was that the confrontation coincided with the start of several PMF leaders' political careers. Although their militias were ostensibly fighting on behalf of the Iraqi state, their close ties to Iran and their overwhelmingly Shia composition made them sources of suspicion in the mostly Sunni-majority areas where the war against IS was waged. The coalition cooperated with some of them, and in November 2016 the Iraqi parliament formally incorporated them into the Iraqi military, but they always retained significant operational autonomy.[132]

The post-military situation created competition between Shia actors in the wake of the May 2018 general elections, which did not afford much space to reintegrate Sunni communities into Iraqi federal institutions. On the contrary, the influence of Shia militias remains a central source of fear for Sunni communities.[133] Neither the United States nor Europe could really affect this balance of power. In other words, the work of the coalition has been undermined by factors that had more to do with the institutional and paramilitary legacy of the U.S. intervention in 2003 than with counterterrorism as such.

The coalition in Iraq has been a collateral victim of U.S.-Iran tensions, a backslide exacerbated by the country's deteriorating political situation. The changing U.S. priority, from the fight against IS to the neutralization of Shia militias, further weakened coalition efforts. Most European member states kept their focus on the fight against IS, and at the same time refused to contribute to the "maximum pressure" policy against Iran. The escalation that started in summer 2019 eventually put non-American coalition members at risk and weakened the coalition even more.

In autumn 2019 the United States started to reduce its overall footprint in Iraq, and it accelerated that process in the first quarter of 2020 with the closure of all bases on Iraqi territory, except for Baghdad and the bases of Erbil and al-Asad. This contraction was accompanied by a significant decrease in the total number of personnel present in Iraq under the coalition, especially in the context of Covid-19.

In the context of high tensions with Iran, the American priority has been to enhance the protection of its forces in a particularly tense security context populated by pro-Iran militias, and to respond to the Trump administration's inclination for a general U.S. military drawdown in the Middle East. But this direction reflects more deeply the desire to transition to the "post–territorial caliphate" phase of the American presence in Iraq. The United States no longer seems to share the fear of a resurgence of IS in the Middle East and considers the situation to be under control.

In the context of a further U.S. withdrawal, the main challenge is to update the set of international programs providing assistance to Iraqi forces. In addition to the U.S.-led coalition providing both lethal support and nonlethal advising at the operational level to help hunt down IS cells, NATO and the European Union provide strategic advice to Iraq's Defense Ministry and Interior Ministry, respectively. Some European states, like France, maintain bilateral military training programs in the context of the IS fight. The UN Assistance Mission for Iraq and the UNDP have also provided training in security sector and justice sector reform—for example, to strengthen local policing.

U.S. allies accepted in February 2020 that the existing NATO training mission in Iraq should play an increasing role by gradually taking over responsibility for training activities previously provided by the coalition. This was meant to enable an American disengagement and hence the transfer of certain support functions (logistics, right-of-way management, strategic evacuation) to other coalition members who are also part of NATO. Now that the United States has reduced its military footprint to 2,500 personnel, Denmark's decision to assume leadership over the mission and send 285 military personnel is meant to demonstrate European willingness to intensify their efforts in order to prevent the reemergence of IS. To be sure, some degree of U.S. military backing (e.g., force protection, airlift, intelligence, base access) will still be required at first if international security assistance is to be sustainable and credible.

A Self-Defeating Policy in Syria

In Syria, the biggest obstacle to political stabilization in the northeast was the initial American refusal to get more heavily involved in the political process. Given limited domestic support for another attempt at regime change, Washington isolated the fight against the Islamic State from the broader Syrian crisis.

The United States initially detached its military intervention against IS from any attempt to fight the Assad regime because of the Obama administration's Syria fatigue. It can be argued that this separation was the only way to secure sufficient American political support for the coalition, and to avoid provoking Russian pushback. It is difficult to speculate regarding what would have happened had the administration made a different policy choice, but it *is* possible to see how the decision that was made ultimately undermined the goal of defeating the Islamic State.

The separation of these two ultimately linked issues—fighting IS and arriving at some sort of political solution in Syria—has indeed been a central weakness of the coalition. It was initially reflected at the bureaucratic level. The coalition has mainly been coordinated through the position created in 2014 of U.S. Special Envoy to the Global Coalition to Counter Daesh/ISIS (SECI). This had the effect of bifurcating U.S. policy toward Syria in terms of geography, mission, and leadership—with the tactical, short-term counterterrorism Islamic State policy in eastern Syria the responsibility of the SECI and the longer-term post-Assad policy elsewhere falling to the Special Envoy for Syria. The latter position replaced the U.S. ambassador role after Washington cut off diplomatic relations with Damascus in 2012.

This bureaucratic divide was later corrected when Ambassador James Jeffrey took over both the SECI and Special Envoy for Syria positions in December 2018. But for the greater part of the fight against the jihadist group, the distinction between the SECI and the Special Envoy led to an absence of clarity regarding the timeline of the U.S. military presence in northeast Syria and the intended political endgame in the area. And although the decision to disconnect the fight against IS from the larger Syria issue was made by the Obama administration, President Trump's intention to withdraw troops from Syria at the end of combat operations compounded the uncertainty and contradictions of American policy, and made clear how limited were the possibilities for European allies to influence the U.S. policymaking process.

Though the relationship between the SECI and its U.S. military counterparts had been close in the early stages of the campaign and pushed the coalition to prioritize military operations against the Islamic State,[134] other parts of the State Department had been in favor of using the anti-IS campaign to pressure Assad and force him to negotiate. European diplomats were not entirely clear on this issue: while several countries did view the anti-IS operation as a way to pressure Assad, their priority was to defeat IS as quickly as possible. In any case, with the operation being largely run by the United States, it was difficult for Europeans to influence its conduct, and large coalition meetings with dozens of countries were not well suited to engage in difficult political discussions. A number of Quint meetings—involving the United States, Britain, Germany, France, and Italy—allowed for more substantial exchanges but did not change the strategy decided by Washington.

The isolation of the anti-IS fight from the Syrian issue had one decisive consequence: the choice of local partner. Although some opposition forces had managed to repel IS attacks in the Aleppo area while fighting against the Syrian regime, the United States decided to make stopping the fight against Assad a prerequisite for American backing. In 2014 and 2015, therefore, Syrian armed opposition groups were not supported if they did not agree to cease the fight against Assad and focus only on IS. In this context, the YPG, the military branch of the Democratic Union Party (PYD)—a Syrian Kurdish group tied to Turkey's Kurdistan Workers Party (PKK)—appeared to be the most effective military partner in the anti-IS campaign. The YPG was politically opposed to the Syrian regime but, unlike all the other armed groups, did not fight it, and maintained relations with it after its withdrawal from northeast Syria in 2012. Since the YPG's territorial goals were limited to the northeast, where most of Syria's Kurdish population lives, it had less incentive than other groups to spend precious resources attempting to topple the government in Damascus.

On the other hand, YPG tensions with Turkey increased after 2015 and the failure of the PKK-Ankara peace talks, after which PYD leaders stopped being authorized to travel to Turkey to negotiate with Turkish officials. The PYD-Turkey dynamic was made even more complicated by tensions between the PYD/YPG and groups from the Free Syrian

Army: the YPG is said to have helped the Syrian regime take over eastern neighborhoods of Aleppo from the FSA in 2016. As a result of this rift, Turkey managed to exclude the PYD from the UN-led process aimed at negotiating an outcome in Syria, which further fragmented the opposition to Assad. By focusing only on the military dimension, the coalition selected military partners who were against the Syrian opposition, which most Western governments were supporting diplomatically in the Syrian crisis. Until today, U.S. military officials do not deny the political ramifications of this choice of partner, but they stress the political limitation of their own mandate given by the White House, which was to focus on the anti-IS fight and remove support for the fight against Assad. They also insist on the quality of their engagement with YPG leaders—especially Gen. Mazloum Kobani Abdi, one of the group's main leaders who serves as commander-in-chief of the Syrian Democratic Forces (SDF). Such figures, in their eyes, proved more reliable and efficient than all the other local leaders they had partnered with, not only in Syria, but also in Iraq and Afghanistan.[135]

In theory, this contradiction could have been addressed through an intense and difficult diplomatic engagement any time between 2015 and 2019 and even in 2014, as members of the coalition were not aligned on Syria the way they were on Iraq. Agreed on the broader goal of forcing the Syrian regime to change its practices or step down, the United States, the Europeans, and the Turks could have designed a new policy mix vis-à-vis Syria, reshaping the UN framework that was supposed to solve the conflict. This could have included security guarantees to Ankara so that Turkey would not have felt obliged to launch three military operations against the YPG;[136] a real separation between the PKK and the PYD as a precondition for increased U.S. support to the YPG after the Kobane battle; and a reshuffle of the Syrian opposition around moderate politicians close to Ankara and non-PYD politicians from the SDF, thereby allowing northeast Syria to join the UN process. This would have implied linking a set of issues, bilateral and international, going much further beyond just the fight against IS.

A first obstacle was that including the SDF (of which the YPG was the central player) within the UN framework would have required the passage of a new resolution to replace UN Security Council Resolution 2254, which outlined a transition process in Syria but did not mention other actors besides the Syrian regime and the Syrian opposition. But Resolution 2254 had been negotiated in a context less favorable to Assad, and Western countries feared that Russia would use the opportunity of a new negotiation to kill the idea of a transition process. This legal obstacle implied that the SDF could not be formally integrated in the UN framework unless it came to an understanding with Turkey to be ultimately merged within the Turkish-backed Syrian opposition (the Syrian National Coalition) controlling the Syrian opposition negotiation committee.

A vicious circle was already in play, however, and difficult to break: the aforementioned bureaucratic divisions between the SECI and the Special Envoy limited the ability to articulate U.S. Syria policy as well as U.S. Turkey policy. The bilateral relationship with Turkey was mostly dealt with through channels outside the anti-IS campaign, without much space to reconcile the two. For instance, at the military level, while the U.S. Central Command (CENTCOM) was doing as much as it could to support the SDF, its partner force against IS, U.S. European Command, was trying to preserve as much as possible the relationship with Turkey, a NATO ally. Similar internal oppositions existed within the State Department.

Different parts of the U.S. system eventually carried out decisions in Syria that initiated a cycle of distrust, ultimately limiting the possibility of compromise with Ankara. For instance, despite U.S. diplomatic assurances to Turkey that the SDF would not advance past the Euphrates' eastern bank, the Defense Department continued supporting the group even as it crossed the river in August 2016 and occupied Manbij, just twenty-five miles from the Turkish border. This confused U.S. signaling led to Turkey's Operation Euphrates Shield campaign to force the SDF back. Such ill-defined commitments in Syria have led to numerous skirmishes of this nature, with U.S. allies attacking U.S.-backed forces.

Turkey's Operation Olive Branch in Afrin was launched in January 2018, after the United States announced in December 2017 the creation of a Kurdish border force, before backtracking.[137] After IS lost its last territory in Syria in March 2019, the timeframe of a U.S. military presence remained unclear, while U.S. officials told their Turkish counterparts that the U.S. presence was limited to the fight against IS. One former senior U.S. military official put it this way: "We were not clear with Turkey. Turkey pushed, and each time we thought doing a bit more would be enough to avoid an offensive."[138] (See figure 2.4 for Turkish campaigns in Syria.)

This context led to contradictions between European and American goals in Syria—the Americans supporting the UN-led negotiation process, notwithstanding the coalition's de facto policy of supporting a force not included in the UN-led process in northeast Syria. In 2016, when tensions occurred between Damascus and the Syrian Democratic Forces, their military leader, Mazloum Kobani Abdi, allegedly proposed to his U.S. counterparts expelling the Syrian regime from the enclaves it had kept in Hasaka since 2012, and requested U.S. air cover to prevent the regime or Russia from bombing the city in retaliation. According to SDF sources, the U.S. military refused, and encouraged Abdi to keep a channel open to the Syrian regime.[139] In 2018, then special envoy Brett McGurk himself is said to have encouraged the SDF to directly strike a deal with the Syrian regime, even as the State Department's policy was to support the opposition to Assad within the UN framework.

As a result of these contradictions, U.S. political engagement in northeast Syria has been limited and slow. State Department senior officials would regularly visit the SDF leadership, but the limited U.S. diplomatic presence in northeast Syria restricted possibilities

Figure 2.4 Turkish Campaigns in Northern Syria

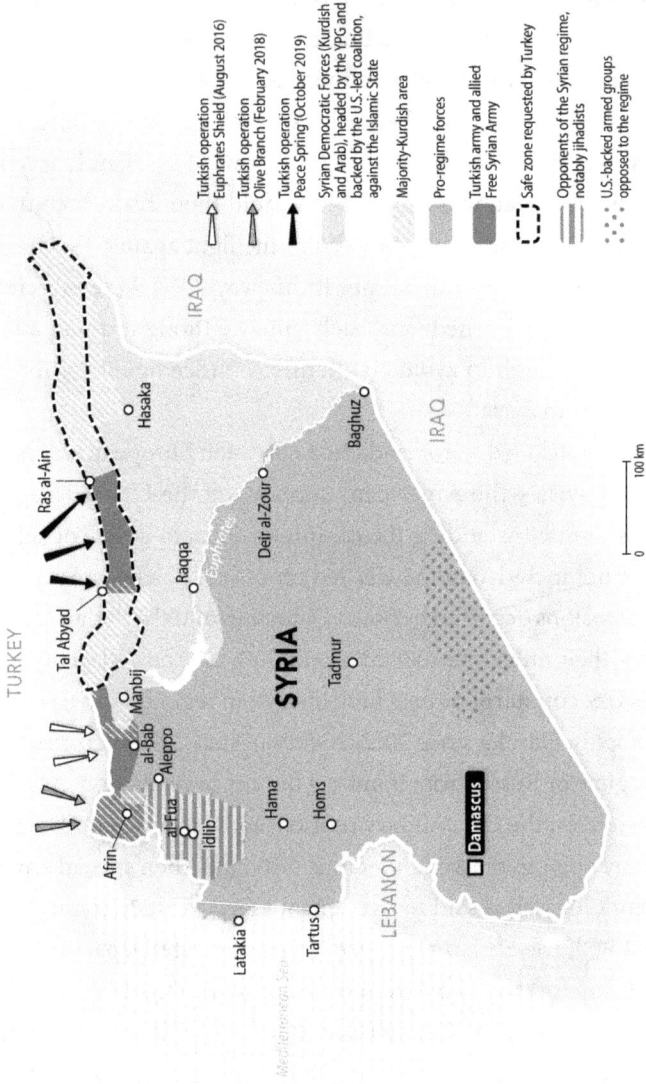

Turkish operation
Euphrates Shield (August 2016)

Turkish operation
Olive Branch (February 2018)

Turkish operation
Peace Spring (October 2019)

Syrian Democratic Forces (Kurdish
and Arab), headed by the YPG and
backed by the U.S.-led coalition,
against the Islamic State

Majority-Kurdish area

Pro-regime forces

Turkish army and allied
Free Syrian Army

Safe zone requested by Turkey

Opponents of the Syrian regime,
notably jihadists

U.S.-backed armed groups
opposed to the regime

for designing sufficient responses to de-escalate with Turkey. U.S. diplomats also seemed to have a limited dialogue with the Turkish-backed Syrian opposition. The State Department therefore struggled to sustain dynamics it had initially pushed for, like the creation of the "Future Party" in northeast Syria, a new Arab-Kurdish political party that was meant to reduce PYD influence, reach out to Syrian opposition parties, and create space for northeast Syria to be integrated in the UN process; but the Future Party never managed to really exist without a strong PYD footprint.[140]

The PYD itself tried to create some political space for itself by engaging with other Syrian political actors. Several PYD officials maintained personal and informal connections with personalities from the Syrian opposition in exile, especially the so-called Cairo group. The PYD also organized several meetings in northeast Syria, for instance in July 2018, with a heterogeneous network of political figures who were not openly opposed to the regime, as well as with people outside Syria. These attempts did not produce substantial outcomes, however, mostly because of the Turkish pressure against opposition figures likely to formally accept the PYD within the "opposition."

France did try to support a political track between Turkey and the PYD between 2018 and 2019, but initially faced difficulties in mobilizing its U.S. counterparts. Parts of the U.S. administration later supported this goal, including Jim Jeffrey and his deputy, William Roebuck. After being appointed Special Envoy for Syria and to the anti–Islamic State coalition in December 2018, Jeffrey tried to work in this direction, proposing a security mechanism with Turkey.[141] The U.S. government as a whole did not exert enough leverage in support of this dynamic, however. And Turkey's Peace Spring operation in October 2019, which saw Turkey-backed forces conducting major military operations to force the SDF out of its northern territory following the partial U.S. withdrawal from northeast Syria, probably closed the window of opportunity.

Another complicating factor was that the dialogue with Turkey throughout this period was only bilateral. The coalition was a forum for briefings and exchanges of information among partners, but was rarely an arena for addressing tensions; despite Turkey's participation, tensions between member states and Turkey were not addressed collectively. The negotiations about Turkey's demand for a safe zone were mostly led by the United States bilaterally, with Washington briefing coalition members depending on their respective involvement in military issues. Thus, a potential takeover of the negotiations by Britain and France in January 2019 was very difficult, as they had not been included in previous negotiations, including about the Manbij safe zone. France had expressed a desire to be involved in the U.S.-Turkey discussions on Manbij; the United States refused, perhaps as a result of Turkish pushback.[142]

The design of the coalition itself turned out to be an obstacle in this context. It was too large for sufficient consultation with partners, but at the same time the wide-ranging goals of member states made tensions inevitable, leading to confusing and often ineffective bilateral negotiations. The U.S.-Turkey bilateral relationship became more decisive for the coalition than coalition meetings—and other bilateral tracks between the United States and its European partners were used to inform Europeans about U.S.-Turkey negotiations rather than to design solutions. (One European official referred to U.S.-Turkey negotiations about a potential safe zone as "a black hole."[143]) With the exception of France,[144] which became more and more vocal about Turkish military operations in northern Syria after the Afrin offensive in January 2018, European countries also probably did not want to link their own bilateral relationship with Turkey to the fate of the coalition. In other words, in order to address what turned out to be a transatlantic challenge in December 2019 at the NATO Summit in London, designing a format enabling discussion among the United States, Turkey, France, Germany, Britain, Italy, and the Netherlands could have helped shift the discussion.

These political shortcomings had direct consequences for stabilization activities. The grueling fight to wrest territory from IS control decimated cities and towns across eastern Syria, leveling entire districts and leaving these "liberated" areas in critical need of major coordinated efforts to stabilize and rebuild. IS undertook a scorched earth strategy, mining cities and roads to an unprecedented level and leaving few options available to the coalition but to resort to airstrikes destroying buildings, which also meant civilian casualties.

Restoring critical infrastructure was essential beyond the initial emergency relief, but the absence of political clarity hampered the potential of existing stabilization programs and limited European contributions. The coalition's stabilization efforts in Raqqa, for example, began at full speed only in January 2018 owing to the extensive risk of explosive devices, but President Trump's first withdrawal statement followed in March. Planning was rendered impossible beyond three months by the fear of a sudden withdrawal of U.S. troops, which, in the end, never happened. Syrians allied with the United States worried that a withdrawal of their forces would lead to the regime returning. Indeed, in light of the abbreviated U.S. timeline, the SDF initiated talks with the Syrian regime to work toward a political settlement on the future of northeast Syria in summer 2018. Even though those talks did not produce any tangible outcome, they reinforced the perception within Syria that regime return was a matter of "when," not "if."

Although stabilization programs are supposed to support a political dynamic, activities in northeast Syria were designed to be apolitical because of the fear of increasing tensions with Turkey, and on account of Ankara's accusation that actors were receiving political support from the PYD. Local coalition partners consistently asked whether the United States would stay and raise political issues related to the broader Syrian crisis, but the State Department team involved in stabilization was not allowed to talk about politics.[145] Early recovery programs funded by the State Department between 2017 and 2019 were specifically designed not to involve the civil councils, the municipal bodies running northeastern Syrian cities, because they were PYD-led, even if this meant teams duplicating the work of these councils and creating friction. Seeing most of the funding channeled outside their institutions, the local administration became more suspicious and distrustful toward international NGOs and implementing partners, which created additional coordination issues.[146]

Against this backdrop, stabilization programs continued to implement early recovery projects, but with extreme uncertainty as to how much longer they could operate owing to financial, legal, and security concerns. The goal of coalition stabilization efforts was not related to the Syrian political process but only to short-term "military stabilization," meaning providing or supporting enough emergency assistance and basic services to end military operations. Though the United States made exceptions and did work with some local councils under PYD influence, European contributions were kept outside the influence of the civil councils.[147] The vetting of local implementing partners slowed the funding process, however, and in many cases led some European countries not to fund projects in northeast Syria at all.

Although European contributions to humanitarian and stabilization efforts have been significant, political uncertainties and internal divisions limited Europe's potential. And the diversity of tools and instruments used by different European actors made internal coordination a challenge. Thus, the European Union has been mostly absent from stabilization efforts in northeast Syria, and member states failed to mobilize existing tools. The United States organized field trips for other European countries; but many Europeans as well as the European Commission remained reluctant to engage stabilization instruments at the bilateral level or in the framework of the European Neighbourhood Policy.

The separation of the fight against the Islamic State from the rest of the Syrian conflict also limited the coalition's stabilization efforts by limiting its ability to coordinate through UN channels. The United

Nations set up in Syria an especially robust system of humanitarian coordination, as part of which it created a platform enabling NGOs to provide assistance to more than ten million Syrians within the country. Yet international law obliges the UN to coordinate with the central government of the host country, which in the Syrian context meant the Assad regime. This has created significant concerns throughout the Syrian conflict regarding aid diversion by regime cronies,[148] and led numerous NGOs to criticize the UN system.[149] Despite this major failure to protect humanitarian assistance from politicization, however, UN agencies have proven to be essential in coordinating a sufficient volume of assistance to non-regime areas like northwest Syria, where four million people depend on humanitarian assistance.

In northeast Syria, this coordination role of the UN has been largely lacking, and tensions between the SDF and Turkey reduced humanitarian access even further. To limit the regime's ability to block assistance to non-regime areas, the UN Security Council established in 2014 a cross-border mechanism[150] allowing the UN to ship assistance from Turkey, Iraq, and Jordan without Damascus's permission. Regime pressure on the UN, however, led it to drastically limit its use of the cross-border point of al-Yarubiya between Syria and Iraq, retaken in 2018 by the SDF. The regime also forbade the UN to work with NGOs not registered in Damascus. This forced all but one NGO to work under the radar without assistance from the UN, and to use the Faysh Khabur border crossing to ship staff and material.

From a humanitarian point of view, northeast Syria has been largely detached from the so-called Whole of Syria mechanism, positioning coalition members as the only donors supporting NGOs in the area. Although diplomatic pressure from coalition members could have changed UN agencies' behavior, bureaucratic distinctions between officials in charge of the fight against IS and those in charge of the humanitarian management of the Syria crisis limited progress. The al-Yarubiya crossing has been used only for medical equipment, and only at a slow pace. In 2019, while almost nine hundred trucks per month were using the border crossing from Turkey to northwest Syria, only five per month entered northeast Syria.[151] Americans and Europeans therefore had to compensate for the UN absence with additional bilateral funding for humanitarian activities in northeast Syria instead of increasing stabilization programs and expanding the scope of international assistance to former IS territories. And a Russian veto at the UN Security Council eventually prevented the renewal of the al-Yarubiya crossing in 2020.

As a result, the areas in Syria where the Islamic State was strongest have been those receiving the least from the international community. The U.S. withdrawal in October 2019 from significant portions of northeast Syria has not only limited humanitarian assistance, but has also prevented any attempt to rehabilitate and reconstruct these areas. Moreover, international sanctions on the regime, put in place owing to the lack of a negotiated outcome, still prevent anyone from investing in or sending reconstruction equipment to the area outside the coalition framework.

The limited resources available to support northeast Syria impacted relationships between the United States, the coalition, and local authorities. The SDF, and its political branch, the Syrian Democratic Council, systematically complained to Western interlocutors about the insufficient support they were receiving, both on account of limited resources and because of the international reluctance to work directly with the PYD. In turn, this situation limited the leverage the coalition might have had on the PYD to develop a more inclusive governance.

Unfinished Business and Missed Opportunities

The lack of a well-designed political track in the coalition's strategy implied that a political alternative to the Islamic State could not be supported. On the Iraqi side, U.S.-Iran tensions as well as rivalries between Shia actors and the political class interested in maintaining the status quo blocked genuine political and institutional reforms. In Syria, given the PYD footprint, the SDF remained by design unable to provide an inclusive political framework or to appease tensions with Turkey. But the self-administration in northeast Syria between 2017 and 2019 and the Iraqi institutions in 2016 and 2018 provided the coalition with opportunities to change this situation.

The political and military achievement of coordinating a coalition of eighty-two countries cannot be underestimated: the territorial defeat of IS would not have been possible without U.S. leadership and contributions. Considerable American resources and lessons learned from fifteen years of counterterrorism cooperation enabled a military success. Given the magnitude of the economic and political problems in Syria and Iraq that led to the rise of IS, it would also not make sense to blame the coalition or the United States alone for not achieving its stabilization goals, or for not solving some of the most complex political problems of the Middle East.

The asymmetry of the U.S.-Europe relationship within the coalition made things more difficult, however, and led to a number of missed opportunities. The territorial defeat of the Islamic State in March 2019 did not prevent the next resurgence of the jihadist group. The number of attacks in Iraq and Syria throughout 2019 and 2020 remained high, with an average of eleven to fifteen per month. In 2020, 3,500 fighters were said to remain underground in Iraq and 4,000 in Syria. Another indicator of the scale of the problem is the remaining number of internally displaced people in both Syria and Iraq. Notwithstanding the slow return of part of them in Iraq, roughly 1.4 million people are still internally displaced there as of March 2021.[152] They live in difficult conditions, which could ultimately feed another cycle of radicalization. The al-Hawl camp, which hosts nearly 65,000 displaced people as of October 2020,[153] including members of IS, understandably attracted a lot of attention, but the situation of large civilian populations remains dangerous beyond that specific example.

The life and shortcomings of the anti-IS coalition confirm that coalition building is a moving process that does not stop after the launch of the coalition. In this case, the coalition's inability to collectively address major tensions like the Turkey-YPG conflict or to rebalance burden sharing along the way ultimately undermined its achievements. It is likely that the U.S. military will sooner or later withdraw from northeast Syria without having entirely stabilized the area liberated from IS.

From the perspective of transatlantic cooperation, then, the fight against IS can be regarded as both an operational success and a politically unsolved problem. The United States and several European countries joined efforts to defeat IS militarily and avert a humanitarian catastrophe in the aftermath of the battle; but imbalances between the U.S. and European military contributions made more equal discussions about the coalition's endgame impossible. President Trump's own management of a campaign his administration was attached to further degraded the transatlantic dialogue. Extensive internal maneuvering and European engagement with President Trump in April 2018 helped delay the American withdrawal until December 2019; but this damage control diplomacy did not suffice, and ultimately further limited the resources available to address extremely complex issues such as Turkey-YPG tensions.

One notable aspect of U.S.-Europe cooperation is that once Washington is in a leadership position, it tends not to want to relinquish control completely, even if it is actually neglecting an operation. One way to prevent this dilemma is to have a clear breakdown of participants' roles and responsibilities clearly defined in the design phase of an undertaking. One successful example of a clear definition of the division of labor was security sector reform in Baghdad, where different partners had responsibility for different parts of the mission: Germany, for example, controlled the intelligence track.

When it agrees at the beginning, the United States is willing to relinquish control. Thus, America left significant portions of the Combined

Joint Task Force–Operation Inherent Resolve, such as the Kurdistan Training Coordination Center, to Spain and Portugal. This division of labor was not found in Syria, because the American strategy in general was not clear, and because European member states were reluctant to intervene militarily in a conflict dominated by other military actors.

From a burden-sharing perspective, one can retrospectively wonder whether a larger European contribution might have reached a sufficient threshold where President Trump would have acquiesced to maintaining troops in position in Syria. Though with respect to stabilization, Saudi Arabian, UAE, German, British, and French funds did replace U.S. taxpayers' money for more than a year (2018–19), the real issue was sending troops on the ground. Europe did try to respond to this need, but did not have the capabilities to replace the United States, especially given the uncertain American timeline and method of withdrawal. Most Europeans refused to commit troops without a guarantee regarding the middle-term presence of key U.S. assets and capabilities. In the end, the fact that the U.S. demand was more for burden substitution than burden sharing created a deadlock for the coalition.

The lack of a political track for the coalition in Syria and Iraq, as well as of a successful political dialogue among allies, was amplified by one issue: the incompatibility between the logic of forming a coalition and the U.S. tendency to bilateralize key decisions. With respect to Syria vis-à-vis Turkey and Iraq vis-à-vis the federal government, the United States maintained a separate track to address political questions, leaving allies mostly in the dark. This bifurcation created a vicious cycle whereby allies were not integrated enough in key discussions to actually take more responsibility. Although this is just another illustration of the military imbalances between the United States and other coalition partners, it also reflects the lack of a true multilateral process. In other words, the United States remains the military superpower, but its habit of ruling coalitions rather than empowering its junior partners undermines its wish to reduce its footprint, leaving even bigger strategic uncertainties than the ones Washington already has.

Iran: Four Years of "Maximum Pressure" and Unsuccessful Diplomacy

The Joint Comprehensive Plan of Action targeting the Iranian nuclear program was one of the most serious points of tension between Europe and the United States under the Trump administration. As opposed to the fight against the Islamic State, where Europe shared U.S. goals despite tactical disagreements, France, Germany, and Britain deeply disagreed with the U.S. decision to leave the JCPOA. This issue is an interesting case study for the transatlantic relationship, because the United States and Europe tried to address these disagreements by means of an intense but largely unsuccessful engagement on a range of issues beyond nuclear proliferation.

The United States and Europe did not disagree on the end goal of the JCPOA, which was to prevent Iran from building a nuclear weapon, but rather on the means of reaching it. The story of the EU-U.S. dialogue on the JCPOA under the Trump administration was one of multiple failed attempts to work out disagreements based on two contradictory goals: President Trump, and a plurality of members of Congress, wanted to cancel a deal they believed was flawed, while the EU-3 (France, Germany, and Britain) wanted to preserve what it considered to be the most robust counterproliferation mechanism possible—and one that constituted a success story for the EU as lead negotiator of the deal. As Dennis Ross put it: "When it comes to Iran, we don't disagree on what the objectives are; we disagree with the means used to deal with the objectives."[154]

EU-3 countries had tried to respond to Washington's concerns and proposed to add to the nuclear framework other provisions, relating to, for example, ballistic missiles and Iranian regional activities. For four years, the EU-3 sought other options and proposed alternatives to Washington while sticking to their defense of the JCPOA as an imperfect

The Iran Nuclear Deal

The Joint Comprehensive Program of Action was signed on July 14, 2015, in Vienna by the P5+1 countries (the five permanent members of the UN Security Council, the United States, Russia, China, France and Britain, plus Germany), as well as the European Union and Iran.

This agreement concluded a round of negotiations opened in 2013 with the election of the comparatively pragmatic President Hassan Rou- hani in Iran, which allowed an initial agreement, first negotiated secretly between the United States and Iran in Oman, on a temporary freeze of Iranian nuclear activities, to be reached in 2013. An agreement was then negotiated from 2014 to 2015 within a framework of broader negotiations, during which the international community accepted for the first time the principle of an Iranian civilian nuclear program and envisaged the lifting of economic sanctions against Iran, in exchange for close control of elements that could facilitate Iranian military activity. The aim was in particular to maintain breakout time for producing the enriched uranium needed for a nuclear weapon at more than one year for a period of ten years.

The agreement included: (1) a reduction in the number of centrifuges from 19,000 to 5,060; (2) a ban on the production of uranium in excess of 3.67 percent, for a maximum quantity of 300 kg, which could be produced only at one site, that of Natanz; (3) a ban on the production of weapons-grade plutonium, which implied an adaptation of the heavy water plant at Arak; (4) closer monitoring by the International Atomic Energy Agency (IAEA); and (5) the lifting of sanctions, with the excep- tion of arms embargoes.

The IAEA confirmed through several reports in 2016 and 2017 that Iran was complying with its commitments.[1]

1   For IAEA reports on Iran, see https://www.iaea.org/newscenter/ focus/iran/iaea-and-iran-iaea-reports.

and insufficient but functioning counterproliferation framework. But joint EU-3–U.S. cooperation, such as meetings and joint statements, diminished, and in the end, the Trump administration's policy and actions were harmful to EU-U.S. ties, and the EU-3 condemned the unilateral U.S. decision to withdraw from the JCPOA.

Early Conciliation Attempts

Despite Iran's legal compliance with the agreement, the Trump administration believed that the spirit of the agreement had not been respected as Iran stepped up its clandestine military operations in Syria and Yemen after the signature of the Iran deal in July 2015. President Trump thereupon took a stance completely opposite to that of his predecessor. Whereas the nuclear agreement relied on economic incentives to encourage the cessation of the nuclear program and launch a constructive regional dialogue, the American objective under Trump was to force Tehran, by damaging Iran's economy, to change its regional strategy. Trump's policy can also be understood with reference to a significant strengthening of the U.S. dialogue with Saudi Arabia, the United Arab Emirates, and Israel, and the concomitant desire to respond to their concerns and support their efforts to contain Iranian influence.

The months following the start of the Trump administration saw an intense cycle of discussions between Europeans and Americans that gave the impression that the United States might stay in the JCPOA even as it exerted increasing pressure on other dimensions of Iran's foreign policy. On February 9, 2017, EU foreign policy chief Federica Mogherini met in Washington with U.S. secretary of state Rex Tillerson and members of Congress, arguing that the JCPOA was vital for European security, owing to Europe's proximity to Iran; she subsequently advised that U.S. officials offered assurances that they would uphold the JCPOA.[155] There were differences among European countries, however, with respect to the best way to press Washington not to leave the deal:

some European officials saw Mogherini's engagement as unhelpful, but could not or would not stop her from visiting Washington.

Meanwhile, Congress worked to launch a new set of sanctions on Iranian non-nuclear activities. On March 23, 2017, Sen. Bob Corker (R-TN) introduced the Countering Iran's Destabilizing Activities Act of 2017, which proposed new sanctions on Iran while targeting Iran's sponsorship of terrorism and its ballistic missile program. President Trump reluctantly certified Iran's compliance with the JCPOA for the second time on July 17, 2017;[156] the next day, the Trump administration announced new non-nuclear sanctions on Iran's "malign activities."[157]

The balance between sticking with the JCPOA and increasing pressure on Iran seemed to decisively change in summer 2017, when the Trump administration started attacking the deal more specifically. Europeans tried to address some U.S. concerns by proposing to add to the JCPOA provisions related to other issues, such as ballistic missiles and regional conflicts. President Macron of France made this proposal to the UN General Assembly on September 19, 2017: "For my part, I would like us to supplement this agreement with work that will help control Iran's ballistic activities, and to govern the situation after 2025 which is not covered by the 2015 agreement. We need to be more demanding, but we should in no way [undo] what previous agreements have secured."[158]

Macron's proposal was rejected by the Iranian leadership, however,[159] and the Trump administration did not show a strong interest in salvaging the deal. On October 13, 2017, Secretary of State Rex Tillerson further pushed against the JCPOA, announcing that the United States "will stay in the JCPOA, but the president will decertify under INARA,"[160] referring to the Iran Nuclear Agreement Review Act. This decertification would not violate the JCPOA in itself, but it allowed Congress to impose sanctions on Iran within sixty days with greater ease. President Trump urged Congress to legislate against the JCPOA's sunset clauses and to add automatic sanctions if Iran were to pass certain "trigger points"; without these amendments, Trump warned, "the agreement will be terminated."[161] Following that announcement, British prime minister Theresa May, French president Emmanuel Macron, and German chancellor Angela Merkel jointly expressed continuing support for the JCPOA.[162] In November 2017, EU foreign policy chief Mogherini again traveled to Washington to speak to legislators and administration officials. She discussed with U.S. congressional representatives "the need for us to have the United States compliant with the deal." She added that she received reassurances from "different sides on the Hill" that legislators are working "to keep the United States compliant with the deal.[163]

On January 12, 2018, the Trump administration said it would issue waivers on nuclear sanctions in order to remain in the JCPOA, but that this would be the last time.[164] President Trump stated that he was waiving the sanctions "in order to secure our European allies' agreement to fix the terrible flaws of the Iran nuclear deal." He added that the administration was engaging with key European allies in seeking to achieve a new supplemental agreement that would "impose new multilateral sanctions if Iran develops or tests long-range missiles, thwarts inspections, or makes progress toward a nuclear weapon."[165] Europeans and Americans worked for months on a side agreement to the Iran deal with Brian Hook, the lead State Department official. French president Macron followed up on his proposal from 2017 and used his visit to Washington in April 2018 and his personal relationship with President Trump to bring the European position to the heads-of-state level. President Trump nevertheless dismissed the efforts of his own administration and announced privately to President Macron his decision to leave the deal.[166] On April 18, 2018, soon after being sworn in as secretary of state, Mike Pompeo met with European leaders and discussed the JCPOA. He confirmed the presidential policy: "absent a substantial fix, absent overcoming the flaws of the deal, [President Trump] is unlikely to stay in that deal."[167]

Ultimately, the U.S. goal to bring about a unilateral renegotiation of the JCPOA could not be reconciled with the European goal to save the JCPOA as such.

The JCPOA's survival after the U.S. withdrawal was further called into question by the Trump administration's policy of "maximum pressure," consisting of gradually reimposing sanctions along with other measures against Tehran: the deployment of an aircraft carrier in the Gulf, the end of the exemptions from sanctions granted to certain countries for imports of Iranian crude oil, the designation of the Revolutionary Guards as a terrorist organization, and the imposition of individual sanctions on Iranian officials.

The European Response: INSTEX

While the Europeans intensively engaged the United States in search of a compromise, they also had to manage a balancing act with respect to the Iranians. They therefore tried early in the process to preserve the economic underpinning of the JCPOA even if all European companies and banks had stopped their attempts to return to doing business with Iran out of fear of U.S. secondary sanctions. A specific bone of contention between Europe and the United States in that context was European attempts to avoid U.S. sanctions. The EU-3 wanted to send a signal to Iran that they were sticking to their economic commitments according to the JCPOA.

Accordingly, several weeks after the U.S. officially left the JCPOA in May 2018, the European Commission announced that it would move forward with a "blocking statute" aimed at preventing European companies and courts from complying with new U.S. sanctions on Iran.[168] On August 6, 2018, EU foreign policy chief Federica Mogherini and the British, French, and German foreign ministers issued a joint statement according to which they remained "determined to protect European economic operators engaged in legitimate business with

Iran" and "expect[ed] Iran to continue to fully implement all its nuclear commitments under the JCPOA."[169] Later that month, the European Commission announced the adoption of a €50 million assistance package for Iran. The package aimed to support Iran in addressing "key economic and social challenges" and to improve EU-Iran "economic and sectoral relations."[170]

These steps did not satisfy the Iranians, however, especially given European companies' reluctance to take any risks. The EU thereupon aimed to design a specific mechanism to enable limited trade with Iran outside the reach of the U.S. Treasury Department—a move more political than trade-related, since whatever framework was devised was never meant to fully compensate for the loss of trade caused by the new U.S. sanctions. On September 24, 2018, Mogherini, along with the foreign ministers of Russia, France, Germany, Britain, and China, discussed establishing a special-purpose vehicle intended "to facilitate payments related to Iran's exports (including oil) and imports"[171]—and to reassure and assist European businesses doing business in Iran in spite of U.S. sanctions.

On January 31, 2019, Britain, Germany, and France established the Instrument in Support of Trade Exchanges (INSTEX) for facilitating transactions with Iran involving nonsanctioned trade, such as in humanitarian, agricultural, and medical goods. Iran registered its own INSTEX counterpart in March,[172] but Iran's foreign minister, Mohammad Javad Zarif, remarked that, "Unless oil goes into INSTEX, it can't be substantial."[173] On the European side, a key problem with INSTEX was that many European companies would not risk any U.S. extraterritorial sanctions and therefore tended to favor overcompliance, despite legal protections afforded by EU rules as well as by technical instruments like INSTEX.

In truth, EU-3 governments had little leverage with respect to companies highly dependent on the U.S. market and with limited prospects in Iran. And although the foreign ministries of the EU-3 understood the strategic nature of the trade incentives for Iran, other parts of their governments did not want to risk market shares in the United States for an uncertain diplomatic gain on the nuclear deal.

For its part, the United States continued imposing new rounds of sanctions—targeting the Supreme Leader's office, for example, on June 24, 2019.[174] On July 31, 2019, the United States sanctioned Iran's foreign minister, Zarif, for acting on behalf of Iran's Supreme Leader.[175]

In July 2019, the Russian Foreign Ministry announced that "Russia is interested in close co-ordination with the European Union on INSTEX."[176] In the same month, EU foreign policy chief Mogherini noted that "the issue of whether or not INSTEX will deal with oil is a discussion that is ongoing among the shareholders."[177] On November 30, 2019, Denmark, Belgium, Finland, Norway, the Netherlands, and Sweden joined the INSTEX barter mechanism.[178] European actors ultimately decided to leave Iranian oil outside of INSTEX's scope, knowingly reducing its attractiveness to the Iranian government.

On January 30, 2020, the Swiss embassy in Tehran announced that a channel they established for humanitarian transactions will soon help "to supply the Iranian population with agricultural commodities, food, medicines and medical equipment."[179] The United States claimed that the Swiss channel was more efficient than INSTEX, but the Swiss channel took a year and a half to be operational and faced pushback from Tehran, as it was presented as an American humanitarian gesture even though the supply was bought by Iran. The humanitarian goals of the Swiss channel could in fact have been achieved through INSTEX, thereby helping to create a space for negotiation, but U.S. opposition to INSTEX prevented such a process.

It is worth noting that the EU-3 limited its communications on INSTEX to a minimum in order not to feed U.S. frustration. There was on February 26, 2020, a mention by the Joint Commission of the JCPOA that reiterated support for the "continuation of key nuclear non-proliferation projects that are an essential part of the JCPOA."[180]

Germany, France, and Britain did announce on March 31, 2020, "that INSTEX has successfully concluded its first transaction, facilitating the export of medical goods from Europe to Iran."[181] The EU-3's goal was above all to maintain the possibility of a process between Iran and the United States—which led Europeans to work quietly on INSTEX and to reject actions that might escalate conflict with Washington, such as retaliatory sanctions against U.S. companies.

The EU also kept invoking INSTEX as an incentive for the Iranians rather than as a direct compensation for the U.S. withdrawal. In July 2020, EU foreign policy chief Josep Borrell wrote, "Having already established measures to protect our companies against extraterritorial U.S. sanctions, we in Europe can do more to satisfy Iranian expectations for legitimate trade."[182] The political nature of INSTEX was clear, however, because it was the Iranian side that showed reluctance to use the full potential of the instrument—during the Covid outbreak in Iran, for example—probably because it was diplomatically more useful for Tehran to continue to blame the Europeans for not compensating them for the cost of U.S. sanctions.[183]

INSTEX is a good example of one of the many missed opportunities in the 2017–20 phase of maximum pressure. Given its limitations, INSTEX was not actually designed to curb the economic effects of U.S. sanctions, but rather to create some negotiation space for the EU-3 with Iran. The U.S. administration could have chosen to maintain its own pressure while agreeing with the EU-3 on a division of labor that would have empowered the Europeans to work out options for de-escalation with Iran. But the administration instead refused to really discuss INSTEX. There was even a strange paradox in Washington: U.S. officials and think tanks tended to criticize INSTEX, but they failed to offer suggestions for how to better operationalize it for both America and Europe. U.S. Treasury undersecretary for terrorism and financial intelligence Sigal Mandelker even threatened a legal challenge from the U.S. against INSTEX.[184]

INSTEX was, as has been noted, at the same time dismissed by the Iranian side as insufficient; Iran repeatedly maintained that the EU had not fulfilled its economic commitment within the JCPOA. Hassan Ahmadian, an Iran expert, noted that European governments failed to "push back against draconian U.S. sanctions and thereby pursue their stated goals," ultimately damaging the reputation of Europe in Iran.[185]

The French Initiative Toward a JCPOA-Plus

A comprehensive deal that addresses the different sets of security threats (the development of a military nuclear program, the development of ballistic missiles, and the pursuit of support for militias in other countries) was theoretically the U.S. administration's policy goal after it withdrew from the JCPOA, but the contents of this deal were never publicly defined. Following the withdrawal, U.S. secretary of state Mike Pompeo presented the new maximum pressure strategy and laid out for Iran a list of twelve demands, but they were mostly maximalist and aspirational. The plan did not propose an operational process of conflict reduction and negotiation. Like its predecessor, the Trump administration did not elaborate regarding the sequence or substance of negotiations whose goal would be wresting difficult regional tradeoffs from Iran, such as stepping back from proxy sponsorship and military activities in Iraq, Lebanon, Saudi Arabia, and Syria.

The EU-3 stuck to its initial position aimed at salvaging the JCPOA, but the U.S.-Iran collision course pushed France to amplify its 2017 proposal to include a new architecture that would include the JCPOA but also allow room to respond to some of the Trump administration's concerns regarding Iranian regional influence and its ballistic missile program. President Macron took several steps in summer 2019 to convince President Trump personally of the benefit of launching a new process.

After a series of meetings between his national security advisor and Iranian officials, President Macron used the G7 meeting in Biarritz in August 2019 as a first step to get his U.S. counterpart to accept the idea of meeting with Iranian president Rouhani. Foreign minister Zarif even flew to Biarritz on short notice to discuss some of the parameters, including a potential U.S. waiver to allow Iranian trade of about $15 billion in exchange for returning to the JCPOA.[186]

On September 10, 2019, U.S. secretary of state Mike Pompeo said that President Trump might meet with President Rouhani at the United Nations with "no preconditions."[187] The second step of this initiative took place on the sidelines of the UN General Assembly. On September 24, Macron advised, after meeting with Rouhani and Trump separately at the UN,[188] "that the conditions in this context for a rapid return to negotiations have been created," but no meeting took place. On September 25, Rouhani stated that Iran would not negotiate while under sanctions and would only talk with the United States if all parties were in compliance with the JCPOA.[189]

On October 2, 2019, President Rouhani confirmed a report that he and President Trump, with the support of President Macron, had agreed to a four-point plan outlining the basis for a restart of U.S.-Iran talks.[190] The plan provided that Iran would never acquire a nuclear weapon and would engage in regional negotiations, including on its ballistic missile program, in exchange for the lifting of U.S. sanctions reimposed on Iran since 2017. But the Trump administration remained opposed to the French plan because it considered the plan a distraction from exerting maximum pressure on Iran. The White House subsequently suspended entry to the United States by senior officials in the Iranian government.[191]

A "5th & Final" Step by Iran

Following the U.S. withdrawal from the JCPOA, Iran began reducing its "commitments step by step."[192] Iran declared on May 8, 2019, that it would no longer bind itself to restrictions on stockpiles of uranium and heavy water reserves; in July, Iran surpassed the 300 kg limit on uranium enriched at 3.67 percent and announced that it had enriched uranium-235 to 4.5 percent, exceeding both stockpile and enrichment percentage limits.[193] In September 2019, President Rouhani confirmed that Iran would remove all "commitments for research and development under the JCPOA."[194]

On October 31, 2019, the United States issued two new sanctions on Iran under Section 1245 of the Iran Freedom and Counter-Proliferation Act of 2012. The first identified Iran's construction sector as falling under either direct or indirect Islamic Revolutionary Guard Corps (IRGC) control; the second identified four materials as being used in Iran's military, ballistic missile, or nuclear programs. The following month, President Rouhani announced that Iran was operating IR-2, IR-4, and IR-6 centrifuges, with plans to start working on IR-9 centrifuges shortly.[195] He soon followed with an announcement that Iran would start injecting uranium gas into 1,044 IR-1 centrifuges at the Fordow facility;[196] the United States responded on November 18, 2019, that it would stop issuing sanctions waivers relating to the Fordow facility.[197] In November, Iran began pouring concrete to construct a second nuclear reactor at Bushehr[198] and breached limits on heavy water stockpiles.[199] European parties repeatedly responded by urging Iran to continue meeting its JCPOA commitments; the United States repeatedly condemned Iran for failing to meet those commitments.

The escalation culminated on January 5, 2020, when the Iranian cabinet announced that it would no longer abide by JCPOA restrictions on uranium enrichment or number of centrifuges.[200] In a tweet, Iranian foreign minister Javad Zarif called the move a "5th & final remedial step."[201] The next day, President Macron, Chancellor Merkel, and British prime minister Boris Johnson issued a joint statement urging "Iran to reverse all measures inconsistent with the JCPOA."[202] Two weeks later, President Rouhani announced that Iran was enriching uranium at a level higher than it did before the JCPOA.[203] On January 20, Foreign Minister Zarif declared, "If the Europeans continue their improper behavior or send Iran's file to the Security Council, we will withdraw from the NPT [Non-Proliferation Treaty]."[204]

The International Atomic Energy Agency reported on March 3, 2020, that Iran had almost tripled its stockpiles of low-enriched uranium since November. In a second report, the IAEA said that it had identified three locations where Iran could be storing undeclared nuclear material or hosting undeclared nuclear activities.[205] Later that month, Iran announced that it was installing a new generation of centrifuges at the Natanz facility;[206] in April, Iran announced that it was "manufacturing 60 advanced centrifuges every day."[207]

At the same time, Iran was making strides in space. On February 9, 2020, the IRGC Aerospace Force commander announced the existence of a new short-range ballistic missile.[208] Iran launched its first military satellite into orbit in April 2020[209] and simultaneously revealed to the public that the IRGC was running a military space program in parallel with its civilian space program.[210] Secretary Pompeo condemned the launch, asserting that "Iran's space program is neither peaceful nor entirely civilian."[211]

At this stage, while diplomatic activity remained intense, the ability of European and American, and also Chinese and Russian, JCPOA stakeholders to reach even a minimal understanding was close to nonexistent.

The Dispute Resolution Mechanism

From the Europeans' perspective, the JCPOA is the only viable framework to prevent Iran from obtaining nuclear weapons, so they try to give Tehran every chance to return to full compliance. The EU-3 had already warned Iran in September 2019 that another breach of the JCPOA would lead to the triggering of a special dispute mechanism.[212]

The dispute resolution mechanism (DRM) is a flexible process that allows any JCPOA party to refer an issue to the Joint Commission for resolution if it believes that another party is failing to meet its commitments. Once triggered, all of the parties—Britain, China, France, Germany, Iran, Russia, and the EU—have approximately one month (or longer, if they agree on an extension) to decide how to deal with the alleged violations.

Again in November 2019, the EU-3 and the European Union affirmed their "readiness to consider…the dispute resolution mechanism"[213] after Iran restarted enriching uranium at the Fordow facility. Iranian parliamentarian Ali Larijani responded in December that if European parties triggered the dispute resolution mechanism, "Iran would be forced to seriously reconsider some of its commitments to the International Atomic Energy Agency."[214] Meanwhile, the United States repeatedly asked European leaders to acknowledge Iran's noncompliance with the JCPOA by engaging the DRM.

Following Iran's fifth-step noncompliance with the JCPOA on January 5, 2020, the EU-3 formally triggered the dispute resolution mechanism nine days later, on January 14.[215] On February 4, EU High Representative Josep Borrell stated that all EU-3 members were agreed on "continuously postponing the dates and the time limits" of the dispute resolution mechanism in order to postpone or avoid referral to the UN Security Council.[216]

The triggering of the DRM happened when it did because competing U.S. and Iranian pressures had already put the nuclear deal in a perilous position, and the DRM was Europe's best option for preserving the EU-3's credibility and trying to avoid further military escalation. European leaders hoped that Tehran's desire to remain in the JCPOA would force it to compromise during the DRM process, thereby laying the foundation for new Iranian negotiations with Washington—initially based on salvaging the JCPOA framework, then broadening to encompass other issues. Yet this approach would have worked only if the Trump administration had provided realistic options that Europe could present as a basis for getting everyone back to the table.

In June, Iranian foreign minister Zarif tweeted that the EU-3 had failed "to fulfill even [their] own JCPOA duties due to total impotence in resisting U.S. bullying." Several weeks later, Iran sent Josep Borrell a letter triggering the DRM for Iran's own reasons, citing concerns about the EU-3's failure to live up to its obligations under the JCPOA.[217]

The DRM is another example wherein the United States and the EU-3 could, without changing their positions, have designed a division of labor to better take advantage of the tools available to the EU-3 in order to restart a negotiation.

Maximum Pressure Policy and Responses

Iranian influence in the Middle East has long been a U.S. concern, and was one of the reasons the United States left the JCPOA. At the same time, the Trump administration's maximum pressure on Iran meant that its JCPOA policy did not always cohere with other policies in countries where Iranian influence was an issue. That is, the United States recognized the threat posed by Iranian regional influence, but U.S. policy was not always designed to combat it, creating a disconnect.

The Trump administration did try to implement its maximum pressure policy with regard to each regional conflict, but the intricacies of each conflict limited the administration's ability to do so. For example, the Trump administration increased its support for Israeli airstrikes against Iranian targets in Syria, but the domestic imperative to reduce military deployments led President Trump to weaken a limited operation in Syria while Iranian forces remained structurally present there. Similarly, the United States supported the Lebanese Armed Forces in an effort to build institutions that would counter Hezbollah influence and took steps to weaken Hezbollah financially, but without engaging in local politics in a way that might have created an alternative to

Hezbollah. The United States has not really tried to address the root causes of Hezbollah's social and institutional control.

Ultimately, the U.S. administration did not design a framework to address Iran's regional influence through diplomatic means. One reason for this absence has been the refusal, on the part of the United States but also by Gulf countries, to directly engage Iran in forums to discuss, for example, the crisis in Yemen or Gulf security. Instead, Washington supported the efforts of the UN envoy in Yemen, but kept supporting the Saudi war effort as well. The United States grows frustrated with Iran's regional influence but has few direct channels with Iran for negotiation.

For Washington, the problem of Iran's regional influence is most acute in Iraq. Whereas the conflicts in Yemen, Syria, and Lebanon have largely played out through proxies, Iraq is the country where the U.S.-Iran rivalry has led to a direct confrontation.

Iran has targeted American lives in Iraq since 2003, but the fight against the Islamic State led to de facto U.S.-Iran coordination from 2014 to 2018. Tensions escalated again, however, in the context of the maximum pressure policy and Iran-backed militias' actions on the ground—and those militias again escalated a campaign of rocket attacks against U.S. interests in Iraq in October 2019.[218] On December 27, the Iranian-backed militia Kataib Hezbollah attacked the K1 base near Kirkuk, killing one American contractor and wounding several others.[219] The United States retaliated with strikes in Iraq and Syria, killing at least twenty-five members of Kataib Hezbollah.[220] On December 31, the U.S. embassy in Baghdad was attacked, evoking memories of both the hostage crisis in Tehran in 1979 and the assassination of Ambassador Christopher Stevens in Benghazi in 2012. The same day, Secretary of Defense Mark Esper announced the deployment of 750 soldiers to the region "in response to recent events in Iraq."[221]

On January 3, 2020, the United States responded by killing Iranian general Qasem Soleimani, the head of Iran's Qods Force, and Abu

Mahdi al-Muhandis, the leader of Kataib Hezbollah, in an airstrike on Iraqi soil. The Department of Defense asserted that the "strike was aimed at deterring future Iranian attack plans."[222] On January 8, Iran retaliated by launching missiles at two bases in Iraq housing U.S. troops;[223] the strikes caused no fatalities but caused brain injuries in more than a hundred U.S. troops.[224] The escalation cycle stopped largely because Iran also accidentally shot down a civilian airliner, Ukrainian International Airlines Flight PS752 just outside Tehran, killing all 176 passengers on board.[225] Rocket attacks against the United States continued, but deadly attacks were halted for several months. On March 11, 2020, however, Iranian-backed militias killed three service members, two American and one British, in a rocket attack on Camp Taji.[226] The United States retaliated by attacking five weapons sites; Iraq criticized the U.S. strikes for killing two police officers, three Iraqi soldiers, and a civilian.[227]

EU-3 countries have been interested in addressing Iran's regional behavior in conjunction with the United States, but disagreements within the transatlantic partnership over strategy in Lebanon, Syria, and Yemen have limited the space for a joint strategy and, ultimately, for a negotiation track with the Gulf and Iran. The four points plan promoted by the French president sought to add regional issues to a larger framework built around the JCPOA, but the United States refused to work within this framework, and Iran's regional influence remained an issue in the transatlantic dialogue without a comprehensive approach to addressing it in Lebanon, Syria, Yemen, or Iraq. Gulf countries also expressed their interest in a regional dialogue after they realized how dangerous the escalation of the maximum pressure/maximum counterpressure strategy was. In June 2019, the UAE's de facto leader, Muhammad bin Zayed, proposed to UN secretary-general António Guterres a framework connecting the P5 countries, Gulf Cooperation Council (GCC) countries, and Iran in order to address regional issues. Guterres deferred to the P5, but the Trump administration rejected the proposal, because it feared it would undermine its maximum pressure approach.

Impact on Maritime Security

During the negotiation of the JCPOA, maritime security was considered unrelated to the nuclear negotiations, but it has become a key issue in U.S.-Iran tensions. An important component of Tehran's "counter–maximum pressure policy" has been maneuvers against tankers in the Strait of Hormuz, through which 40 percent of the world's oil passes. Though the issue drew particular attention in May 2019 following the sabotage suffered by Japanese and Norwegian oil tankers and inflicted by equipment that the United States considered to be Iranian, harassment of commercial vessels had been a concern prior to that. A similar situation had already occurred between 1984 and 1987, when Tehran responded to an Iraqi attack on its oil terminals by attacking Kuwaiti and other tankers transporting Iraqi oil. The United States responded by reflagging Kuwaiti tankers to the U.S. Navy, enabling a rescue by the navy in the event of an Iranian attack.[228]

Numerous incidents have occurred more recently in the Strait of Hormuz, specifically involving U.S. military and IRGC ships on July 15 and 25 and on September 10, 2017. Subsequently, U.S.-Iran verbal escalation occurred in spring 2018, and after Iran conducted a military drill in the Persian Gulf in September 2018, verbal threats were exchanged that fall and winter.

In spring 2019, U.S. officials insisted that there had been an increase in Iranian threats against the United States and other international actors and announced that the country was sending additional capabilities to the area, including the USS *Abraham Lincoln* carrier strike group, a bomber task force, the USS *Arlington*, and a Patriot battery; Iranian officials responded by asking U.S. forces to leave the area. On May 12, 2019, the UAE announced that four commercial ships had been subjected to sabotage in Fujairah that the United States attributed to Iran. On June 13, two internationally flagged and operated tankers were struck by explosions in the Gulf of Oman; though the Iranian foreign minister denied any Iranian involvement and hinted at possible manipulation to place the blame on Iran, the United States attributed the attack to Tehran. On the same day, the U.S. military described an unsuccessful attack against one of its drones over the Gulf of Oman and announced the deployment of a thousand additional troops to the region.

A U.S. drone was shot down by the IRGC on June 20; President Trump revealed the next day that he had canceled a retaliation strike against Iran because of the disproportionate human casualties it would have inflicted relative to the loss of a drone. The EU-3 reacted to this incident by warning against the risks of miscalculation while reaffirming their commitment to the JCPOA.[229] But a British vessel was itself targeted three weeks later, on July 11.

Another incident, on July 18, involved a U.S. vessel and an Iranian drone.[230] U.S. Central Command announced on July 19 that it was "developing a multinational maritime effort, Operation Sentinel, to increase surveillance of and security in key waterways in the Middle East so as to ensure freedom of navigation."[231] Incidents involving tankers in the Strait of Hormuz continued in August,[232] and the United States applied pressure on its partners to block access of Iranian tankers to their ports.[233] On September 14, Iran launched a drone and cruise missile strike that damaged Saudi oil facilities at Khurais and at the world's largest oil processing center, the state-owned Aramco oil processing installation in Abqaiq—an attack that disrupted more daily oil supply than any other event in history. The shutdown of these facilities resulted in a loss of about 5.7 million barrels a day, constituting over half of Saudi Arabia's output at the time and roughly 6 percent of the world's total supply.[234]

On September 19, 2019, Saudi Arabia and the UAE joined the International Maritime Security Construct (IMSC), an entity that monitors activity in the Persian Gulf, Gulf of Oman, Gulf of Aden, and southern

Red Sea and aims at deterring Iranian hostile activities in the area.[235] The United States announced the deployment of additional troops to Saudi Arabia on September 20; France, Germany and Britain condemned Iran for the Aramco attack "in the strongest terms" on September 23.[236] An Iranian tanker was attacked in the Red Sea on October 19, but Saudi Arabia denied being involved.[237] (Other incidents took place in early 2020.) The Coalition Task Force (CTF), under the IMSC, launched Operation Sentinel on November 7: the original participants were Australia, Bahrain, Saudi Arabia, the UAE, Britain, and the United States, [238] with Lithuania signing on later. The CTF sentinel transferred leadership of the IMSC to Britain in January 2020.[239]

Many other European countries refused to join the U.S.-led IMSC operations, despite the American attempt to form a larger international coalition to support its maritime mission.[240] Some were concerned about joining a mission under which they would not have control over the rules of engagement. The U.S. special representative for Iran, Brian Hook, insisted that "the IMSC is separate from our maximum pressure campaign,"[241] but the Europeans feared they could potentially find themselves in the middle of an escalation between the United States and Iran—even as they were concerned about maritime security and freedom of movement.

On July 23, 2019, French foreign minister Jean-Yves Le Drian explained his reluctance to contribute to an operation focused on maritime security but also part of the maximum pressure effort. He announced the launch of a separate European initiative (European Military Awareness in the Strait of Hormuz, or EMASOH) to monitor and observe maritime security in the Gulf. He further clarified that "this is the opposite of the American initiative which is about maximum pressure to make Iran go back on a certain number of objectives." Le Drian continued, "In that respect, we should even go further and think about a joint securitisation approach in the Gulf, diplomatically speaking. This way, we'll really be in a logic of de-escalation."[242]

Differences among the EU-3 slowed down the start of the European mission, however, because Britain ultimately joined the U.S. mission and because of Germany's reluctance to contribute military assets. Other EU member states showed interest, including Denmark,[243] Greece, and the Netherlands,[244] and did contribute military assets. In addition, Belgium, Germany, Italy, and Portugal jointly announced that they "politically support the creation of a European-led maritime surveillance mission in the Strait of Hormuz."[245] The French-led EMASOH operation was launched from the French military base in Abu Dhabi in January 2020,[246] and all participants emphasized the specific goals of the operation in terms of maritime surveillance and linked it to European diplomatic efforts on behalf of regional stability. In parallel, France announced in January 2020 that it was sending to Saudi Arabia a Jaguar Task Force, responsible for operating a radar system for detecting hostile aerial activities, to contribute to reassurance measures after the Abqaiq attack and the mounting tensions in the Persian Gulf. This move triggered additional Iranian criticism.[247]

Tensions remained high in spring 2020, with new incidents and harassment in March and April,[248] but they eventually diminished, leading CENTCOM commander Kenneth McKenzie to declare in June 2020 that "since the IMSC's founding, there have not been any Iranian attacks on maritime shipping in the area and there haven't even been any serious confrontations with Iranian maritime forces in the area of the Strait of Hormuz...our presence makes deniable attacks less likely to succeed. So they've chosen not to try. [T]he exposure of Iranian activities is a powerful tool and it's a non-kinetic and a de-escalatory tool that we routinely employ," he added. "A clear result of the IMSC has been a...drawdown in tensions."[249]

As with INSTEX, the United States and Europe had the same strategic goals when it came to maritime security: freedom of movement and trade in the Strait of Hormuz. Owing to the Trump administration's pursuit of maximum pressure, however, there could be no solution to tactical-level disagreements. The issue of maritime security showed once more the variable ramifications of European capabilities and political will. Though the United States and Europe were both concerned about freedom of trade, opposition to the maximum pressure policy led to the launch of another mission, which could have been seen as complementary to the U.S. one, but ended up being criticized by Washington because of the political point behind it. At the same time, some member states still contributed to the U.S. mission and broke European unity in favor of their own bilateral relations with the United States. At the end, the collective transatlantic response displayed more division than unity, which ultimately undermined the leverage of both Europe and the United States. As with INSTEX, there could have been a smarter division of labor; instead, having separate American and European maritime missions added to the frustrations of both.

"Snapback" Sanctions

The next incidence of transatlantic friction regarding Iran occurred at the UN Security Council. On April 30, 2020, U.S. special representative for Iran Brian Hook said that the Trump administration planned to prevent the expiration of a UN embargo that blocked arms sales with Iran. The Security Council originally imposed the embargo in 2007; under the JCPOA, it was scheduled to expire in October 2020. Special Representative Hook asserted that the White House is "prepared to use every diplomatic option available to us" to prevent the embargo's expiration.[250] The move was backed by the U.S. Congress: on May 4, over three-quarters of House members signed a letter urging the Trump administration to renew the embargo.[251] In an opinion piece in the May 13, 2020, *Wall Street Journal*, Hook conveyed the administration's resolve: "If American diplomacy is frustrated by a [Security Council] veto…the U.S. retains the right to renew the arms embargo by other means."[252]

In June 2020, the United States circulated a draft resolution to UN Security Council members that would permanently extend the arms embargo.[253] At a Security Council meeting, Secretary of State Pompeo argued that "renewing the embargo will exert more pressure on Tehran to start behaving like a normal nation."[254] On July 1, Washington announced that it would soon request a Security Council vote on the draft resolution. Then U.S. ambassador to the UN Kelly Craft affirmed that "[w]e want to give the council the opportunity to talk through the [arms embargo] renewal…But we will use every measure, every tool, and if that means a snapback, that's exactly what we'll do, we'll be initiating it."[255]

Not surprisingly given the European frustration with the American maximum pressure policy, this push from Washington was definitively rejected by the EU-3, on both legal and political grounds. On August 20, the EU-3 reiterated that the United States was no longer a member of the JCPOA following its May 2018 withdrawal. In response to the U.S. resolution, the EU-3 made clear that "[w]e cannot therefore support this initiative, which is incompatible with our current efforts to support the JCPOA."[256] In response, Secretary of State Pompeo accused the EU-3 of "siding with the ayatollahs."[257] On August 25, the UN Security Council president observed that the council was "not in [a] position to take further action" on the U.S. bid, triggering a thirty-day period for the Security Council to debate the topic. In a clear acknowledgment of the way in which Washington had approached the Iran issue between 2017 and 2020, Ambassador Craft declared, "Let me just make it really, really clear: the Trump administration has no fear in standing in limited company on this matter."[258]

On September 8, Secretary Pompeo tweeted: "Iran's uranium stockpile is reportedly more than 10 times the limit set by the JCPOA. The E3 and other nations must wake up to the reality that the nuclear deal is history and should join us in imposing strong sanctions. Pressure and comprehensive talks are the only path forward."[259] Pompeo's reference to the need for comprehensive talks suggested an admission that the

maximum pressure policy had not in itself brought Tehran to the negotiating table. He asserted that the nuclear deal was over, but at the same
time invoked the same rationale that underpins the JCPOA: reducing
economic pressure in exchange for nuclear concessions. Nevertheless,
on September 20, the United States went ahead and imposed "snapback"
sanctions on Iran—essentially unilaterally, given that all the other P5+1
members considered the move illegal.[260]

The fight for the JCPOA has divided and weakened both Europe
and the United States. As one analyst put it, "In a Trumpian world…
Europe has lost much of its charm for Tehran."[261] This has also prevented the United States from halting Iran's nuclear program. The
maximum pressure strategy, based mostly on sanctions and lacking a
real negotiations framework, has created a paradoxical situation: it has
increased the risk of a proliferation crisis while refusing to address it
through an actual strategy. Even on issues where there was agreement
with the Europeans—like acknowledging that the JCPOA was not
enough—no real division of labor could be devised between the EU-3
and the United States.

Transatlantic Disconnects

Issues related to "U.S. leadership," "burden sharing," European division,
and risk aversion have continued to shape the transatlantic dialogue
with respect to the Middle East despite changes in the strategic environment impelled by the Arab Spring.

U.S. fatigue was poorly aligned with a European willingness to
support democratic transitions in Tunisia, Egypt, Libya, and Syria
while managing migration- and terrorism-related risks. President
Barack Obama did intervene in Libya and against the Islamic State,
but the dynamics of coalitions of the willing were now reversed, and
the coalitions were more fragile than in the past. After criticizing or

reluctantly following Washington in 2003, Europeans found themselves urging the United States to lead and stay committed militarily in the region. President Trump called for more burden sharing with allies but disengaged from political processes in the region. At both the military and diplomatic levels, Western countries collectively failed to create a sufficient ground presence to support the transition in Libya or push back against Iranian and Russian intervention in Syria.

Even when they had overlapping interests—as with respect to counterproliferation and counterterrorism—European and American officials could not coordinate well enough to create sufficient collective leverage. After President Obama conducted secret negotiations with Iran without European participation, he eventually concluded the JCPOA, aided by the other members of the P5+1 (Britain, China, France, Russia, and Germany). But President Trump withdrew the United States from the deal in 2018, despite several EU-3 proposals addressing American concerns.

Meanwhile, within the anti-IS coalition, early disagreements about the fight against Syria's president, Bashar al-Assad, as well as Turkish concerns about the People's Defense Units (YPG), have not been overcome. In Iraq, the United States and Europe did not push back early enough against the September 2017 Kurdish referendum, thereby forfeiting post-IS momentum, and failed to forestall an increase in intra-Shia rivalry following Iraq's May 2018 elections.

Western assistance to Libya since the 2011 fall of Muammar Qadhafi has been limited by security concerns as well as a lack of coordination. Despite the successful negotiation of the Skhirat Agreement in 2015, which sought to reunify Libyan institutions, clear tactical disagreements existed within each Western country, pitting diplomats against the security establishment regarding how best to combine counterterrorism operations with support for the UN process. On the assumption that Libyan National Army head Khalifa Haftar—who opposed the internationally backed government that emerged from Skhirat—could be put under civilian supervision, Washington, Paris, and Rome tried at different times to include him in the political process. But Haftar's other supporters—Egypt, the UAE, and Russia—helped him evade Western pressure.

Under U.S. pressure, Europe did take more action through some of its member states or at the EU level: military contributions, kinetic and nonkinetic, to the fight against the Islamic State in Syria, Iraq, and Libya; maritime activities in Libya to monitor the arms embargo and disrupt human smuggling and trafficking (Operation Irini), along with EMASOH initiatives to protect trade routes; financial support to Tunisia; and billions of dollars in humanitarian aid in Syria, Iraq, and Yemen—as well as multiple diplomatic initiatives vis-à-vis Iran, Syria, Libya, and Lebanon. European countries failed to persuasively present these activities to Washington, however, as examples of alternative burden sharing.

The outcome of transatlantic cooperation between 2011 and 2021 is problematic with respect to both European and U.S. interests. Operational cooperation between the United States and some European countries has improved in certain cases; but the political dialogue over tensions in the Middle East has deteriorated significantly. One former European official pithily summarized the course of the relationship: "Under Bush, Europeans agreed less with the U.S. but were more consulted. Under Obama, they agreed more but were less consulted. Under Trump, they disagree and are barely consulted."[262]

Notes

1   Ben Smith, "Obama's Berlin Speech," *Politico*, July 24, 2008,
     https://www.politico.com/blogs/ben-smith/2008/07/obamas-berlin-
     speech-010499.

2   William J. Burns, *The Back Channel: A Memoir of American Diplomacy
     and the Case for Its Renewal* (New York: Random House, 2019), 87.

3   Ibid.

4   Ibid., 87.

5   Emile Hokayem, interview by author, August 25, 2020.

6   Kim Ghattas, "How Does the U.S. View Tunisia's Revolt?" BBC, January
     16, 2011, https://www.bbc.com/news/world-us-canada-12200851.

7   "Statement by the President on Events in Tunisia," National
     Archives and Records Administration, January 14, 2011, https://
     obamawhitehouse.archives.gov/the-press-office/2011/01/14/
     statement-president-events-tunisia.

8   Juan Tovar, "The Foreign Policy of the United States Following the Arab
     Spring," in *Political Change in the Middle East and North Africa: After the
     Arab Spring* (Edinburgh: Edinburgh University Press, 2017), 330.

9   Burns, *The Back Channel*.

10   Alister Bull and Patricia Zengerle, "Obama Hopes Mubarak Will Make
     'the Right Decision,'" Reuters, February 3, 2011, https://www.reuters.
     com/article/us-egypt-usa/obama-hopes-mubarak-will-make-the-right-
     decision-idUSTRE71175920110204; Tovar, "The Foreign Policy of the
     United States," 329.

11   Sharon Otterman, "Egypt's Leaders Signal Commitment to Civilian
     Rule," *New York Times*, February 21, 2011, https://www.nytimes.
     com/2011/02/22/world/africa/22egypt.html.

12   "It must be said, for all of us, this (Arab) 'spring' was a surprise. For too
     long, we thought that authoritarian regimes were the only bulwarks
     against extremism in the Arab world. For too long, we have used the
     Islamic threat as a pretext to justify complacency toward governments
     that trample on freedom and hamper the development of their
     countries." Alain Juppé, remarks at the colloquium "Printemps Arabe:
     Enjeux et Espoirs d'un Changement," l'Institut du Monde Arabe, April

16, 2011, https://www.vie-publique.fr/discours/181887-declaration-de-m-alain-juppe-ministre-des-affaires-etrangeres-et-europ.

13   Tovar, "The Foreign Policy of the United States," 328.

14   Eduard Soler i Lecha and Pol Morillas, *Middle Power with Maghreb Focus: A Spanish Perspective on Security Policy in the Southern Neighbourhood* (Berlin: Friedrich Ebert Stiftung, 2020), 10, available at http://library.fes.de/pdf-files/id/ipa/16307-20200722.pdf.

15   Charles Thépaut, *Can the EU Pressure Dictators? Reforming ENP Conditionality After the Arab Spring*, EU Diplomacy Paper (Bruges: College of Europe, June 2011), https://www.coleurope.eu/system/files_force/research-paper/edp_6_2011_thepaut.pdf?download=1.

16   "EU's Response to the 'Arab Spring': The State-of-Play After Two Years," European Commission, February 8, 2013, https://ec.europa.eu/commission/presscorner/detail/de/MEMO_13_81.

17   "The EU's Response to the 'Arab Spring,'" European Commission, December 16, 2011, https://ec.europa.eu/commission/presscorner/detail/en/MEMO_11_918.

18   Ibid.

19   Ibid.

20   Ellen Boccuzzi and Jan Cartwright, "One Year On, the Arab Spring Continues to Inspire and Challenge," *Frontlines*, USAID (January/February 2012), https://2012-2017.usaid.gov/news-information/frontlines/democracy-human-rights-governance/one-year-arab-spring-continues-inspire.

21   USAID Office of the Inspector General, "Survey of USAID's Arab Spring Challenges in Egypt, Tunisia, Libya, and Yemen," April 30, 2015, https://oig.usaid.gov/sites/default/files/2018-06/8-000-15-001-s.pdf.

22   Thepaut, *Can the EU Pressure Dictators?* https://www.coleurope.eu/system/files_force/research-paper/edp_6_2011_thepaut.pdf?download=1.

23   Ibid.

24   "The EU's Response," December 16, 2011. https://ec.europa.eu/commission/presscorner/detail/en/MEMO_11_918.

25   Ibid.

26   Ibid.

27   Boccuzzi and Cartwright, "One Year On, the Arab Spring,"
     https://2012-2017.usaid.gov/news-information/frontlines/democracy-
     human-rights-governance/one-year-arab-spring-continues-inspire.

28   Ibid.

29   Irene Fernández-Molina, "EU and EU Member States' Responses to the
     Arab Spring," in *Political Change in the Middle East and North Africa: After
     the Arab Spring* (Edinburgh: Edinburgh University Press, 2017), 330.

30   Patrick Cockburn, "Bahrain Protesters Driven out of Pearl Square
     by Tanks and Tear Gas," *Independent*, March 17, 2011, https://www.
     independent.co.uk/news/world/middle-east/bahrain-protesters-
     driven-out-pearl-square-tanks-and-tear-gas-2244165.html.

31   Burns, *The Back Channel*.

32   Alessandro Marrone, *Security Policy in the Southern Neighbourhood: A
     View from Rome* (Rome: Friedrich Ebert Stiftung, 2020), 4, available at
     http://library.fes.de/pdf-files/bueros/rom/16768-20200421.pdf.

33   Simon Tisdall, "Germany Blocks Plans for Libya No-Fly Zone,"
     Guardian, March 15, 2011, https://www.theguardian.com/world/2011/
     mar/15/germany-blocks-libya-no-fly-zone.

34   Burns, *The Back Channel*.

35   Ibid.

36   Conor Friedersdorf, "How Obama Ignored Congress, and Misled
     America, on War in Libya," *Atlantic*, September 13, 2012, https://
     www.theatlantic.com/politics/archive/2012/09/how-obama-ignored-
     congress-and-misled-america-on-war-in-libya/262299/.

37   Former NSC official, interview by author, August 2020.

38   Former NSC official, interview by author, August 5, 2020.

39   Ibid.

40   "Libya and the New Global Disorder: A Conversation with Ghassan
     Salamé," Carnegie Endowment for International Peace, October 15,
     2020, https://carnegieendowment.org/2020/10/15/libya-and-new-
     global-disorder-conversation-with-ghassan-salam-event-7439.

41   Former NGO staff member based in Libya, interview by author, August
     2020.

42   Former U.S. official, interview by author, August 14, 2020.

43 Report of the UN Panel of Experts, 2015, https://www.
securitycouncilreport.org/un_documents_type/sanctions-committee-
documents/?ctype=Libya&cbtype=libya.

44 "UK Man Raped by Libyan Cadets Sues MoD for Negligence," *Guardian*,
March 7, 2016, https://www.theguardian.com/uk-news/2016/mar/07/
uk-man-raped-by-libyan-cadets-sues-mod-for-negligence.

45 "Foreign Office: Britons Should Leave Benghazi Immediately,"
Guardian, January 25, 2013, https://www.theguardian.com/world/2013/
jan/24/britons-leave-benghazi-libya-foreign-office.

46 Mattisan Rowan, "Libya Timeline: Since Qaddafi's Ouster,"
U.S. Institute of Peace, July 1, 2019, https://www.usip.org/
publications/2019/07/libya-timeline-qaddafis-ouster.

47 Soler i Lecha and Morillas, *Middle Power with Maghreb Focus*, 9,
available at http://library.fes.de/pdf-files/id/ipa/16307-20200722.pdf.

48 See "Déclaration de M. Jean-Yves Le Drian,..." *Vie Publique*, https://
www.vie-publique.fr/discours/275572-jean-yves-le-drian-08072020-
politique-etrangere.

49 Including Seifallah bin Hussein, leader of an al-Qaeda offshoot
in Tunisia, who was reportedly killed in a strike on Ajdabiya in
June 2015. See Patrick J. Lyons, "Libya: America's First, and Latest,
Target," *New York Times*, February 19, 2016, https://www.nytimes.
com/interactive/2016/02/19/world/africa/Lybia-us-wars-timeline.
html; Rowan, "Libya Timeline," https://www.usip.org/libya-timeline-
qaddafis-ouster; Aidan Lewis, "Islamic State Shifts to Libya's Desert
Valleys After Sirte Defeat," Reuters, February 10, 2017, https://www.
reuters.com/article/us-libya-security-islamicstate/islamic-state-
shifts-to-libyas-desert-valleys-after-sirte-defeat-idUSKBN15P1GX;
and Thomas Joscelyn and Bill Roggio, "U.S. Resumes Strikes Against
Islamic State in Libya," *Long War Journal*, September 30, 2017, https://
www.longwarjournal.org/archives/2017/09/us-resumes-strikes-against-
islamic-state-in-libya.php.

50 Nathalie Guibert, "La France Mène des Opérations Secrètes en Libye,"
Le Monde, February 24, 2017, https://www.lemonde.fr/international/
article/2016/02/24/la-france-mene-des-operations-secretes-en-
libye_4870605_3210.html.

51   Lyons, "Libya: America's First," https://www.nytimes.com/
     interactive/2016/02/19/world/africa/Lybia-us-wars-timeline.html.

52   "Manchester Attack: Militia to 'Co-operate' on Extradition," BBC,
     November 2, 2017, https://www.bbc.com/news/uk-england-
     manchester-41838638.

53   Former U.S. official, interview by author, August 14, 2020.

54   Former NSC official, interview by author, September 2020.

55   David D. Kirkpatrick, "The White House Blessed a War in Libya, but
     Russia Won It," *New York Times*, updated June 18, 2020,
     https://www.nytimes.com/2020/04/14/world/middleeast/libya-russia-
     john-bolton.html.

56   Agence France-Presse, "Trump Discussed 'Shared Vision' in Phone
     Call to Libyan Warlord Haftar," April 19, 2019, available at https://www.
     france24.com/en/20190419-libya-trump-haftar-phone-call-tripoli.

57   Ben Fishman and Conor Hiney, "What Turned the Battle for Tripoli?"
     PolicyWatch 3314, Washington Institute for Near East Policy, May
     6, 2020, https://www.washingtoninstitute.org/policy-analysis/
     what-turned-battle-tripoli.

58   Fernández-Molina, "EU and EU Member States' Responses to the Arab
     Spring," 311.

59   Ibid.

60   John Irish, "France, Partners Planning Syria Crisis Group: Sarkozy,"
     Reuters, February 4, 2012, https://www.reuters.com/article/
     us-syria-france/france-partners-planning-syria-crisis-group-sarkozy-
     idUSTRE8130QV20120204.

61   "UN-Backed Action Group Agrees on Measures for Peaceful
     Transition in Syria," *UN News*, June 30, 2012, https://news.un.org/
     en/story/2012/06/414532-un-backed-action-group-agrees-measures-
     peaceful-transition-syria.

62   Anne Barnard and Nick Cumming-Bruce, "After Second Round of
     Syria Talks, No Agreement Even on How to Negotiate," *New York
     Times*, February 15, 2014, https://www.nytimes.com/2014/02/16/world/
     middleeast/after-second-round-of-syria-talks-no-agreement-even-on-
     how-to-negotiate.html.

63 UN Secretary-General, "Note to Correspondents: Vienna
    Communiqué on Syria," October 30, 2015, https://www.un.org/sg/en/
    content/sg/note-correspondents/2015-10-30/note-correspondents-
    vienna-communique-syria.

64 Nick Cumming-Bruce and Somini Sengupta, "Syria Talks Are
    Suspended," *New York Times*, February 3, 2016, https://www.nytimes.
    com/2016/02/04/world/middleeast/syria-peace-talks-geneva-
    de-mistura.html.

65 John Hudson, "John Kerry Consults with Russians on Syria Less
    Than 48 Hours After Suspending Ties," *Foreign Policy*, October 5,
    2016, https://foreignpolicy.com/2016/10/05/john-kerry-consults-with-
    russians-on-syria-less-than-48-hours-after-suspending-ties/.

66 Michael Gordon, "U.S. and Russia Reach Deal to Destroy Syria's
    Chemical Arms," *New York Times*, September 14, 2013, https://www.
    nytimes.com/2013/09/15/world/middleeast/syria-talks.html.

67 Burns, *The Back Channel*.

68 Carla Humud and Christopher Blanchard, *Armed Conflict in Syria:
    Overview and U.S. Response* (Congressional Research Service, July
    2020), https://fas.org/sgp/crs/mideast/RL33487.pdf.

69 Mark Mazzetti and Matt Apuzzo, "U.S. Relies Heavily on Saudi Money
    to Support Syrian Rebels," *New York Times*, January 23, 2016,
    https://www.nytimes.com/2016/01/24/world/middleeast/us-relies-
    heavily-on-saudi-money-to-support-syrian-rebels.html.

70 Mark Mazzetti, Adam Goldman, and Michael Schmidt, "Behind the
    Sudden Death of a $1 Billion Secret CIA War in Syria," *New York
    Times*, August 2, 2017, https://www.nytimes.com/2017/08/02/world/
    middleeast/cia-syria-rebel-arm-train-trump.html.

71 Helene Cooper, "Few U.S.-Trained Syrians Still Fight ISIS, Senators
    Are Told," *New York Times*, September 16, 2015, https://www.nytimes.
    com/2015/09/17/world/middleeast/isis-isil-syrians-senate-armed-
    services-committee.html.

72 Lead Inspector General for Overseas Contingency Operations,
    "Quarterly Report and Biannual Report to the United States Congress,
    December 17, 2014–March 31, 2015," April 30, 2015, p. 31, https://media.

defense.gov/2017/Apr/13/2001732265/-1/-1/1/FY2015_LIG_OCO_OIR_
Q2_REPORT_MAR2015.PDF.

73   Helene Cooper, "Few U.S.-Trained Syrians Still Fight ISIS, Senators
     Are Told," *New York Times*, September 16, 2015, https://www.nytimes.
     com/2015/09/17/world/middleeast/isis-isil-syrians-senate-armed-
     services-committee.html.

74   U.S. Department of Defense, "Request for Additional FY2017
     Appropriations Overseas Contingency Operations," March 2017,
     https://comptroller.defense.gov/Portals/45/Documents/defbudget/
     fy2017/marchAmendment/FY2017_CTEF_J-Book_March_
     Amendment_Final.pdf.

75   "Obama Warns Syria Not to Cross 'Red Line,'" CNN, August 21, 2012,
     https://www.cnn.com/2012/08/20/world/meast/syria-unrest/index.html.

76   Steven Erlanger and Stephen Castle, "Britain's Rejection of Syrian
     Response Reflects Fear of Rushing to Act," *New York Times*, August 29,
     2013, https://www.nytimes.com/2013/08/30/world/middleeast/syria.html.

77   Patrick Wintour, "Ex–UN Syria Envoy Says He Quit to Avoid Having
     to Shake Assad's Hand," *Guardian*, November 5, 2019, https://www.
     theguardian.com/world/2019/nov/05/ex-un-syria-envoy-says-he-quit-
     to-avoid-having-to-shake-assads-hand.

78   Senior European official, interview by author, May 2020.

79   Michael Knights, interview by author, June 2020.

80   "Spain," Global Coalition Against Daesh, December 6, 2019, https://
     theglobalcoalition.org/en/partner/spain/.

81   U.S. Department of Defense, "FY 2019 Quarter 4 Cost of War Update as
     of September 30, 2019," https://fas.org/man/eprint/cow/fy2019q4.pdf.

82   U.S. Department of Defense, "Special Report: Operation Inherent
     Resolve," accessed November 19, 2020, https://dod.defense.gov/OIR/.

83   U.S. Department of State, "Briefing with Assistant Secretary for Near
     Eastern Affairs David Schenker on Iraq and Middle East Issues," April
     9, 2020, https://www.state.gov/briefing-with-assistant-secretary-for-
     near-eastern-affairs-david-schenker-on-iraq-and-middle-east-issues/.

84   U.S. Department of Defense, "Fiscal Year 2016 Budget Request,"
     February 2015, https://comptroller.defense.gov/Portals/45/Documents/
     defbudget/fy2016/FY2016_Budget_Request_Overview_Book.pdf.

85   U.S. Department of Defense, "Fiscal Year 2018 Budget Request,"
     May 2017, https://comptroller.defense.gov/Portals/45/Documents/
     defbudget/fy2018/fy2018_Budget_Request_Overview_Book.pdf.

86   "CHAMMAL: Le Canon CAESAR En Première Ligne Contre Daech,"
     Ministère des Armées (French Ministry of Armed Forces), November
     26, 2018, https://www.defense.gouv.fr/operations/actualites2/
     chammal-le-canon-caesar-en-premiere-ligne-contre-daech.

87   "Bataille de Mossoul: Qui Participe à la Reconquête?" *L'Obs*, October
     17, 2016, http://tempsreel.nouvelobs.com/monde/20161017.OBS9927/
     bataille-de-mossoul-qui-participe-a-la-reconquete.html.

88   Julien Licourt, "Premières Opérations Depuis Le Charles-De-
     Gaulle Avant L'offensive Sur Mossoul," *Le Figaro*, September 30,
     2016, https://www.lefigaro.fr/international/2016/09/30/01003-
     20160930ARTFIG00055-irak-la-coalition-debute-son-offensive-sur-
     mossoul.php.

89   "French Soldier Killed in Iraq-Syria Military Zone, Élysée Palace
     Says," France 24, September 23, 2017, https://www.france24.com/
     en/20170923-french-soldier-killed-iraq-syria-military-zone.

90   "Mali, Syrie…Les Opérations Extérieures, un Défi pour Emmanuel
     Macron," *Le Journal du Dimanche*, May 19, 2017, https://www.lejdd.
     fr/International/mali-syrie-les-operations-exterieures-un-defi-pour-
     emmanuel-macron-3335711.

91   "'Hundreds' More UK Troops to Be Sent to Iraq—Michael Fallon,"
     BBC, December 13, 2014, https://www.bbc.com/news/uk-30464272.

92   Jon Vale, "This Is How Much the Ministry of Defence Spent
     Fighting ISIS in the Past Three Years," *Daily Mirror*, October 20,
     2017, https://www.mirror.co.uk/news/world-news/how-much-
     ministry-defence-fighting-11374906. A different source estimates
     the cost to be around £1.75 billion: see Chris Cole, "Cost of UK Air
     and Drone Strikes in Iraq and Syria Reach £1.75 Billion," *Drone
     Wars UK*, February 26, 2018, https://dronewars.net/2018/02/26/
     cost-of-uk-air-and-drone-strikes-in-iraq-and-syria-reach-1-75-billion/.

93   AWACS stands for airborne early warning and control system.

94   Training areas included handling "Milan" antitank weapons, tactical
     and command-and-control processes, administration of medical aid,

maintenance of equipment, handling of CBRN defense equipment, explosive ordnance disposal, and international humanitarian law.

95   "How Italy Supports the Global Coalition Against Daesh," Global Coalition Against Daesh, June 21, 2019, https://theglobalcoalition.org/en/how-italy-supports-the-global-coalition-against-daesh/.

96   Courses conducted in favor of the Peshmerga have been: Basic Infantry Training, Folgore Anti-Tank System Training, Use of Mortars and Artillery, Snipers' Course, First Aid, Counter- IED.

97   Netherlands Ministry of Defense, "Militaire Bijdrage Nederland in Irak," https://www.defensie.nl/onderwerpen/missie-in-irak-en-oost-syrie/militaire-bijdrage.

98   Michael Knights, interview by author, June 2020.

99   Operation Inherent Resolve, "Iraq Ministry of Defense Deploys Elite Force," December 4, 2019, https://www.inherentresolve.mil/Releases/News-Releases/Article/2032361/iraq-ministry-of-defense-deploys-elite-force/.

100 Michael Knights, interview by author, June 2020.

101 Dexter Filkins, "A Bigger Problem than ISIS?" *The New Yorker*, December 26, 2016, https://www.newyorker.com/magazine/2017/01/02/a-bigger-problem-than-isis.

102 Ibid.

103 Michael Knights, interview by author, June 2020.

104 Saif Hameed, "Italian Engineers Need Two Months on Mosul Dam Before Starting Repairs: Ministry," Reuters, March 14, 2016, https://www.reuters.com/article/us-mideast-crisis-iraq-dam-idUSKCN0WG10G.

105 Retired senior military official who has been involved with Operation Inherent Resolve, interview by author, November 2019.

106 Michael Knights, interview by author, June 2020.

107 U.S. Department of Defense, *Quadrennial Defense Review 2014*, 37, https://archive.defense.gov/pubs/2014_Quadrennial_Defense_Review.pdf.

108 "The Strengthening of French Special Forces: The Future of War or the Consequence of the Crisis" (in French), public report from the French Senate 52513, May 2014, http://www.senat.fr/rap/r13-525/r13-525_mono.html#fnref8.

109 Dan Lamothe, "There Are Four Times as Many U.S. Troops in Syria as Previously Acknowledged by the Pentagon," *Washington Post,* December 6, 2017, https://www.washingtonpost.com/news/checkpoint/ wp/2017/12/06/there-are-four-times-as-many-u-s-troops-in-syria-as-previously-acknowledged-by-the-pentagon/.

110 Lara Seligman, "Britain, France Agree to Send Additional Troops to Syria," *Foreign Policy*, July 9, 2019, https://foreignpolicy. com/2019/07/09/britain-france-agree-to-send-additional-troops-increase-syria-us-withdrawal-uk/.

111 Ben Riley-Smith, "Revealed: Theresa May Considered Sending 1,000 UK Troops to Syria After Trump Withdrawal," *Telegraph*, November 27, 2019, https://www.telegraph.co.uk/politics/2019/11/27/ revealed-theresa-may-considered-sending-1000-uk-troops-syria/.

112 French official, interview by author, May 2020.

113 Retired senior military official who has been involved with Operation Inherent Resolve, interview by author, November 2019.

114 U.S. congressional staffer, interview by author, December 2019.

115 Diyar Guldogan, "Denmark to Send $7.3M to Clear Mines in Syria," Anadolu Agency, October 6, 2019, https://www.aa.com.tr/en/ middle-east/denmark-to-send-73m-to-clear-mines-in-syria/1603906.

116 France Ministry for Europe and Foreign Affairs, "Post-Daesh Iraq: France's Engagement," January 15, 2019, https://www.diplomatie.gouv. fr/en/country-files/iraq/post-daesh-iraq-france-s-engagement/.

117 "'Every Crisis Concerns Us to Some Extent,'" deutschland.de, March 29, 2019, https://www.deutschland.de/en/topic/politics/ crisis-prevention-and-stabilisation-interview-with-ekkehard-brose.

118 "Briefing with David Schenker on Iraq and Middle East Issues," https:// www.state.gov/briefing-with-assistant-secretary-for-near-eastern-affairs-david-schenker-on-iraq-and-middle-east-issues/.

119 Maher Chmaytelli and Ahmed Hagagy, "Allies Promise Iraq $30 Billion, Falling Short of Baghdad's Appeal," Reuters, February 13, 2018, https://www.reuters.com/article/us-mideast-crisis-iraq-reconstruction-ku/allies-promise-iraq-30-billion-falling-short-of-baghdads-appeal-idUSKCN1FY0TX.

120 "France," Global Coalition Against Daesh, https://theglobalcoalition.
     org/en/partner/france/.

121 "Netherlands," Global Coalition Against Daesh, https://
     theglobalcoalition.org/en/partner/netherlands/.

122 "Spain," Global Coalition Against Daesh, https://theglobalcoalition.
     org/en/partner/spain/.

123 "The EU and Iraq," European External Action Service,
     July 9, 2019, https://eeas.europa.eu/headquarters/
     headquarters-homepage_en/32427/The%20EU%20and%20Iraq.

124 U.S. Department of State, "U.S. Relations with Syria," May 6, 2020,
     https://www.state.gov/u-s-relations-with-syria/.

125 "Syria," European Civil Protection and Humanitarian Aid Operations,
     European Commission, June 30, 2020, https://ec.europa.eu/echo/
     where/middle-east/syria_en.

126 German foreign office official, interview by author.

127 Charles Thépaut, "U.S. Withdrawal from Syria Makes Countering
     ISIS More Difficult," *The Hill*, October 16, 2019, available
     at https://www.washingtoninstitute.org/policy-analysis/
     view/u.s.-withdrawal-from-syria-makes-countering-isis-more-difficult.

128 Max Greenwood, "Trump Freezes $200M in Syria Recovery Funds:
     Report," *The Hill*, March 31, 2018, https://thehill.com/homenews/
     administration/381086-trump-freezes-200m-in-syria-recovery-funds-
     report.

129 Michael Knights, interview by author, June 2020.

130 Senior Spanish official, interview by author, June 2020.

131 European official, interview by author, August 2020.

132 Issam Saliba, "Iraq: Legislating the Status of the Popular Mobilization
     Forces," *Global Legal Monitor*, Library of Congress, December 7,
     2016, https://www.loc.gov/item/global-legal-monitor/2016-12-07/
     iraq-legislating-the-status-of-the-popular-mobilization-forces/.

133 U.S. military official, interview by author, August 12, 2020.

134 Retired senior military official who has been involved with Operation
     Inherent Resolve, interview by author, November 2019.

135 Former U.S. military officials, interviews by author, November 2019
     and August 2020.

136 Euphrates Shield in al-Bab in August 2016; Olive Branch in Afrin in February 2018; Peace Spring in Tal Abyad in October 2019.

137 Wladimir van Wilgenburg, "U.S. Backtracks on Syrian 'Border Guard' Plan After Turkey Threatens Efrin," *Defense Post*, January 18, 2019, https://www.thedefensepost.com/2018/01/18/us-syria-border-security-force-turkey-efrin/.

138 Former senior U.S. military official, interview by author, November 2019.

139 SDF military official, interview by author, December 2018.

140 Sardar Mullah Darwish, "Leader Defines Principles of New Future Syria Party," Al-Monitor, June 6, 2018, https://www.al-monitor.com/pulse/originals/2018/05/future-syria-party-rojava-turkey-pressure.html.

141 Semih Idiz, "Turks Skeptical over Accord with U.S. for Syrian 'Safe Zone,'" Al-Monitor, August 15, 2019, https://www.al-monitor.com/pulse/originals/2019/08/turkey-united-states-syria-turks-skeptical-over-safe-zone.html.

142 French official, interview by author, May 2020.

143 European official, interview by author, May 2020.

144 "Emmanuel Macron Warns Europe: NATO Is Becoming Brain-Dead," *Economist*, November 7, 2019, https://www.economist.com/europe/2019/11/07/emmanuel-macron-warns-europe-nato-is-becoming-brain-dead.

145 Former U.S. stabilization officer, interview by author, October 2019.

146 International NGO staffer, interview by author, September 2019.

147 French officials, interview by author, December 2019.

148 Human Rights Watch, "Rigging the System," June 28, 2019, https://www.hrw.org/report/2019/06/28/rigging-system/government-policies-co-opt-aid-and-reconstruction-funding-syria.

149 Emma Beals and Nick Hopkins, "Aid Groups Suspend Cooperation with UN in Syria Because of Assad 'Influence,'" *Guardian*, September 8, 2016, https://www.theguardian.com/world/2016/sep/08/aid-groups-un-syria-concern-assad-united-nations.

150 Through the adoption of UN Security Council Resolution 2165 (2014), and its subsequent renewals, 2191 (2014), 2258 (2015), 2332 (2016), 2393 (2017), 2449 (2018), 2504 (2020), 2533 (2020), and 2585 (2021), the Security Council has authorized UN agencies and their partners to use

routes across conflict lines and the border crossings at Bab al-Salam, Bab al-Hawa, Ramtha, and al-Yarubiya to deliver humanitarian assistance, including medical and surgical supplies, to people in need in Syria. The Syrian government is notified in advance of each shipment, and a UN monitoring mechanism has been established to oversee loading in neighboring countries and to confirm the humanitarian nature of consignments.

151 UN Office for the Coordination of Humanitarian Affairs, "Syrian Arab Republic: United Nations Cross-Border Operations Under UNSC Resolutions 2165/2191/2258/2332/2393/2449 (July 2014 to December 2019)," December 31, 2019, https://www. humanitarianresponse.info/en/operations/stima/infographic/ syrian-arab-republic-united-nations-cross-border-operations-under-3.

152 UN Office for the Coordination of Humanitarian Affairs, "About OCHA Iraq," https://www.unocha.org/iraq/about-ocha-iraq.

153 UN Office for the Coordination of Humanitarian Affairs, "Syrian Arab Republic: North East Syria: Al Hol Camp," October 11, 2020, available at https://bit.ly/35ntmAt.

154 Dennis Ross, interview by author, June 10, 2020.

155 Felicia Schwartz, "Trump Administration Committed to Upholding Iran Deal, EU Official Says," *Wall Street Journal*, February 10, 2017, https://www.wsj.com/articles/u-s-europe-in-agreement-on-russia-sanctions-eu-official-says-1486755982.

156 Peter Baker, "Trump Recertifies Iran Nuclear Deal, but Only Reluctantly," *New York Times*, July 17, 2017, https://www.nytimes. com/2017/07/17/us/politics/trump-iran-nuclear-deal-recertify.html.

157 Karen DeYoung, "U.S. Slaps New Sanctions on Iran, After Certifying Its Compliance with Nuclear Deal," *Washington Post*, July 18, 2017, https:// www.washingtonpost.com/world/national-security/us-certifies-that-iran-is-meeting-terms-of-nuclear-deal/2017/07/17/58d0a362-6b4a-11e7-b9e2-2056e768a7e5_story.html.

158 "United Nations General Assembly—Speech by M. Emmanuel Macron, President of the Republic (19.09.17)," Ministry for Europe and Foreign Affairs, accessed November 20, 2020, https://www.diplomatie. gouv.fr/en/french-foreign-policy/united-nations/news-and-events/

united-nations-general-assembly/unga-s-72nd-session/article/united-nations-general-assembly-speech-by-m-emmanuel-macron-president-of-the.

159 Ahmad Majidyar, "Iranian Leaders Reject Macron's Proposal to Supplement Nuclear Deal," Middle East Institute, September 19, 2017, https://www.mei.edu/publications/iranian-leaders-reject-macrons-proposal-supplement-nuclear-deal.

160 Krishnadev Calamur, "The Questions Raised by Trump's Iran Deal Decision," *Atlantic*, October 13, 2017, https://www.theatlantic.com/international/archive/2017/10/iran-deal-trump/542862/.

161 Ibid.

162 "Timeline of Nuclear Diplomacy with Iran," Arms Control Association, September 2020, https://www.armscontrol.org/factsheets/Timeline-of-Nuclear-Diplomacy-With-Iran.

163 Nicole Gaouette, "EU Diplomat Says U.S. Lawmakers Want to Honor Iran Deal," CNN, November 7, 2017, https://www.cnn.com/2017/11/07/politics/mogherini-us-iran-deal/index.html.

164 White House, "Statement by the President on the Iran Nuclear Deal," January 12, 2018, https://www.whitehouse.gov/briefings-statements/statement-president-iran-nuclear-deal/.

165 Ibid.

166 Gardiner Harris and Stanley Reed, "Roiling Markets, U.S. Insists World Must Stop Buying Iranian Oil," *New York Times*, June 26, 2018, https://www.nytimes.com/2018/06/26/world/middleeast/us-iran-oil-sanctions-.html.

167 Lesley Wroughton and Robin Emmott, "On First Day, Pompeo Charms NATO but Warns on Iran, Defense Spending," Reuters, April 26, 2018, https://www.reuters.com/article/us-nato-foreign-pompeo/on-first-day-pompeo-charms-nato-but-warns-on-iran-defense-spending-idUSKBN1HY0CA.

168 "EU to Reactivate 'Blocking Statute' Against U.S. Sanctions on Iran for European Firms," Deutsche Welle, May 17, 2018, https://www.dw.com/en/eu-to-reactivate-blocking-statute-against-us-sanctions-on-iran-for-european-firms/a-43826992.

169	UK Foreign & Commonwealth Office, "Joint Statement on the Re-Imposition of U.S. Sanctions on Iran," gov.uk, August 6, 2018, https://www.gov.uk/government/news/joint-statement-on-the-re-imposition-of-us-sanctions-on-iran.

170	"European Commission Adopts Support Package for Iran, with a Focus on the Private Sector," European Commission, August 23, 2018, https://ec.europa.eu/commission/presscorner/detail/en/IP_18_5103.

171	"Timeline of Nuclear Diplomacy," https://www.armscontrol.org/factsheets/Timeline-of-Nuclear-Diplomacy-With-Iran.

172	Ibid.

173	Demetri Sevastopulo, "Kremlin Throws Weight Behind EU Effort to Boost Iran Trade," *Financial Times*, July 18, 2019, https://www.ft.com/content/3aa3e7ee-a8b7-11e9-984c-fac8325aaa04.

174	U.S. Department of State, "Executive Order to Impose Sanctions on the Office of the Supreme Leader of Iran," June 24, 2019, https://www.state.gov/executive-order-to-impose-sanctions-on-the-office-of-the-supreme-leader-of-iran/.

175	U.S. Department of the Treasury, "Treasury Designates Iran's Foreign Minister Javad Zarif for Acting for the Supreme Leader of Iran," July 31, 2019, https://home.treasury.gov/news/press-releases/sm749.

176	Sevastopulo, "Kremlin Throws Weight Behind EU Effort," https://www.ft.com/content/3aa3e7ee-a8b7-11e9-984c-fac8325aaa04.

177	Ibid.

178	Reuters, "Six More Countries Join Trump-Busting Iran Barter Group," *Guardian*, December 1, 2019, https://www.theguardian.com/world/2019/dec/01/six-more-countries-join-trump-busting-iran-barter-group.

179	"Swiss Humanitarian Channel to Iran Launches with Medical Shipments," BBC, January 30, 2020, https://www.bbc.com/news/world-middle-east-51314171.

180	"JCPOA: Chair's Statement Following the Meeting of the Joint Commission," European External Action Service, February 26, 2020, https://eeas.europa.eu/headquarters/headquarters-homepage/75190/jcpoa-chairs-statement-following-meeting-joint-commission_en.

181 "Iran Receives European Medical Gear amid Coronavirus Crisis," Al Jazeera, March 31, 2020, https://www.aljazeera.com/ economy/2020/03/31/iran-receives-european-medical-gear-amid-coronavirus-crisis/.

182 Josep Borrell, "Saving the Iran Nuclear Deal," *Japan Times*, July 20, 2020, https://www.japantimes.co.jp/opinion/2020/07/20/commentary/ world-commentary/saving-iran-nuclear-deal/.

183 European official, interview by author, April 2020.

184 Rick Noack, "Will the White House's Bullying of Europe over Iran Work?" *Washington Post*, May 30, 2019, https://www.washingtonpost. com/world/2019/05/30/europes-controversial-plot-bypass-us-sanctions-iran/.

185 "Strengthening European Autonomy Across MENA," in *Mapping European Leverage in the MENA Region*, European Council on Foreign Relations, November 2019, https://www.ecfr.eu/special/ mapping_eu_leverage_mena/.

186 David E. Sanger, Steven Erlanger, and Adam Nossiter, "France Dangles $15 Billion Bailout for Iran in Effort to Save Nuclear Deal," *New York Times*, September 2, 2019, https://www.nytimes.com/2019/09/02/world/ middleeast/iran-france-nuclear-deal.html.

187 "U.S. President Trump Could Meet with Iran's Rouhani at U.N. with No Preconditions: Pompeo," Reuters, September 10, 2019, https:// www.reuters.com/article/us-usa-iran-un/us-president-trump-could-meet-with-irans-rouhani-at-un-with-no-preconditions-pompeo-idUSKCN1VV2D7.

188 "UN General Assembly 2019: All the Latest Updates," Al Jazeera, September 30, 2019, https://www.aljazeera.com/news/2019/9/30/ un-general-assembly-2019-all-the-latest-updates.

189 "Iran President Hassan Rouhani's Full Speech to the UN General Assembly," YouTube video, 22:40, posted by "PBS NewsHour," September 25, 2019, https://www.youtube.com/watch?v=OpibxAg5Erk.

190 Sarah Dadouch, "Iranian President Backs French Plan to Restart Talks with the U.S.," *Washington Post*, October 2, 2019, https://www. washingtonpost.com/world/middle_east/iran-president-backs-french-plan-to-restart-talks-with-the-us/2019/10/02/db1cb39e-e4f9-11e9-b403-f738899982d2_story.html.

191   White House, "Proclamation on the Suspension of Entry as Immigrants and Nonimmigrants of Senior Officials of the Government of Iran," September 25, 2019, previously available (page no longer live) at https://www.whitehouse.gov/presidential-actions/proclamation-suspension-entry-immigrants-nonimmigrants-senior-officials-government-iran/.

192   President of the Islamic Republic of Iran, "President at the Session of CBI General Assembly," accessed November 20, 2020, http://president.ir/en/113398.

193   Kelsey Davenport, "Iran Newly Breaches Nuclear Deal," Arms Control Association, December 2019, https://www.armscontrol.org/act/2019-12/news/iran-newly-breaches-nuclear-deal.

194   President of the Islamic Republic of Iran, "President After the Meeting of Three Branches' Heads," September 5, 2019, http://president.ir/en/111155.

195   "Iranian President Announces Installation of IR-9 Centrifuge Soon," *Azer News*, October 15, 2019, https://www.azernews.az/region/157272.html.

196   "Iran's Rouhani Announces Another Step Away from 2015 Nuclear Deal," Al Jazeera, November 5, 2019, https://www.aljazeera.com/news/2019/11/05/irans-rouhani-announces-another-step-away-from-2015-nuclear-deal/.

197   Daphne Psaledakis, "U.S. to No Longer Waive Sanctions on Iranian Nuclear Site," Reuters, November 18, 2019, https://www.reuters.com/article/us-usa-iran/u-s-to-no-longer-waive-sanctions-on-iranian-nuclear-site-watching-irans-protests-pompeo-idUSKBN1XS2DG.

198   Mohsen Ganji, "Iran Begins Pouring Concrete for 2nd Nuclear Power Reactor," Associated Press, November 10, 2019, https://apnews.com/article/bc0bbdeb85e34b3f92ba57b0f99f0516.

199   Davenport, "Iran Newly Breaches," https://www.armscontrol.org/act/2019-12/news/iran-newly-breaches-nuclear-deal.

200   Islamic Republic News Agency, "Iran Takes Final Step by Abandoning JCPOA Restrictions," January 5, 2020, https://en.irna.ir/news/83622509/Iran-takes-final-step-by-abandoning-JCPOA-restrictions.

201   Javad Zarif (@JZarif), "As 5th & final REMEDIAL step under paragraph 36 of JCPOA, there will no longer be any restriction on

number of centrifuges[.] This step is within JCPOA & all 5 steps are reversible upon EFFECTIVE implementation of reciprocal obligations[.] Iran's full cooperation w/IAEA will continue," post on Twitter, January 5, 2020, 2:10 p.m., https://twitter.com/JZarif/status/1213900666164432900.

202 Élysée, "Joint Statement from President Macron, Chancellor Merkel and Prime Minister Johnson," January 6, 2020, https://www.elysee.fr/en/emmanuel-macron/2020/01/06/joint-statement-from-president-macron-chancellor-merkel-and-prime-minister-johnson.

203 Alex Ward, "Iran Says It's Now Enriching Uranium at Levels Higher Than Before Nuclear Deal," Vox, January 16, 2020, https://www.vox.com/world/2020/1/16/21069361/iran-nuclear-uranium-enrichment-rouhani-trump.

204 Babak Dehghanpisheh, "Iran Says It Will Quit Global Nuclear Treaty if Case Goes to UN," Reuters, January 19, 2020, https://www.reuters.com/article/us-iran-nuclear/iran-says-it-will-quit-global-nuclear-treaty-if-case-goes-to-un-idUSKBN1ZJ0ML.

205 Kiyoko Metzler and David Rising, "UN Agency: Iran Nearly Triples Stockpile of Enriched Uranium," Associated Press, March 3, 2020, https://apnews.com/article/40f58d4d8114a774c7771a68345d6b0f.

206 "Iran Produces New Generation of Centrifuges," *Tehran Times*, March 27, 2020, https://www.tehrantimes.com/news/446338/Iran-produces-new-generation-of-centrifuges.

207 Ibid.

208 "Iran Shows Missile, Launches Satellite Which Fails to Reach Orbit," Al Jazeera, February 9, 2020, https://www.aljazeera.com/news/2020/2/9/iran-shows-missile-launches-satellite-which-fails-to-reach-orbit.

209 Associated Press, "Iran Fails to Launch Satellite in Orbit," *New York Times*, April 22, 2020, https://www.nytimes.com/2020/04/22/world/middleeast/iran-satellite-launch.html.

210 Samuel Hickey, "Iran's Military Satellite Launch: What Just Happened?" Center for Arms Control and Non-Proliferation, May 4, 2020, https://armscontrolcenter.org/irans-military-satellite-launch-what-just-happened/.

211 U.S. Department of State, "Iran's Space Program Is Dangerous, Not Peaceful," April 25, 2020, previously available (page no longer live) at https://www.state.gov/irans-space-program-is-dangerous-not-peaceful/.

212 "Iran Nuclear Deal: EU Nations Warn Tehran over Breaches," BBC, September 27, 2019, https://www.bbc.com/news/world-middle-east-49849448.

213 UK Foreign & Commonwealth Office, "Joint Comprehensive Plan of Action on Iran: France, Germany, UK and EU Joint Statement After 11 November IAEA Report," gov.uk, https://www.gov.uk/government/news/joint-statement-by-the-foreign-ministers-of-france-germany-united-kingdom-and-the-eu-high-representative-on-the-jcpoa.

214 Patrick Wintour, "Iran Threatens to Step Back from UN Nuclear Watchdog," *Guardian*, December 1, 2019, https://www.theguardian.com/world/2019/dec/01/iran-threatens-to-step-back-from-un-nuclear-watchdog?utm_source=AM+Nukes+Roundup.

215 UK Foreign & Commonwealth Office, "E3 Foreign Ministers' Statement on the JCPoA: 14 January 2020," gov.uk, press release, January 14, 2020, https://www.gov.uk/government/news/e3-foreign-ministers-statement-on-the-jcpoa-14-january-2020.

216 "Iran: Remarks by High Representative/Vice-President Josep Borrell at the Press Conference During His Visit to Tehran," European External Action Service, accessed February 4, 2020, https://eeas.europa.eu/headquarters/headquarters-homepage/73972/iran-remarks-high-representativevice-president-josep-borrell-press-conference-during-his-visit_en.

217 Lorne Cook, "EU Says Iran Has Triggered Nuclear Deal Dispute Mechanism," *Washington Post*, July 3, 2020, https://www.washingtonpost.com/world/middle_east/eu-says-iran-has-triggered-nuclear-deal-dispute-mechanism/2020/07/03/9eeb33de-bd7d-11ea-97c1-6cf116ffe26c_story.html.

218 Kyra Rauschenbach, "U.S.-Iran Escalation Timeline," Critical Threats Project, accessed January 13, 2020, https://www.criticalthreats.org/analysis/US-iran-escalation-timeline.

219 Shawn Snow, "Several American Troops Wounded and a U.S. Contractor Killed in Rocket Attack on Kirkuk Base," *Military*

Times, December 27, 2019, https://www.militarytimes.com/
flashpoints/2019/12/28/several-american-troops-wounded-and-a-us-
contractor-killed-in-rocket-attack-on-kirkuk-base/.

220 "Kataib Hezbollah: Iraq Condemns U.S. Attacks on Iran-Backed
Militia," BBC, December 30, 2019, https://www.bbc.com/news/
world-middle-east-50951742.

221 U.S. Department of Defense, "SD Statement on Deployment of 82nd
Airborne Division," December 31, 2019, https://www.defense.gov/
Newsroom/Releases/Release/Article/2048934/sd-statement-on-
deployment-of-82nd-airborne-division/.

222 U.S. Department of Defense, "Statement by the Department of Defense,"
January 2, 2020, https://www.defense.gov/Newsroom/Releases/Release/
Article/2049534/statement-by-the-department-of-defense/.

223 "Iran Attack: U.S. Troops Targeted with Ballistic Missiles," BBC,
January 8, 2020, https://www.bbc.com/news/world-middle-east-
51028954.

224 Mihir Zaveri, "More Than 100 Troops Have Brain Injuries from Iran
Missile Strike, Pentagon Says," *New York Times*, February 10, 2020,
https://www.nytimes.com/2020/02/10/world/middleeast/iraq-iran-
brain-injuries.html.

225 "Iran Plane Crash: What We Know About Flight PS752," BBC, January
14, 2020, https://www.bbc.com/news/world-middle-east-51047006.

226 Barbara Starr et al., "2 Americans and 1 British National Killed in
Rocket Attack on Base in Iraq," CNN, March 11, 2020, https://www.cnn.
com/2020/03/11/politics/americans-killed-iraq-rocket-attack/index.html.

227 Alissa J. Rubin and Eric Schmitt, "U.S. Airstrikes Kill Iraqi Soldiers and
Police, Iraqi Officials Say," *New York Times*, March 13, 2020, https://
www.nytimes.com/2020/03/13/world/middleeast/iraq-military-us-
airstrike.html.

228 Robin Wright, "A Tanker War in the Middle East—Again?" *The
New Yorker*, June 14, 2019, https://www.newyorker.com/news/
our-columnists/a-tanker-war-in-the-middle-eastagain.

229 UK Foreign & Commonwealth Office, "E3 Joint Statement on Iran,"
gov.uk, June 24, 2019, https://www.gov.uk/government/speeches/
e3-statement-on-iran.

230 White House, "Remarks by President Trump at a Flag Presentation Ceremony," July 18, 2019, https://www.whitehouse.gov/briefings-statements/remarks-president-trump-flag-presentation-ceremony/.

231 U.S. Central Command, "U.S. Central Command Statement on Operation Sentinel," July 19, 2019, https://www.centcom.mil/MEDIA/STATEMENTS/Statements-View/Article/1911282/us-central-command-statement-on-operation-sentinel/utm_source/hootsuite/.

232 Tasnim News Agency, "Iran's IRGC Captures Foreign Ship Smuggling Fuel in Persian Gulf," August 4, 2019, https://www.tasnimnews.com/en/news/2019/08/04/2068699/iran-s-irgc-captures-foreign-ship-smuggling-fuel-in-persian-gulf.

233 U.S. Department of State, "Middle East Peace and Security," previously available (page no longer live) at https://www.state.gov/middle-east-peace-and-security.

234 Frank Verrastro, "Attack on Saudi Oil Infrastructure: We May Have Dodged a Bullet, at Least for Now…," Center for Strategic and International Studies, September 18, 2019, https://www.csis.org/analysis/attack-saudi-oil-infrastructure-we-may-have-dodged-bullet-least-now.

235 UAE Ministry of Foreign Affairs, "UAE Joins International Coalition for Maritime Security," September 20, 2020, https://www.mofaic.gov.ae/en/mediahub/news/years/2019/9/20/20-09-2019-uae-maritime-security; Saudi Press Agency, "The Kingdom of Saudi Arabia Joins the International Maritime Security Construct," September 18, 2019, https://www.spa.gov.sa/viewstory.php?lang=en&newsid=1970536.

236 UK Prime Minister's Office, "Joint Statement by the Heads of State and Government of France, Germany and the United Kingdom," gov.uk, September 23, 2019, https://www.gov.uk/government/news/joint-statement-by-the-heads-of-state-and-government-of-france-germany-and-the-united-kingdom.

237 Iran Ministry of Foreign Affairs, "Spokesman's Reaction to Attack on Iranian Tanker in Red Sea," October 11, 2019, https://bit.ly/3wz28mj.

238 U.S. Naval Forces Central Command, "United Kingdom Commander Takes Control of CTF Sentinel," January 30, 2020, https://www.cusnc.navy.mil/Media/News/Display/Article/2069359/united-kingdom-commander-takes-control-of-ctf-.

239 U.S. Naval Forces Central Command, "Lithuania Joins the International Maritime Security Construct," March 26, 2020, http://www.cusnc.navy.mil/Media/News/Display/Article/2125964/lithuania-joins-the-international-maritime-security-construct/.

240 U.S. Department of State, "Secretary of State Michael R. Pompeo with David Rubenstein, President of the Economic Club of Washington, DC," July 29, 2019, previously available (page no longer live) at https://www.state.gov/secretary-of-state-michael-r-pompeo-with-david-rubenstein-president-of-the-economic-club-of-washington-d-c/.

241 U.S. Central Command, "United Kingdom Commander Takes Control of CTF Sentinel," January 30, 2020, http://www.centcom.mil/MEDIA/NEWS-ARTICLES/News-Article-View/Article/2069565/united-kingdom-commander-takes-control-of-ctf-sentinel/.

242 Reuters, "France, Germany, Britain Working on Maritime 'Observation' Mission in Gulf: Le Drian," July 23, 2019, https://www.reuters.com/article/us-mideast-iran-france/france-germany-britain-working-on-maritime-observation-mission-in-gulf-le-drian-idUSKCN1UI1WO.

243 Denmark Ministry of Foreign Affairs, "Denmark Sends Officers and Frigate to the Strait of Hormuz," December 12, 2019, http://um.dk/en/news/newsdisplaypage/?newsID=1CDA3A13-8D04-45AF-9CE6-9A3A62746579.

244 Government of the Netherlands, "Dutch Deployment in the Strait of Hormuz," November 29, 2019, https://www.government.nl/latest/news/2019/11/29/dutch-deployment-in-the-strait-of-hormuz.

245 France Ministry of Europe and Foreign Affairs, "European Maritime Awareness in the SoH (EMASOH): Political Statement by the Governments of Belgium, Denmark, France, Germany, Greece, Italy, the Netherlands, and Portugal," January 20, 2020, http://www.diplomatie.gouv.fr/en/french-foreign-policy/european-union/news/article/european-maritime-awareness-in-the-soh-emasoh-political-statement-by-the.

246 Reuters, "France Says Abu Dhabi to Host HQ for European Naval Mission for the Gulf," November 24, 2019, http://www.reuters.com/article/us-emirates-france/france-says-abu-dhabi-to-host-hq-for-european-naval-mission-for-the-gulf-idUSKBN1XY0AO.

247 Reuters, "France Deploys Radar System in Saudi Arabia to 'Reassure' Kingdom," January 17, 2020, http://www.reuters.com/article/us-iran-usa-france/france-deploys-radar-system-in-saudi-arabia-to-reassure-kingdom-idUSKBN1ZG1HC.

248 U.S. Naval Forces Central Command, "IRGCN Vessels Conduct Unsafe, Unprofessional Interaction with U.S. Naval Forces in Arabian Gulf," April 15, 2020, http://www.cusnc.navy.mil/Media/News/Display/Article/2151642/irgcn-vessels-conduct-unsafe-unprofessional-interaction-with-us-naval-forces-in/.

249 U.S. Central Command, "Gen. McKenzie Interview Transcript, Aspen Security Forum, June 18, 2020," June 19, 2020, http://www.centcom.mil/MEDIA/Transcripts/Article/2226655/gen-mckenzie-interview-transcript-aspen-security-forum-june-18-2020/.

250 U.S. Department of State, "Briefing with Special Representative for Iran and Senior Advisor to the Secretary Brian Hook on Depriving Iran of the Weapons of War," April 30, 2020, previously available (page no longer live) at https://www.state.gov/briefing-with-special-representative-for-iran-and-senior-advisor-to-the-secretary-brian-hook-on-depriving-iran-of-the-weapons-of-war/.

251 Eliot Engel et al., letter to Secretary of State Mike Pompeo, May 4, 2020, https://foreignaffairs.house.gov/_cache/files/9/e/9e07750b-34b2-4687-98f2-eec2acf00d10/E10ACB7928A8BD5CB48A15510084A49D.arms-embargo-final-pdf.pdf.

252 Brian Hook, "We're Ready to 'Snap Back' Sanctions," *Wall Street Journal*, May 13, 2020, https://www.wsj.com/articles/were-ready-to-snap-back-sanctions-11589410620.

253 David Wainer, "U.S. Seeks Indefinite Arms Embargo on Iran in UN Resolution," Bloomberg, June 22, 2020, https://www.bloomberg.com/news/articles/2020-06-23/u-s-seeks-indefinite-arms-embargo-on-iran-in-un-resolution.

254 U.S. Department of State, "Secretary Michael R. Pompeo at the UN Security Council on the Iran Arms Embargo," June 30, 2020, previously available (page no longer live) at https://www.state.gov/secretary-michael-r-pompeo-at-the-un-security-council-on-the-iran-arms-embargo/.

255 David Wainer, "U.S. to Seek UN Vote on Iran Arms Embargo This Month, Craft Says," Bloomberg, July 1, 2020, https://www.bloomberg.com/news/articles/2020-07-01/u-s-to-seek-un-vote-on-iran-arms-embargo-this-month-craft-says?utm_source=AM+Nukes+Roundup.

256 France Ministry of Europe and Foreign Affairs, "Communiqué des Ministres des Affaires Étrangères de La France, de L'Allemagne et du Royaume-Uni," August 20, 2020, https://www.diplomatie.gouv.fr/fr/dossiers-pays/iran/evenements/article/communique-des-ministres-des-affaires-etrangeres-de-la-france-de-l-allemagne-et.

257 "Iran Nuclear Deal: European Nations 'Siding with Ayatollahs'—Pompeo," BBC, August 21, 2020, https://www.bbc.com/news/world-middle-east-53847650.

258 "UNSC Dismisses U.S. Demand to Impose 'Snapback' Sanctions on Iran," Al Jazeera, August 25, 2020, https://www.aljazeera.com/news/2020/8/25/unsc-dismisses-us-demand-to-impose-snapback-sanctions-on-iran.

259 Secretary Pompeo (@SecPompeo), "Iran's uranium stockpile is reportedly more than 10 times the limit set by the JCPOA. The E3 and other nations must wake up to the reality that the nuclear deal is history and should join us in imposing strong sanctions. Pressure and comprehensive talks are the only path forward," post on Twitter, September 8, 2020, 12:18 p.m., https://twitter.com/SecPompeo/status/1303367064892116998.

260 Carol Morello, "U.S. Insists 'Snapback' Sanctions Against Iran Are in Force, but Most of the World Says That's Illegal," *Washington Post*, September 20, 2020, https://www.washingtonpost.com/national-security/us-insists-snapback-sanctions-against-iran-are-in-force-but-most-of-the-world-says-thats-illegal/2020/09/20/d9f2bbf2-fb65-11ea-830c-a160b331ca62_story.html.

261 Hassan Ahmadian, "Iran," in *Mapping European Leverage in the MENA Region*, European Council on Foreign Relations, December 2019, https://ecfr.eu/special/mapping_eu_leverage_mena/iran.

262 Former senior European official, interview by author, July 2020.

3

The New Middle East Geopolitics

A prerequisite to thinking about the future of transatlantic cooperation in the Middle East is to reflect on the state of the region itself, extending to its own perceptions and expectations regarding the United States and Europe as well as other international actors. Those perceptions and expectations have, of course, been shaped in part by the limits and weakening of that cooperation in the decade since the Arab Spring uprisings.

The Local Dynamics

The difficulty of mitigating the negative consequences of the Arab uprisings has contributed to various local dynamics that have changed the political landscape in the Middle East and North Africa.

Fragmentation, State Collapse, and the Quest for Dignity

The Middle East in 2021 is characterized by fragmentation resulting from the collapse of state structures and the domination of militias, as well as by sustained pressure from the region's populations for more dignified treatment by their rulers.

The uprisings of 2011 resulted from mismanagement of the problems long plaguing Arab societies: demographic pressures, rising unemployment, the global financial crisis of 2007–8, the food crisis of 2008,[1] resource shortages, and tensions between traditional family structures and the individual aspirations of a younger generation. But the conditions leading to the 2011 uprisings have not fundamentally changed, and have even worsened to some extent. The demographic challenge, for example, remains. As one European analyst explains: "It should be abundantly clear that the biggest security threat facing the states of the Mediterranean, who are partners of the 'southern neighborhood' within the framework of the European Neighbourhood Policy, is the socioeconomic situation combined with accelerating demographic growth. More specifically, even if the latter is slowed, for the next 20 years around 60% of local populations will be under 30 years of age."[2]

New difficulties have made matters worse. The bankruptcy of the Iraqi, Syrian, Libyan, and Yemeni states is profound, while continued resistance to change from the strongest clans has engendered continual violence,[3] embracing both mobilizations against the heads of regimes and the resistance of patronage networks. The crises within these states' governments predate 2011, but the phenomenon has since taken on much greater proportions. And the transformation of corrupt sectarian political systems demanded by demonstrators in Iraq and Lebanon will be difficult, because pro-Iran actors are likely to resist reforming a system they benefit from. In each of these countries, the appointment of apolitical expert governments has sometimes represented a compromise between the street and the relevant political actors, but these governments often lack the resources and political capital to carry out structural reforms.

Regional conflicts allow regimes that are still in power to avoid dealing with internal problems that have caused their neighbors to go bankrupt. So the fight against the Islamic State, like the so-called war on terror, has diverted attention from the problems endemic to these countries. Arab authoritarianism was therefore not defeated by the uprisings of 2011, but it has a more fragmented political base today than before 2011. In fact, authoritarian leaders are increasingly brutal as they know that their power is fragile in the face of socioeconomic conditions that are even more dire than in 2011.

Burying the concept of the state in Arab countries would nevertheless be a mistake. The limitations and critiques of the state are in reality based not on its legitimacy but rather its dysfunction, and the monopoly that some people exercise over its resources. The "strong state" or "deep state" is certainly at its limits in the region, but Arab populations do not appear to wish to get rid of some form of statehood, however limited it may be. State structures persevere in Egypt, Algeria, Jordan, Tunisia, and Morocco; and even in countries in crisis, political actors continue to position themselves in relation to state institutions. People, it might be said, want less regime and more state: protestors, for example, tend to ask for *more* social and economic interventions from the state. Moreover, an alternative model to the state seems difficult to create when societies are already in crisis and political tensions run very high.

The search for a truly traditional model of governance is likewise limited, insofar as it suggests that the tribal or sectarian past might somehow have been ignored and could thus be legitimately reintroduced as an alternative to the state. But the state structures that emerged from colonization did not ignore these traditional political dynamics. Rather, they integrated them into the state, notably through clientelism. While the Iraqi disaster highlights the dangers of state-building attempts from the outside, the issues of decentralization and state reform and transformation remain.

The challenge seems to be to develop original modes of decentralization and federation. Multiple voices in the region stress that it is neither possible nor desirable today to "restore" pre-2011 governance. But it *might be* possible to initiate national dialogues that would enable local actors to establish functional constitutional organizations without denying either a sense of national unity or the existence of religious and ethnic solidarities. The failures of most Arab states in the twentieth century do not stem from shortcomings inherent in the idea of a state within the region, but from the refusal of those in power to rule their societies in a nonviolent manner.

A second factor that feeds on and amplifies fragmentation and state collapse in the region is the *paramilitarization* of Arab politics. The lack of faith in state structures has given new political space to nonstate actors who exploit identity politics based on tribes, religious communities, and other minorities.

This phenomenon reflects an empowerment of different sets of actors accompanying a fragmentation of the political order. In Syria, Iraq, and Libya, the existing security structures did not evaporate, but became detached from each other. The careers of Saddam Hussein's officers who went on to become Islamic State commanders, or of deserters from the Qadhafi regime who now head militias in Libya, show how state apparatuses fed into armed conflict in different ways.

These routes blur the boundary between state and nonstate actors. The fact that both the Iraqi and Syrian states seem now more effectively defended by militias than by state forces reflects the development of so-called state militias that weaken the state while defending it. The fifty or so Shia militias of the "Popular Mobilization" (notably, the Badr Organization, Asaib Ahl al-Haq, Iraqi Hezbollah, and the Sadrists of Saraya al-Salam) also claim political roles and compete with the regular army.

The militias participate in both the dismantling and the reshaping of the state, with the aim of transforming it into an entity they can control. IS, for example, tried to form a "refuge state" to attract international jihadism, based on the existing local institutions of the territories it conquered; other Syrian jihadist groups are betting on the establishment of proto-state zones under Salafi governance; and the Democratic Union Party (PYD) hopes to control a largely decentralized region in northeast Syria. In Lebanon, Hezbollah controls the state and blocks it from reforming itself; the Iraqi state uses Shia militias based on a sectarian logic; and competition between militias, whether Islamists or anti-Islamists, for access to national resources is paralyzing the political reunification of Libyan institutions.

Parallel to these political and military trends, Arab societies continue to live with and adapt to globalization while cultivating their own various ethnic and religious identities. Artistic creation, digital communication, and civil society engagement, meanwhile, follow their own logics and often redraw the mental maps of populations, often in conjunction with their diasporas around the world. The recent hype about the Arab trends on the Clubhouse app is just the latest example of a constant process of reshaping virtual and actual spaces for expression and connection.[4] Through scattered collectives or local associations, civil society in the Arab world remains active.

Some Arab societies are attracted to post-Western globalization—one shaped by American and European modernity, but increasingly diversified through Asian, Turkish, and African influences and examples. There are still a variety of links with Europe and America, but they are no longer seen as the exclusive drivers of development. Some Arab youth, moreover, have the necessary tools to escape their societies, physically or digitally, and to pursue projects away from regional politics.

The wave of spontaneous movements in 2019 in Algeria, Sudan, Lebanon, and Iraq demonstrated that the roots and spirit of the 2011 uprisings are still alive and well, even if they take unique forms in each country. These populations continue to demand less corruption, more public services, and more dignified treatment by those in power. These are calls for more rule of law. These demands are frequently repressed, but they cannot be eliminated. Whether through riots or via peaceful mobilization, people regularly reaffirm their aspirations. It is particularly interesting to note that if the sectarian systems in Iraq and Lebanon largely prevented the spread of the Arab Spring in 2011, by the end of 2019, the unresolved paralysis and corruption of these same systems provoked the most massive mobilizations these two countries have experienced in several decades.

The Impact of Covid-19

In considering the aftermath of the pandemic, the spread of the 2007–8 financial crisis in the United States and Europe to North Africa could provide a window into some of the consequences a global recession might produce in the coming years. While less exposed to international financial markets, non–oil producers in the region are more vulnerable to external shocks and foreign economic cycles. Thus, between 2007 and 2010, the downturn in Europe led to a 60 percent drop in the trade balance of goods from North African countries. Similarly, Egypt and Tunisia saw their tourism revenue decrease by 5 percent, their foreign direct investment by 31 percent, and remittances by 6 percent. Similar trends are likely in the wake of the pandemic.[5]

The International Monetary Fund (IMF) projected that the global recession would cause countries in the Middle East region to see their real GDP shrink by 5 percent in 2020—though it did predict a partial rebound of 3.2 percent in 2021.[6] By December 2020, UNICEF estimated that the equivalent of 11 million full-time jobs in the Middle East had been lost due to Covid-19,[7] an especially devastating figure for a region in which unemployment already plunged 27 percent for youth in 2019,[8] and where the demographic challenge is even greater today than in 2011.

In the 2000s, the main issue for governments in this region was absorbing millions of young workers entering the workforce each year. In 2011, out of the region's 398 million people, 189 million were between the ages of fifteen and forty, with that figure rising by 18 million in 2020,[9] compounding that challenge. Arab societies today must also support more elderly people, whose numbers will have more than doubled, from twenty million in 2011[10] to forty million, by 2030.[11] Family solidarity remains a strong cultural norm in Arab societies but will be heavily tested, both by pandemic-related confinement and by the lingering economic consequences of the pandemic.

A global recession will likely have a still more dramatic impact on refugees in the region. This is because the number of people affected by conflicts and reliant on UN assistance is even greater today than in 2011. For instance, the United States and Europe together currently provide 90 percent and 45 percent of the billions of dollars of UN assistance, respectively, for Syria and Yemen.[12] Assuming these Western contributions are even partially reduced by a recession in the period ahead, the consequences for Yemen, Syria, Lebanon, Jordan, and even Turkey are likely to be dramatic.

As in the run-up to 2011, when the 2007 drought in Syria pushed waves of rural workers to the south and to the suburbs of Damascus, environmental change will add to regional tensions. As of 2018, two-thirds[13] of the 448 million inhabitants[14] of North Africa and the Middle East already suffered from insufficient water resources. The region does not have the means to sustain economic growth commensurate with its surging population, raising the specter of cascading public health issues, uncontrolled urbanization, and competition between countries over access to water.

IMF and World Bank programs,[15] technical assistance, and equipment supplied by UN agencies brought some immediate relief to countries in the region in 2020.[16] Governments across the region have also taken public health measures including lockdowns, social distancing, and donning of masks and protective gear; Morocco, for its part, has organized local production of masks and vaccine rollout efficiently. The GCC countries and Egypt have announced stimulus packages to contain the initial economic shocks, but other countries have been unable to afford comparable measures. Arab countries will need to find new drivers of growth as post-pandemic economic fallout globally reduces traditional sources of development assistance.

Beyond financial resources, political fragility will weaken governments' response. Heads of state have recently changed in Oman, Algeria, and Tunisia; Egypt, Jordan, and Morocco have faced social unrest and security challenges, while conflict continues unabated in Yemen, Syria, and Libya. Protestors in Algeria, Lebanon, and Iraq proved in 2019 that the 2011 quest for dignity was far from over. Lockdowns have allowed authorities to reduce social movements, for example, in Iraq and Algeria, but this is unlikely to solve underlying political and institutional tensions, as the demonstrations throughout 2021 in Lebanon showed.

Even oil-producing countries are more vulnerable than in 2011. They have suffered from a precipitous decline in prices since 2014; and prices hit a spectacular historic negative in mid-2020. Arab oil-producing states could well lack the fiscal room for maneuver that they used to contain the Arab Spring through massive social spending (up to $130 billion in Saudi Arabia in 2011[17]); they have started issuing sovereign bonds.[18] The oil blockade imposed by Khalifa Haftar on Libya's oil production has reduced output to below 100,000 barrels per day in 2020, compared with 1.8 million in 2010. Algeria had a limited public debt by the end of 2020 but held only twelve months of reserves in foreign currency. Politically and economically, Iraq has not recovered from the war against the Islamic State, and suffers both from governmental instability and from insufficient investments in its oil sector.

Societal resilience has already played a role in mitigating the effects of local Covid outbreaks: individuals and civil society organizations are providing support to communities in every country amid the pandemic.[19] But local solidarity is unlikely to be enough. Public healthcare and capacities to produce medical equipment remain weak throughout the region, owing to excessive state centralization, public service cuts, and partial liberalization benefiting mostly regime affiliates since the 1990s. The number of hospital beds in each country indicate that very few countries could handle a massive outbreak.[20]

Pandemic consequences will also vary internally and across the region on account of income disparities: the Arab world, where the top 10 percent own 65 percent of wealth, is the world's most unequal region by income.[21] So Covid patients from the top 10 percent are likely to find excellent private hospitals in the Gulf or in some other Arab capitals. Many of the 100 million people already living in poverty, on the other hand, may suffer economic consequences from the pandemic or contract the virus without ever knowing it.[22]

The New Strategic Landscape and Non-Western Influences

Local dynamics create even more instability when they are magnified by chaotic regional and international competition.

The Missing Regional Order

For the first time in almost a century, Middle East politics is dominated primarily by regional actors and no longer by international powers (as was the case in the twentieth century). The United States, Russia, China, and Europe all remain present and active, but are no longer willing to invest in the region, nor do they have the means to claim decisive influence on its affairs. Crises and their resolution depend on local and regional arrangements more than on international powers.

Observers are in this context quick to regularly appoint a new "leader" of regional politics. Qatar, Turkey, Saudi Arabia, Iran, and the United Arab Emirates, along with Russia outside the region, have been, one after the other, described as the "new" masters of the Middle East game, before the limitations of their power become evident. There is no longer any hegemony in North Africa and the Middle East, and regional powers often neutralize each other through one-off incidents. Ultimately, these confrontations leave no real space for a new regional security architecture.

The regional chessboard is too fragmented and the local players too volatile for any one power to be able to sustainably manipulate the region for its own benefit. Local actors may gain control of particular resources without generating any resultant domination; instead, local and international actors are forced to deal with regional, confessional, ethnic, and tribal divisions that are in most cases beyond the reach of their influence.

Several regional lines of tension influence local conflicts. The "cold war" between Iran and Saudi Arabia is a primary element of tension in the Middle East and has multiple ramifications—evident, for example, in the role played by Hezbollah in Lebanon, the Houthi insurrection in Yemen, or the importance of the Shia militias, more or less close to Tehran, in Iraq. Whether or not it is desired by all or some of the actors in Tehran and Riyadh, any incident that degenerates can provoke escalation.

The opposition of the United Arab Emirates, Egypt, and to a lesser extent Saudi Arabia to any form of political Islam also plays a role in several conflicts, as in Libya and Yemen. On the other hand, the willingness of Qatar and Turkey to promote Islamist forces has led to their providing major financial and political support for several groups, such as Hamas and Libyan Islamist militias. The opposition to political Islam is likely to continue to structure external interventions in many local political arenas, but that can evolve—because regional leaders are largely pragmatic, and have shown that they are able to compromise on the more ideological dimensions of their foreign policy, depending on their strategic needs. The Turkish outreach to Egypt in 2021 is a notable example.

The process of normalization between Israel and Arab countries has the potential to redraw a number of geopolitical lines in the region—and one way or another, it will deeply affect the Palestinian question. Arab countries might leverage it to improve the lives and rights of Palestinians, but may be limited by Israeli domestic politics, the paralysis of the

Palestinian Authority in Ramallah, or the growing power of Hamas. On the other hand, the trade and technological potential of the cooperation made possible by normalization may also have a structural impact on regional economic integration. The entire process, in any case, will be subject to the hybrid conflict between Israel and Iran and the renegotiation of the Iran nuclear deal.

Among the many factors impacting the transatlantic ability to cope with this new regional context, the roles of Russia and China are also key. Speaking about the diplomatic balance of power in the Middle East after the Cold War, a former European diplomat recalled that "Russia and China did not really 'exist' in the 1990s and 2000s. In the Madrid process, the United States cochaired with Russia to give them a status, but they no longer existed as a diplomatic force in the Middle East. Today, the question of how to deal with the Europeans may arise, but the question of how to get along with the Russians and fight the Chinese is a priority."[23] Referring to a new phase of strategic rivalry between the United States and China and, to a lesser extent, Russia, the Trump and Biden administrations have indeed made Great Power competition their priority.

Washington's China Nemesis

China's economic presence is felt throughout the region, but Beijing remains mainly focused on strengthening its commercial position in the Gulf and North Africa—and China's market share in the Maghreb has risen from 2.5 percent in 2000 to more than 15 percent in 2015, half of which is in Algeria. In the Middle East, China is mostly active in a few states concentrated in the Gulf, working as an investor in infrastructure and energy and as a contractor.

The Middle East is a critical source of energy for Beijing, as the Gulf states supply China with roughly 44 percent of its oil imports and 9 percent of its natural gas imports.[24] China surpassed the United States as the world's biggest net oil importer in 2017; America became a net *exporter* of oil in 2019. The region serves as a place to invest, and as a significant destination for Chinese capital and workers: increasingly, the Middle East is becoming a centerpiece of President Xi Jinping's Belt and Road Initiative. China has invested more than $123 billion in the Middle East and North Africa since the launch of the BRI, and China is now the Middle East's largest source of foreign investment, including with respect to many U.S. allies.[25]

At first glance, China does not appear to want to intensively engage militarily in the Middle East, even when its immediate interests are at stake. Beijing reacted cautiously after the attack on Saudi oil installations in October 2019, for example, even though China is the largest buyer of Saudi oil, which constitutes roughly 16 percent of Chinese oil imports.[26] In the wider region, China supports some Russian positions of principle (such as state sovereignty), even going so far as to offer training to the forces of the Syrian regime in 2017 to reinforce the Russian narrative as to the legitimacy of Bashar al-Assad. Chinese strategy has begun to shift, however. Diplomatic and military interests follow economic ones, as can be seen in China's growing naval and diplomatic presence through special envoys on a variety of issues (ranging from Syria to the Israeli-Palestinian conflict). China has signed comprehensive strategic partnerships with Algeria, Egypt, Iran, Saudi Arabia, and the UAE,[27] and Egypt is already China's third-largest trading partner in Africa.[28]

Recently, China has tried to exercise more leadership, such as through diplomatic conferences on Syria. According to Michael Singh, managing director of The Washington Institute, China's policy is self-correcting and evolving.[29] An example of this is the Israeli-Palestinian conflict, with respect to which China initially tried to appear neutral but has recently realigned itself away from the Palestinians to deepen ties with the Israelis. As China increasingly tries to project an image of itself as a major player and an alternative to the United States in the

Middle East, it has deepened its economic ties and embedded itself in the infrastructure of the region.

China has also ramped up its military engagement. In 2011, China's first expeditionary naval operation took place in Libya, to evacuate Chinese citizens there. Since then, China has opened its first naval base in Djibouti, and Chinese ships and fighter aircraft have stopped in the region and worked with local actors to address the threat posed by Chinese foreign terrorist fighters who joined jihadist groups.[30] President Xi has underscored that the Belt and Road Initiative requires a stable environment. Xi later said that because certain countries along the Silk Road experience "conflict, turbulence, crisis and challenge," there must be a "common, comprehensive, cooperative and sustainable…security environment built and shared by all."[31]

China has also increasingly tried to frame itself as an alternative to the United States. According to Karen Young, until recently a fellow at the American Enterprise Institute, "Framing the discussion of China's rise or role in the Middle East to a zero-sum game of choosing either US or Chinese patronage and partnership has served rhetorically only to increase China's stature among the region's political leadership."[32] As some American experts have stressed, the direction in the Trump administration (and, since then, in the Republican Party generally) pointed to disengaging from the Middle East, and China is capitalizing on that trend to promote its own status in the region. China stresses the vacuum that will be created if the United States disengages, even if it recognizes that Beijing cannot provide a security umbrella itself.

Beyond the actual Chinese economic and military footprint, a key issue for the Middle East is whether Chinese and American interests are compatible or contradictory. Some experts believe that the rhetoric of Great Power competition creates a false dichotomy between the two countries, given that America's deep security presence, its soft power and stature in the region, and its web of allies mean that China cannot truly serve as an alternative to the United States at this point. Even in areas like investment where China focuses much of its effort, private investment from the United States consistently exceeds Chinese investment over time. For analysts who consider the United States the still dominant power in the Middle East, the Belt and Road Initiative and other Chinese strategies in the region will not significantly change that.

Others argue that U.S. and Chinese interests in the Middle East are actually quite similar, even if the two countries differ with respect to how to achieve these interests.[33] Given China's reliance on the Gulf for oil and natural gas, it wants to keep Gulf states stable and exporting. And even though the United States has become less dependent on the Middle East for its energy needs, America and its allies are still susceptible to the global market volatility that would occur if there was disruption to this supply. Thus, both China and the United States have a stake in a strong, stable Gulf—and both countries' vulnerability to terrorist attacks by global or homegrown Islamist extremists enhances their interest in Middle East stability. To date, however, these shared interests have not resulted in strategic convergence.

On the other hand, some American experts see China's presence in the region as ipso facto counter to U.S. interests. They point to growing hard power competition in the Middle East, and warn that if the United States does not treat it seriously it will lose, because Beijing is trying to make Washington appear unreliable to allies—even more so as the United States continues to disengage from the region—all toward the broader goal of chipping away at American power and becoming the dominant power in the region. Finally, they emphasize the growing partnership between Russia and China to combat the United States in the Middle East. They regard other analysts as too focused on the shared Chinese-American interest in stability as against Russia's interest in *in*stability, and insist that the real threat is Russia-China convergence.

Ali Wyne, a senior analyst at the Eurasia Group, and Colin Clarke, a senior fellow at the Soufan Center, argue that Russia and China will likely continue to increase their influence across the Middle East, particularly if U.S. blunders allow them to invest in the Middle East with small, low-cost initiatives yielding high returns. They cite America's maximum pressure strategy, which led to deeper Tehran-Beijing ties. Wyne and Clarke hold that it is unclear whether either China or Russia is looking to become a "security heavyweight" in the region, particularly as they assess the failed U.S. strategy in the Middle East over the past two decades. Moreover, they argue, the larger China's Middle East footprint grows, the more likely it will become enmeshed in the region's squabbles. It will become more difficult for China to insist on its policy of noninterference.[34]

In the end, the reality of China's role in the Middle East lies somewhere between the two predominant caricatures of Chinese involvement in the region as depicted by observers. One camp characterizes China's involvement as purely economic and therefore benign; the other side represents China's intentions as trying to supplant the United States and dominate the region. It is possible that Beijing might be exploiting U.S. mistakes in the region to achieve limited economic goals at the moment, rather than displaying a comprehensive strategy for the region.

In the end, China does not seem to be exporting a governance model to the region, although its model is more attractive for some than a Western one; Beijing is more preoccupied with preventing others from trying to export *their* governance model to China. It is, rather, exporting goods and services, and acting to ensure market access, stability of energy supplies, and cooperative relationships across the region.

Russia's Role, Actual and Intended

Russia remains identified within both U.S. government and foreign policy circles as a rival, whereas Europeans tend to see Russia as a difficult but inevitable interlocutor. Whether the issue is Syria or Israel, Russia indeed appears to be at the center of many diplomatic and military equations in the region through skillful triangulation maneuvers—positioning itself as an intermediary between opposing parties. Moscow has in fact succeeded in establishing a series of three-way relationships that dominate the main conflicts in the Middle East: a triangle between Iran, Turkey, and Russia within the framework of the Moscow-brokered Astana format to manage northwest Syria; a triangle between Iran, Israel, and Russia wherein Moscow acts as an intermediary so as to avoid a complete escalation between Tehran and Tel Aviv; a triangle between Jordan, the Syrian regime, and Russia to negotiate the reopening of the border between Syria and Jordan; and a triangle between Egypt, Turkey, and Russia in Libya. The objective has been to raise Russia's international status: in the Middle East in particular, but especially vis-à-vis the United States.

Moscow's centrality is above all the result of American disengagement; but it is also the result of a tactical calculation on Moscow's part, and its willingness to take risks that have paid off so far. Russia is often perceived as the only international player ready to follow through on its commitments. Benefiting from high oil prices, Russia has since 2005 been conducting a policy of reengagement in the region—both to regain its traditional levers there, by offering alternatives to American hegemony, and in order to find new economic outlets. Russia's dependence on hydrocarbons has also led it to move closer to the dominant countries within OPEC, notably Saudi Arabia, even if this leads to regular confrontations, like the "oil war" of 2020.

In the region's pre-2011 state of affairs, Moscow was a medium-sized trading partner; as a military partner, it was living predominantly on past glories. The Russian reaction to the uprisings in 2011 changed this dynamic given Moscow's determination to oppose foreign-backed regime change and thus protect its strategic interests. Russia was also motivated by a desire to manifest a relationship of equals with the United States, as well as by domestic counterterrorism imperatives. Fear of Islamist extremism, especially from Chechnya, undergirded Vladimir Putin's uncompromising stance toward all forms of religious activism and opposition. With regard to the rejection of regime change, Moscow's position has been unchanging, but the nature and form of that commitment will evolve in accordance with strategic requirements aimed at making Moscow an indispensable interlocutor for Washington.

Moscow's Syria policy has transformed Russia into the most credible foreign power in the region, owing as well to its role in several Middle East crises. In this context, Moscow has cultivated its relations with all the countries of the region, especially in the Gulf, in order to reap the benefits of its credibility on the Syrian dossier. Russia's position in Syria is not as comfortable as it appears, however: Russia has nurtured numerous policy ambiguities in order to place itself at the center of the situation. Moscow has, for instance, let Western countries assume that it could get the Syrian regime to compromise, and it has entertained the notion that it could be a pragmatic interlocutor in addressing Turkish and Israeli security concerns. But if Moscow emerges from these ambiguities, it will be at some cost to itself—including the risk of a stronger Turkish reaction, as in Idlib in March 2020, when the Turkish army inflicted significant losses on the forces of the Syrian regime.

In other words, Moscow has no interest in a resolution of the various crises in the region, as their resolution would mean a loss of at least some of its influence. The paradox is that Moscow feeds on crises whose persistence limits the benefits, including economic benefits, that Russia could eventually derive from established partnerships. On the other hand, Russia has comparatively little to offer countries in the Middle East, whether in economic or security terms. Crisis management—and, by definition, crisis extension—is one of the few cards Moscow has to play in the region. The Russian reassertion in Syria and Libya feeds on a well-established geopolitical tradition of seeking access to the Mediterranean. But for several years this quest has been pursued by Russia with the new tools of "hybrid" warfare: a combination of conventional means (military cooperation with Damascus to close the airspace of western Syria, extension of the Tartus naval base, use of military police to freeze the fronts of the Syrian civil war, recourse to special forces) and nonconventional means (deniable operations from Russia-backed Wagner Group mercenaries in Libya as well as Syria; disinformation; cyberattacks).

In that respect, Moscow is a central actor but does not offer a real alternative beyond security cooperation. Russia's pragmatism also fits the new regional competition, characterized by more opportunistic and militarized behaviors. Moscow is not in a position to really compete structurally with Washington but can still make significant political and commercial gains when it provides strategic military equipment or places itself as a mediator. However, beyond the optical effect linked to the memory of the Cold War when Moscow was the equal competitor of Washington, what Russia might offer today is meaningful only if Washington is absent. The United States has 128 operational military bases in the Middle East, compared to Russia's two naval facilities in Syria. Russian trade with the Middle East is fifteen times less than American trade with Middle East countries.

Russia's objectives, however, go well beyond the area: Moscow uses its positions in the region to strengthen its *global* standing. The various Russian actions—whether in Syria, Libya, or Egypt—entail calculated risks designed to allow Vladimir Putin to influence the international agenda without getting bogged down. Russian military interventions, whether they be ground operations in Syria from September 2015 to February 2016 or airstrikes launched from Iran into Syria in summer 2016, are maneuvers limited in time and scope, each aimed at resetting a balance of power that was becoming unfavorable to Bashar al-Assad, and therefore to Russia.

In this context, Moscow has an interest in cultivating relations with all the countries of the region, especially in the Gulf. Russian authorities have deepened leadership relationships and contacts with security services so as to reap the benefits of their enhanced credibility achieved by standing with their Syrian ally. Russia's position in the region, however, depends fundamentally on its Iranian ally. Even if it talks to everyone, Russia does not have the means to build far-reaching partnerships if several important relations between Iran and Arab countries remain so hostile.

The Turkish Conundrum

Though it is doubtful that Europeans can play a role in bilateral relations between the United States and Gulf countries or the United States and Israel, each of the recent episodes of tension in the region (Syria, Libya, eastern Mediterranean) made clear that relations with Turkey are a challenge both for the EU and for NATO. Turkey's adventurism has surpassed its incursion into northeast Syria and now includes its presence in Libya, its Blue Homeland strategy for maritime control in its neighborhood, and its violations of Iraqi sovereignty.

Since 2016 and the failed coup against Erdogan, Turkey has transformed its foreign policy. Ankara's support of the Arab Spring uprisings had already gradually evolved into support for Islamist revolutionary forces as vehicles of Turkish soft and hard power. After 2016, Ankara amplified this dynamic and combined it with another dimension, namely partnering with Russia to push a revisionist agenda aiming at renegotiating sovereignty and territorial borders in the Caucasus and the Mediterranean. The Turkish president also turned away from Turkey's European perspective and, by forming a parliamentary alliance with ultranationalists, put an end to the policy of openness toward Turkish Kurds, as well as to the peace process of engagement with the Kurdistan Workers Party (PKK). And though Turkey had been one of the main supporters of the Syrian opposition after 2011, Ankara has gradually recalibrated its support, backing certain Syrian groups and using them as proxies for Turkish foreign policy; this is notably the case with respect to the establishment of a buffer zone in northern Syria. Turkey also capitalized on sending Islamist militias to Libya in

2020, in order to sign an agreement with the Libyan government on maritime delimitations in the Mediterranean.

The partnership with Moscow was motivated by the singular role played by Russia among the regional actors in the Middle East since the beginning of the Syrian conflict. The Russia-Turkey partnership was formed after Russia used heavy sanctions against Turkey in the aftermath of the downing of a Russian jet by the Turkish military in 2015. This show of force from Moscow opened a new phase in bilateral relations, especially given Western hesitation in supporting Ankara in northwest Syria and the Western decision to work with the Democratic Union Party (PYD) in northeast Syria. The two countries have, since 2016, developed an efficient dynamic of "brutal entente,"[35] consisting of using proxies on the ground to raise tensions, so as then to be able to pose as guarantors of various truces. In Syria as in Libya, but also in the Nagorno-Karabakh area, the combination of a strong military presence on the ground and blocking maneuvers or duopoly management of diplomatic negotiations has strengthened both Vladimir Putin and Recep Tayyip Erdogan, despite the episodes of tension between the two countries. For Moscow as for Ankara, the levers obtained in these North African or Middle East crises can be directly exploited in negotiations with European countries—on the migration issue, for example, or on maritime delimitations in the eastern Mediterranean.

Even if Erdogan has softened his tone and sought more diplomatic engagement since Joe Biden's election as U.S. president, Turkey will likely pose one of the most pressing Middle East policy issues for both the United States and Europe. Turkey's new policies have put it at odds with Europe—particularly with France, Cyprus, and Greece—creating a new transatlantic dynamic and shaking the security architecture of many European countries that are traditionally more concerned about Russia than the Middle East. At the same time, Turkey's anchoring in NATO is extremely important to the United States so as to prevent Turkey's weaponization by Russia, and for other reasons.

Perceptions and Expectations
of the United States and Europe

The local, regional, and international changes that have transformed the Middle East in the last decade have predictably had a profound impact on the region's perception of the United States, perceived as weakened, and of the EU, perceived as weak.

In an informal survey conducted in 2020 by the *Fikra Forum* of The Washington Institute of ten writers of Sudanese, Iraqi, Tunisian, Syrian, Jordanian, and Egyptian nationality, respondents were split as to whether or not the United States had lost influence in the Middle East since 2011. Those who thought the United States had lost influence cited the rise of Russia and China as alternative sources of foreign support, the lack of a clear U.S. position on Middle East issues, and the U.S. failure to respond to changes in the region, such as the Arab Spring.

Respondents were also split as to whether *Europe* had lost influence in the Middle East since 2011. Those who believed that Europe *had* lost influence responded that whether or not the loss was a good or bad thing for the Middle East depended on which country one was speaking of. Those who believed Europe as a whole had lost influence pointed to Europe's reluctance to intervene militarily or take a strong stance in many Middle East conflicts. Some also cited Europe's prioritization of its own interests over building relationships in the Middle East.

The vast majority of respondents considered the United States to still be the most influential country in the Middle East and North Africa today. Most believed that U.S.-Europe cooperation in the region could be beneficial to their countries in sectors such as education, technical assistance, the economy, trade, democracy strengthening, and the military. Several respondents commented that such cooperation would be important in containing the influence of Iran, Russia, Turkey, and China. One wrote that U.S.-Europe cooperation benefits the region by preventing a single power from monopolizing influence, thereby creating "an atmosphere of moderation, international understanding and credibility." Another pointed out that transatlantic cooperation could combat Iranian-backed terrorism, but might be hampered by differing U.S. and European viewpoints on Iran. Still another recommended that both the United States and Europe need to incorporate the concerns of Middle East residents within their definition of their own self-interest.

For many in the region, European influence also depends on Europe's ability to demonstrate independence from the United States. This would, in theory, imply that transatlantic coordination is in itself damaging to European influence. A closer look suggests, however, that it is Europe's lack of tactical autonomy rather than its shared strategic goals with the United States that is creating frustration. It is Europe's difficulty in reacting independently that is perceived as a sign of weakness, rather than U.S.-EU cooperation as such. On the other hand, Europe's perceived weakness opens avenues for mediation from which both Europe and the United States could benefit: in Yemen and Iraq, for example, where European ambassadors have been the only ones able to meet with Muqtada al-Sadr.[36] Europe can exploit its own strengths vis-à-vis the region: thus, the EU's economic and cultural power as well as its financial support to Egypt afford Europe some leverage in Cairo, even if countries like Saudi Arabia and the UAE have greater influence.[37]

The analysts from the region that the *Fikra Forum* surveyed did not seem to rule out Western action in the Middle East, but rather questioned its coherence vis-à-vis actors who have been more consistent in pursuing their agenda in the region. They would welcome a constructive role for the United States and Europe, and do not see "withdrawing" as a solution, given the vacuum it creates for other actors.

***

Ultimately, the changes that have occurred in the region have had practical consequences for both the United States and Europe. State collapse and political fragmentation have made it more difficult for Western countries to build relationships of solid cooperation with local actors; and the more assertive foreign policy of regional powers has made it harder to channel Western priorities through traditional Western allies. The perception of a less involved United States undermines the West's negotiation positions in the region and amplifies the tendency of regional actors to hedge their bets between the United States, Europe, Russia, and China. And there is the related observation that actors like Russia or Turkey seize strategic opportunities, while the United States and Europe often hesitate and are slow to react. The perception of weakness by the West is not about absolute power, therefore, but about the willingness to act.

One paradox is that the notion of Great Power competition would require the United States to refill the vacuum it left in the Middle East in the first place. To date, Russia, Iran, and to some extent Turkey have benefited the most from U.S. fatigue in the region. The Middle East is supposed to be one of the many areas of competition between China and the United States, but there is more confusion than clarity as to how the region fits into this framework. Many of the world's most immediate foreign policy crises take place there, which often leads to a gap between daily policymaking and the larger geopolitical framework. The American foreign policy community will have to grapple with whether the Middle East is a distraction from Great Power competition or an arena where that competition is playing out.

"Great Power competition" might just be a fancy name, in fact, to describe a new and more open phase of globalized competition. In the Middle East, as elsewhere, the recipe for power might not be so new: a combination of long-term relationships, diplomacy, economic leverage, and hard power. The real question is whether global powers will have the attention span, patience, and resources to commit to this hard work in an era of lingering pandemic, sharply escalating climate worries, and fractious domestic politics. For the United States, this may present an unwelcome change of paradigm. As an Emirati expert put it, "The U.S. used to be the only shareholder in Gulf security; now it is an important shareholder but not the only one anymore."[38] And for Europe, the question is whether it wants to be a shareholder at all.

Notes

1   Global prices for grain staples rose significantly from mid-2005 to 2008, triggering a food crisis that affected developing nations in particular. See "Causes of the 2007–2008 Global Food Crisis Identified," *Science for Environmental Policy* (European Commission), January 20, 2011, https://ec.europa.eu/environment/integration/research/newsalert/pdf/225na1_en.pdf.

2   Constantinos Filis, *Troubled Waters in the Eastern Mediterranean? A Greek Perspective on Security Policy in the Southern Neighbourhood* (Berlin: Friedrich Ebert Stiftung, 2020), 4, available at http://library.fes.de/pdf-files/id/ipa/16306.pdf.

3   H. Bozarslan, "The Arab World Between 2011 and 2014: From Revolutionary Configurations to the State of Violence," in *Authoritarianism in the Middle East*, ed. J. Karakoc (London: Palgrave Macmillan, 2015).

4   "Clubhouse Gives Arabs a Space to Speak Freely," *Economist*, April 3, 2021, https://www.economist.com/middle-east-and-africa/2021/04/03/clubhouse-gives-arabs-a-space-to-speak-freely.

5   See Charles Thépaut, "The Lessons of the Arab Springs," *Orient XXI*, May 25, 2020, https://orientxxi.info/magazine/The-Lessons-of-the-Arab-Springs.

6   International Monetary Fund, *Regional Economic Outlook: Middle East and Central Asia* (Washington DC: October 2020), mreo1020-full-report.pdf.

7   UNICEF, "Middle East & North Africa Region: COVID-19 Situation Report No. 13," February 28, 2021, https://bit.ly/3xvB6wt.

8   World Bank, "Middle East and North Africa Human Capital Plan," n.d., http://pubdocs.worldbank.org/en/907071571420642349/HCP-MiddleEast-Plan-Oct19.pdf.

9   "Middle East's Demographic Earthquake: The Generation Fuelling Protests," *Financial Times*, February 10, 2020, https://www.ft.com/content/03274532-21ce-11ea-b8a1-584213ee7b2b.

10 World Bank, "Population Ages 65 and Above, Total—Middle East & North Africa," n.d., https://data.worldbank.org/indicator/SP.POP.65UP.TO?locations=ZQ.

11 UNICEF, "MENA Generation 2030," April 2019, https://data.unicef.org/resources/middle-east-north-africa-generation-2030/.

12 See Charles Thépaut and Calvin Wilder, "Expanding Humanitarian Assistance to Syrians: Two Deadlines Approaching," PolicyWatch 3456, Washington Institute for Near East Policy, March 23, 2021, https://www.washingtoninstitute.org/policy-analysis/expanding-humanitarian-assistance-syrians-two-deadlines-approaching, and Financial Tracking Service, "Yemen 2019," UN Office for the Coordination of Humanitarian Affairs, https://fts.unocha.org/appeals/675/summary.

13 *Beyond Scarcity: Water Security in the Middle East and North Africa* (Washington DC: World Bank, 2018), https://www.worldbank.org/en/topic/water/publication/beyond-scarcity-water-security-in-the-middle-east-and-north-africa.

14 World Bank, "Middle East & North Africa," https://data.worldbank.org/region/middle-east-and-north-africa.

15 International Monetary Fund, "Joint Ministerial Committee of the Boards of Governors of the Bank and the Fund on the Transfer of Real Resources to Developing Countries," April 17, 2020, https://bit.ly/3gEP8VK.

16 UN Development Program, "Arab States Step Up Response to Coronavirus," March 30, 2020, https://www.undp.org/content/undp/en/home/stories/arab-states-step-up-response-to-coronavirus.html.

17 Guido Steinberg, "Kein Frühling Am Golf: Bpb," Bundeszentrale für Politische Bildung, October 24, 2011, https://www.bpb.de/internationales/afrika/arabischer-fruehling/52401/saudi-arabien-und-seine-nachbarn.

18 Yousef Saba and Davide Barbuscia, "Franklin Templeton Grabs More Gulf Government Debt amid Oil Crash," Reuters, April 15, 2020, https://www.reuters.com/article/us-franklin-templeton-bonds-gulf/franklin-templeton-grabs-more-gulf-government-debt-amid-oil-crash-idUSKCN21X278.

19 Rayhan Uddin, "Coronavirus: Kindness Spreads as Middle East Scrambles to Contain Deadly Virus," Middle East Eye, March 22, 2020, https://www.middleeasteye.net/news/coronavirus-kindness-spreads-middle-east-iran-iraq-lebanon.

20   Scott Peterson and Taylor Luck, "Why Coronavirus Clampdown Is Proving Risky for Arab Regimes," *Christian Science Monitor*, April 9, 2020, https://www-csmonitor-com.cdn.ampproject.org/c/s/www.csmonitor.com/layout/set/amphtml/World/Middle-East/2020/0409/Why-coronavirus-clampdown-is-proving-risky-for-Arab-regimes.

21   Facundo Alvaredo, Lydia Assouad, and Thomas Piketty, "Measuring Inequality in the Middle East, 1990–2016: The World's Most Unequal Region?" *Review of Income and Wealth* (2018), available at http://piketty.pse.ens.fr/files/AAP2019RIW.pdf.

22   "Coronavirus Pandemic Threatens to Plunge Millions in Arab Region into Poverty and Food Insecurity," *UN News*, April 1, 2020, https://news.un.org/en/story/2020/04/1060822.

23   Michel Duclos, interview by author, August 2020.

24   U.S. Energy Information Administration, "Country Analysis Executive Summary: China," September 30, 2020, https://www.eia.gov/international/content/analysis/countries_long/China/china.pdf.

25   Jonathan Fulton, "After Aramco Attacks, China's Middle East Interests Are at Stake," Atlantic Council, September 20, 2019, https://www.atlanticcouncil.org/blogs/iransource/after-aramco-attacks-chinas-middle-east-interests-are-at-stake/.

26   U.S. Energy Information Administration, "China's Crude Oil Imports Surpassed 10 Million Barrels per Day in 2019," March 23, 2020, https://www.eia.gov/todayinenergy/detail.php?id=43216.

27   "Strengthening European Autonomy Across MENA," in *Mapping European Leverage in the MENA Region*, European Council on Foreign Relations, November 2019, https://www.ecfr.eu/special/mapping_eu_leverage_mena/.

28   Adel Abdel Ghafar, "Egypt," in *Mapping European Leverage in the MENA Region* European Council on Foreign Relations, December 2019, https://ecfr.eu/special/mapping_eu_leverage_mena/egypt.

29   Michael Singh, "U.S. Policy in the Middle East amid Great Power Competition," Reagan Institute Strategy Group, March 30, 2020, available at https://www.washingtoninstitute.org/policy-analysis/us-policy-middle-east-amid-great-power-competition.

30   Ibid.

31 Daniel R. Russel and Blake H. Berger, "Weaponizing the Belt and Road Initiative," Asia Society Policy Institute, September 2020, https://bit.ly/3gs0VYE.

32 Karen Young, "The False Logic of a China-U.S. Choice in the Middle East," Al-Monitor, June 29, 2020, https://www.al-monitor.com/pulse/originals/2020/06/false-logic-china-us-choice-mideast-economic-political-power.html.

33 Michael Singh, "China in the Middle East: Following in American Footsteps?" London Middle East Institute, June 1, 2018, available at https://www.washingtoninstitute.org/policy-analysis/view/china-in-the-middle-east-following-in-american-footsteps.

34 Ali Wyne and Colin P. Clarke, "Assessing China and Russia's Moves in the Middle East," *Lawfare Blog*, September 17, 2020, https://www.lawfareblog.com/assessing-china-and-russias-moves-middle-east.

35 Marie Jégo and Benoît Vitkine, "Entre Vladimir Poutine et Recep Tayyip Erdogan, l'Entente Brutale," *Le Monde*, May 21, 2021, https://www.lemonde.fr/international/article/2021/05/21/entre-poutine-et-erdogan-l-entente-brutale_6081047_3210.html.

36 Renad Mansour, "Iraq," in *Mapping European Leverage in the MENA Region*, European Council on Foreign Relations, December 2019, https://ecfr.eu/special/mapping_eu_leverage_mena/iraq.

37 Adel Abdel Ghafar, "Egypt," in *Mapping European Leverage in MENA*, European Council on Foreign Relations, December 2019, https://ecfr.eu/special/mapping_eu_leverage_mena/egypt.

38 Emirati expert, interview by author, November 2019.

4

Heading in Opposite Directions

Based on the preceding assessment of local and regional dynamics, the discussion now turns to the current debate in the United States and Europe about the Middle East, its significance regarding the interests of both parties, and their leverage in the region.

Strategic Soul-Searching, Beginning in Southern Europe?

The evolution of European foreign policy in the Middle East, highlighted in the three case studies in chapter 2 (Arab Spring, anti-IS campaign, and JCPOA), must also be put into a larger strategic context. The debate over the EU role in the world evolved significantly during the Trump administration, and Trump's policy toward the Middle East and toward Europe played an important role in this. According to Michel Duclos, "American policy has greatly weakened Europe in the Middle East: Obama, because his Iran, Syria, and Libya policies have more or less marginalized Europeans, while Trump has continued this process by undermining them on the JCPOA."[1]

As the European Council on Foreign Relations points out, the result in 2019 was that "turmoil in the Middle East and north Africa directly affects Europeans. Yet their influence in the region has never been weaker."[2] As the three case studies highlighted, divisions and transatlantic dysfunction significantly limited Europe's ability to shape political outcomes, even on priority issues such as fighting terrorism. Based on a large number of interviews inside and outside Europe, the council identifies three principal European weaknesses: the ability of external actors to play on European disunity; Europe's dependence on U.S. foreign policy; and Europe's inability to exploit all its leverage.

The growing number of issues related to the Middle East inspired soul-searching on various levels among analysts and decisionmakers in Europe, along with a quest for solutions. Different political dynamics framed this discussion. The most visible and clearly articulated has been the sustained advocacy of French president Macron on behalf of concepts like "European strategic autonomy." This advocacy was based on a larger rationale that the EU had to prove to its citizens that it could protect them and protect the continent—thereby pushing back against populist claims that the EU was merely a big free market. Between 2017 and 2020, Macron made numerous speeches in which he set forth what he wished to be a new strategy for Europe: strengthening a European pillar within NATO as an answer to U.S. demands for burden sharing, an approach that could equally be used by Europe to protect its borders from threats Washington might not be willing to address as it had before.

> Only Europe can…guarantee genuine sovereignty or our ability to exist in today's world to defend our values and interests. European sovereignty requires constructing, and we must do it. Why? Because what constructs and forges our profound identity, this balance of values, this relation with freedom, human rights and justice cannot be found anywhere on the planet. This attachment to a market economy, but also social justice. We cannot blindly entrust what Europe represents, on the other side of the Atlantic or on the edges of Asia. It is our responsibility to defend it and build it within the context of globalization.[3]

Applied to the Middle East, this rationale was intended to afford Europe more leverage on issues like the fight against terrorism and its root causes, many of them related to instability in Syria, Iraq, and

Libya. In a way, the French perspective has been to look at these crises as confirming the lack of European foreign policy strength. To address these challenges, the French logic advocated using these crises as test cases for a more assertive Europe, the underlying fear being that if Europe failed to act quickly, it might not resist the shocks caused by international crises. This rationale explains a number of French foreign policy moves—in Libya, for example, or in northeast Syria and the eastern Mediterranean.

Germany gradually developed a similar trend of reasoning, though it has not always been so clearly articulated. The 2015 refugee crisis transformed the German perspective on the southern flank of Europe: the need for Germany to take more responsibility in addressing some of the root causes of these migrations gained traction despite a strong noninterventionist tradition. Germany had been a major contributor to humanitarian and development assistance for years, but was still very cautious when it came to diplomatic or military initiatives. The 2015 shock associated with receiving a sudden influx of migrants served those within the German government who favored being more assertive outside Europe, especially in the southern neighborhood of the EU, even as a preference for a transatlantic approach within EU procedures was maintained. The trauma of the Trump administration's policy toward Germany, and toward Europe in general, imparted an additional impetus to Germany, as illustrated by Angela Merkel's words in 2018:

> Let's be honest—Europe is still at the very start when it comes to a common foreign policy. However, this is what we will need for our own survival because the nature of conflicts has changed completely since the end of the Cold War. A great many global conflicts are taking place on Europe's doorstep. And it is not the case that the United States of America will simply protect us. Instead, Europe must take its destiny in its own hands. That is our job for the future.[4]

The trajectory proposed by Germany has been more of an incremental process than a clearly conceptualized one. The trend is clear, however, and German authorities have been steadily more and more vocal about it. In June 2020, the German foreign minister Heiko Maas had already gone further:

> What we are proposing is to keep Europe functioning in a world in which the global balance is shifting rapidly—away from Europe... This brings me to the term "European sovereignty"...I understand the worries expressed by the critics, their concerns about losing sovereignty or even about isolating European from American security. But that is not what's meant. European sovereignty, as I understand it, means that Europe can act independently and decide to pool its resources in areas where the individual states have long since lost their ability to shape globalisation to the major powers."[5]

This did not lead to a dramatic shift from Germany's positions, but rather, to a more visible approach, whereby Berlin became more active and flexible. While Germany tended to favor inclusive processes and consensual formats, its diplomacy impelled it to join the "small group" on Syria, and Germany presented its own mediation process on Libya, to include only a limited number of European member states and North African countries. This process has sometimes been messy—with public disagreements, for example, between the foreign minister, Heiko Maas, and the defense minister, Annegret Kramp-Karrenbauer, on the idea of a safe zone in northern Syria.[6] At the heart of these problems, of course, lies Germany's historical reluctance to resort to military power—but also a political system that is based on collective deliberations within each party and within the governing coalition, making it difficult to agree on quick and strong positions.

Another contribution to this debate came from European institutions themselves. The new European Commission appointed in 2019, led by President Ursula von der Leyen, defined as one of its key priorities creating a stronger Europe in the world. Though in 2014 her predecessor Jean-Claude Juncker had announced a "political commission," von der Leyen has promised that hers would be a "*geo*political commission." The newly appointed high representative Josep Borrell emphasized that Europe had to "relearn the language of power."[7] He stressed that the EU had "the instruments to play power politics. Our challenge is to put them together [in] the service of one strategy."[8] Borrell also stressed the importance for the EU of investing in its southern neighborhood.[9] This push was seen positively by member states like Spain, which insists that the EU needs stronger instruments and has advocated for a more ambitious EU Multiannual Financial Framework.[10]

Silences are often more important than statements, however, in European politics; actors who remain silent can be more decisive than those who speak up. A number of European member states have, for their part, remained silent or skeptical about the consensus that has slowly appeared among France, Germany, and EU institutions about the need to build a more geopolitical Europe, starting in the Middle East. Some states, mostly Eastern European, are hesitant because they fear European autonomy will be perceived as antagonistic toward the United States; similarly, states like Spain, pragmatic and Atlanticist, are cautious about expressing support for any initiatives perceived as hostile to the U.S. presence in Europe.[11] Historically neutral states, such as Austria, Ireland, and Cyprus, are skeptical on the grounds that a more geopolitical Europe would lead to a more assertive defense posture. And other states, like Italy and Portugal, are resistant for economic reasons.[12]

These different developments in the European discourse regarding foreign policy, and the pushback against them, confirm a key connection between two issues. First, although security concerns regarding Russia have been evident since the Cold War, security concerns originating in Europe's southern neighborhood are more broadly acknowledged than they used to be: because of migration and terrorism, Middle East politics is no longer just an issue for Mediterranean members of the EU. Second, discussions about strengthening EU foreign policy in the region are shaped by the evolution of transatlantic relations, and by the way in which Europeans relate their NATO commitment to the ability to react to security challenges in the Middle East.

The issue of European unity on foreign policy, therefore, comes down to two questions. Are European countries more satisfied with a lowest-common-denominator foreign policy, through which Europeans migrate freely between smaller coalitions, or do they wish to act as a bloc and give priority to solidarity, even in the absence of consensus? And how do they articulate the political and military role of NATO in this context?

In many cases, the default option for most member states remains pursuing foreign policy mostly through their bilateral relations with Washington, rather than focusing on European strategic interests in the Middle East. Long-term efforts toward a more powerful Europe remain slow because of national policies in the short term. Divisions between France, Italy, Britain, and Germany on Libya and the organization in 2019 by Poland of a summit on Iran contrary to some EU-3 positions[13] are just some examples. The vision of an end state for EU foreign policy will probably always vary among European actors. There is a growing consensus, however, that the status quo is not viable. Europe's lack of influence on issues like the Syrian conflict "should trigger a wake-up call," according to one senior diplomat. "Something needs to be done."[14]

Developments over the last few years did not produce immediate tangible progress, therefore, but did induce a change of mindset, along with real developments at the strategic level. Beyond the EU-3's unwavering position on the JCPOA, which was not a given, France and Germany launched two major industrial projects, for a joint fighter jet and tank. And many European leaders began to acknowledge that the policies of the Trump administration had real consequences for European security.

It is worth remembering that France and Germany had proposed a permanent, structured cooperation on defense issues in 2015 but faced a strong pushback from other member states. After the early signals from the Obama administration, however, along with the repeated warnings of the Trump administration about withdrawing from the Middle East and Africa and, especially, the lack of a coordinated response from Europeans, several EU member states began engaging with other European countries on defense while preserving the potential of a reset with the United States in case of a change of administration. This allowed some limited progress. For instance, Italy started investing more in European projects that could theoretically allow stronger actions in the southern neighborhood of Europe, like Permanent Structured Cooperation,[15] the European Defence Fund,[16] and the French-led European Intervention Initiative,[17] which has an explicit focus on Mediterranean security.[18]

The biggest obstacle to a more geopolitical Europe, however, might not always be divergent interests. The fact that European debates are often public, or at least not kept secret, gives disproportionate visibility to disagreements when they arise. In the case of Libya, Rome, Berlin, and Paris largely addressed their differences before the Berlin conference, but European media coverage kept focusing on those differences, which were probably less decisive on the ground than was Russian intervention, or the U.S. reluctance to define a clear policy. In those cases, the emphasis on the need to address European discord can be a mere excuse not to deal with the real issue: the collective European reluctance to be more forceful in hard security situations. "Often the political will to go one or two steps further is simply not there."[19]

The real issue Europeans have to deal with, therefore, is maybe not disunity as such, but risk aversion. Though Europe was never the actor that would do "the heavy lifting," some experts believe Europe was somewhat more willing to act in the late 1990s and early 2000s than it is today.[20] They note that there is currently an unwillingness to incur the costs—and they call on Europe to show that "we're willing to not only put our money, but our boots, where our mouth is."[21] While all European states are afraid of a new migration wave that could be produced by further destabilization in the Middle East or North Africa, very few seem willing to invest in policies that could be risky in such a complex environment. In Syria and Libya, it was collective weakness, lack of military capabilities, and fear of escalation that determined European inaction more than conflicting goals or analysis relative to the situation in Syria or the understanding of Russian and Turkish policies.

The EU position has actually been stable and consistent, but was short of hard security tools. In a conflict zone with failed or nonexistent state structures, finding local partners is always risky, and few Europeans are willing to make risky bets. Risk aversion is difficult to overcome, and can be cured only after violent crises, or through a gradual process of reassurance. The JCPOA gave much hope to European diplomats about what could be collectively achieved, but other success stories are necessary, also in the field of hard security. "We need the political will to get our hands dirty, [while] always keeping in mind that many tools and options are available before the military option or putting boots on the ground."[22] This is how the French moves in the Mediterranean to show solidarity with Greece and Cyprus can be understood. By sending Rafale fighter jets to the area in August 2020, Paris answered the call of Athens, after a number of Turkish maneuvers in the disputed maritime areas, as a way of showing concrete European solidarity and sovereignty.[23] Other member states, like Germany, felt uncomfortable with the move, while Spain opted for a mediation initiative—all reflections of a larger disagreement about the method, speed, and scope of European geopolitical assertiveness.

Ultimately, these disagreements and differences should not always be a problem for the EU as long as they can be well articulated. President Macron and Chancellor Merkel explained their approach in the eastern Mediterranean during a joint press conference in August 2020:

My wish is that Europe's action (on Turkey) is efficient as a whole...
This requires a coordination with Germany that leverages our
respective strengths," Macron said. Merkel added, "There are different possibilities of action. You can help our European partners,
as France did, by sending a ship and promising support. On the
other side we have tried to get the dialogue between Turkey and
Greece going again...Out of these different parts there should result
a common larger project, and thus I believe, you can't weigh these
different (France's and Germany's) actions against each other."
Macron went on: "This is complementary. Facing disinhibited
regional powers, diplomacy without red lines and a military presence doesn't work, at least not very long. But a military presence
without a diplomatic solution is counterproductive, as it just leads
to escalation. You have to do both things, and that's what we do."
Merkel replied to this with "Exactly!"[24]

These kinds of good cop/bad cop strategies have rarely been designed
in the open, and it remains to be seen how systematic they can be,
especially outside the context of a direct threat to the EU border, like
in the eastern Mediterranean. There is nevertheless a need for a smarter
division of labor exploiting the assets of each member state in the
context of a broader European strategy.

The Missing Element in European Foreign Policy Making

When it comes to the EU, the process is often as important as the
substance. The idea of a division of labor is therefore largely dependent on a broader debate about the formation of EU foreign policy. A
number of European policy discussions related to the Middle East
have been highly dependent on institutional settings and formats. The
current European system rewards obstruction more than action: some
issues have, for example, been determined by the rule of unanimity

at the European Council regarding matters of foreign policy. In some cases, countries can gain international leverage via their ability to be an intermediary enabling access to the EU, or can even block European decisions. Thus, the development of the Greek-Egyptian relationship after 2013 and the coup against Mohamed Morsi pushed Athens to facilitate EU-Egypt relations.[25] Hungary's relationship with Israel has benefited from its blocking role in Brussels, even as Budapest has no vital interest at stake. The opposition of Hungary to any kind of sanction against Israel has pushed other member states to explore options outside the format of the EU27, as the twenty-seven member states of the European Union are known. Another example is the JCPOA, with respect to which the central role of the EU-3 has helped maintain a stable and cohesive position despite the U.S. administration's attempt to change the European position by pressuring other European countries.

These examples show that even if, in theory, EU foreign policy is still discussed on a consensual basis, in practice there is already a multiple-track European foreign policy. A number of member states are deeply opposed to the notion of a two-track Europe, but European foreign policy cannot be strengthened if it is limited to the results of discussions among twenty-seven countries; there has to be a discussion about other means of action.

A key issue for EU foreign policy is to depart from the notion that decisionmaking processes for European domestic decisions are relevant when it comes to foreign policy. A process whereby twenty-seven member states all decide on everything is simply not effective in foreign policy and, most importantly, limits the ability of Europe to act quickly and decisively. "The 27 group is workable to work on large conclusions or frameworks. Anything more specific or more tactical is not feasible in such a large framework."[26] In addition, a blunt reality has to be acknowledged: not all member states are willing and able to act on all foreign policy issues. Certain relationships, like those with the United States, China, or Russia, are obviously essential to all member states and can only be dealt with unanimously, but a key gap in the European foreign policy toolbox relates to international crisis management.

There are mechanisms to pool resources quickly once a European political position exists, but there is no mechanism to arrive at such a position quickly, especially during a foreign policy crisis with a hard security component. Any natural division of labor that might take account of member states' history, geography, and capabilities to respond to a foreign policy crisis is never really discussed or acknowledged at the EU level. In the end, the debate about EU foreign policy is paralyzed by those arguing that countries acting on their own in this vacuum are harming European unity versus those who believe there is currently no alternative to reacting quickly to a crisis. A growing number of experts therefore make the case that "smaller, more flexible, coalitions should now become prominent vehicles for policy."[27]

The paradox is that, in reality, many small frameworks, like the P3 (the United States, France, and Britain), the Quint (France, Germany, Italy, Britain, and the United States), the Quad (France, Germany, Britain, and the United States), the EU-3, the Nordic countries, the Visegrad Group (Czech Republic, Hungary, Poland, and Slovakia), and others are already in place for dialogue and consultation. Yet with the exception of the EU-3 in the JCPOA context, it is almost a taboo in Brussels to talk about using them, or argue for their operationalization as a vanguard of EU foreign policy. Successful examples of such collective action exist—for example, when permanent and nonpermanent European members of the UN Security Council make joint statements related to the agenda of the Council. The challenge is, therefore, not only to mainstream the use of smaller frameworks but also to make such frameworks capable of joint action, rather than serving only as forums for discussion.

The logic of certain tools like European Permanent Structured Cooperation, created in the area of defense to allow a group of EU member states "willing and capable" to work on joint projects, could be replicated in the area of diplomacy. "European contact groups," which would, under the coordination of the European External Action Service (EEAS), play a leading role in the political management of geopolitical crises, could be developed as vanguards to which other EU member states would give mandates in order to generate quick European geopolitical reactions before having larger consultations with all member states. A key element for the success and relevance of such flexible formats is their ability, under EEAS control, to combine instruments of soft and hard power. While the EU Civil Protection Mechanism[28] allowed for a quick European civilian response to the August 2020 Beirut port explosion, other tools, like EU Battlegroups (forces intended to be quickly deployable abroad) or the European Intervention Initiative (designed to improve military planning among thirteen EU countries), could be activated through the European contact groups.

These contact groups could be formed on an ad hoc basis with the coordination of the EEAS, but they could also be complemented by other ideas that have been mentioned in recent years, like that of a European security council, mentioned in different versions by both Chancellor Merkel and President Macron. While questions remain unanswered about what the relationship of this council would be to the EU's existing Political and Security Committee, one possibility would be to make this security council a smaller version of the Political and Security Committee (a dedicated format of the executive branch of the EU), to convene on very short notice so that "willing and capable" member states who wish to respond beyond issuing statements could react to international crises. The EEAS, which also chairs the Political and Security Committee, could decide when to convene the security council and at which level (senior officials or foreign ministers).

From the EU-3 Model to European Contact Groups

The best illustration of the rationale under which these contact groups could function has been the EU-3—so the evolution of the EU-3 format will have important implications for the future of EU foreign policy. The EU-3 became even more relevant in the context of Brexit, as it enabled effective coordination with Britain despite its withdrawal from the EU. Between July 2016 and June 2020, the EU-3, sometimes with additional partners, issued twenty-six statements on various foreign policy issues, most of them concerning Middle East–related issues.[29]

Paris and Berlin are committed to the EU-3 format and to cooperation with London in the Middle East, but for different reasons. While Paris sees it as a quicker and more effective way to drive European foreign policy, Berlin sees it as a way to balance French initiatives with a British counterweight, while giving more weight to Germany in foreign policy and without changing the unanimity rules governing the common foreign and security policy of the EU.

At the same time, according to one analysis, "Brexit has altered the balance of power within the EU, giving Spain and Italy a more prominent position, provided that Madrid and Rome manage to preserve a minimum level of internal political stability."[30] While the EU-3 as a format has been controversial for other member states worried by the prospect of the EU-3's simply taking over Europe's foreign policy, many member states acknowledge the leading role that Paris, London, and Berlin need to play in pushing for European action.[31] The EU-3 role, therefore, remains key, and building a larger coalition requires subtle intra-European diplomacy.

A key issue will be, on the one hand, how Paris, Berlin, Rome, and Madrid, as well as Warsaw and other capitals, build small coalitions and contact groups; on the other hand will be how London balances its coordination with Paris and Berlin with a more independent policy—especially toward the United States, but also toward actors like Turkey.

The temptation to salvage what remains of the "special relationship" with Washington has already resulted in conflicts with the EU-3, for instance about what Donald Trump called the "deal of the century" in the Middle East,[32] or when London joined the U.S. maritime mission in the Strait of Hormuz while the Europeans launched their own operation. Other member states are also likely to build renewed bilateral channels with London with regard to foreign policy, and Britain might struggle to stay active on all fronts at the same time. Joint visits and maneuvers by Italy, France, and Germany in the context of the Berlin process on Libya served as an example of an alternative "EU-3" relevant in the Libyan context.

Ultimately, a decisive factor will be how EU institutions manage the variable geometry of European foreign policy. The "geopolitical" commission has yet to find operational solutions to coordinate processes that will remain messy and complicated depending on the issue at stake. While building consensus will remain the natural goal of EU institutions, their ability to seize opportunities presented by Middle East crises to demonstrate assertiveness and efficiency will be key to establishing the relevance of a more collective approach in foreign policy that is based not just on statements and middle-term financial assistance, but also on relevant quick reactions.

The American Consensus on Middle East Minimalism

Dynamics in the Middle East, along with the related European dilemmas, are all the more significant given the changing nature of U.S. foreign policy. As the above case studies showed, the reluctance to intervene militarily observed under President Obama was confirmed under President Trump, even if the style and method differed, often dramatically. Obama sought to limit conventional operations, following the costly Iraq war, and he therefore invested in a combination of diplomatic engagement and more remote military tools, such as drone strikes and the "by, with, and through" approach to working with local partners. Trump, meanwhile, could be characterized as a neo-isolationist concerned about ending "by, with, and through" operations and focused on investing mostly in transactional diplomacy.

The key question for 2021 and beyond is what the Biden administration's approach to the region will be. A close look at the Democratic campaign in 2020, as well as at the intellectual discussions within the foreign policy community—along with an analysis of the administration's early steps—confirms that the United States is unlikely to reengage in the Middle East as it has over the past thirty years.

The 2020 Campaign and the Democratic Primaries

Foreign policy is usually not a central topic in U.S. presidential campaigns. Yet a number of issues related to the Middle East appeared in the 2020 campaign, mostly because decisions made by President Trump stirred controversy, and turned foreign policy issues into campaign items with which Democratic candidates cautiously engaged. The Democratic Party's posture in 2020, therefore, was largely a reaction to Donald Trump's Middle East foreign policy—which was essentially a combination of calls for withdrawal of military assets from the region combined with the use of economic sanctions. There were some notable exceptions (often driven by internal pressure from the Pentagon), when U.S. troops were in danger or when reassurance was necessary, such as with Saudi Arabia after the Abqaiq attack, but these exceptions were mostly limited in time and scope. Much of the Democratic campaign discourse, rather, was grounded in reactions to Trump's policies and the contradictions within them.

Beyond reactions to news cycles, the Democratic presidential field was characterized by very different foreign policy postures. Joe Biden, Kamala Harris, and Pete Buttigieg argued for a return to or reinvigoration of a more traditional foreign policy, while Bernie Sanders and Elizabeth Warren tended to frame their foreign policy as defining a new path and highlighting a struggle against autocracy. Biden and Buttigieg insisted on restoring U.S. leadership while Sanders and Warren favored military restraint, significantly reducing the defense budget and shifting the conversation away from geopolitical rivalries and toward a focus on "inequality, economic policy, and democracy" along with climate change.[33]

Unsurprisingly, Iran has been a central issue among Middle East–related topics. Most major Democratic candidates favored a return to the JCPOA with some suggestion of conditionality (e.g., if Iran returns to full compliance). There was consensus among the major candidates during the debates in favor of reassessing the American relationship with Saudi Arabia and ending assistance to the Saudi war effort in Yemen. During the primaries, Biden specifically pledged to "reevaluate our relationship with Saudi Arabia to ensure it is fully aligned with American values and priorities"[34] and also said that he would treat Saudi Arabia as "the pariah that they are,"[35] but without singling out the crown prince. Kamala Harris, then a senator, cosponsored legislation requiring a public report into the murder of Jamal Khashoggi and frequently voted against arms sales to Saudi Arabia.[36]

In an article published during the campaign, former Biden advisor Daniel Benaim (now deputy assistant secretary for the Arabian Peninsula in the State Department) described the Democratic debate on the U.S.-Saudi relationship as a contest between so-called resetters and rethinkers. Resetters, Benaim says, see the value in a close U.S.-Saudi relationship and advocate a "tough love" approach to shaping the kingdom's behavior.[37] Rethinkers argue for a more fundamental change to the U.S.-Saudi relationship and question the overall value the United States is getting out of any close ties to Saudi Arabia. Resetters lean toward a more "forward-looking deterrence," whereas rethinkers favor "a punitive reckoning."[38] Benaim advocated ending U.S. support to the Saudi airstrikes campaign in Yemen and placing a moratorium on major arms sales.

The Democratic candidates also differed on subjects such as the ideal force posture in the Middle East. While all candidates called for the end of "endless wars" and a smaller military footprint, Biden and Buttigieg made a distinction between large-scale military interventions and small-scale special operations—which may be the U.S. force posture of the future.[39] Biden supports a "counterterrorism plus" strategy whereby a small number of U.S. Special Forces would train and bolster local troops fighting terrorist groups.[40] "Smaller-scale missions are sustainable militarily, economically, and politically," Biden has written, "and they advance the national interest."[41] Meanwhile, Sanders and Warren voiced greater skepticism with regard to military involvement on any scale and emphasized nonmilitary tools.[42]

The candidates offered different visions on the Israeli-Palestinian issue. They diverged on whether they would consider moving the U.S. embassy in Israel back to Tel Aviv, with Biden and Buttigieg indicating they would not, Sanders indicating he would be open to it, and Warren taking an ambiguous position. Biden refused calls to condition Israeli military aid on no settlement expansion,[43] while Buttigieg, Sanders, and Warren were open to the idea. When asked if Israeli annexation would complicate the U.S. relationship with Israel, Secretary of State Antony Blinken contended during the campaign that annexation "complicates…the prospect of achieving a two state solution in the Middle East, and that outcome, two states for two people, represents the best way and probably the only way that you'll have a secure future for Israel as a Jewish and democratic state and a state for the Palestinians…any unilateral action by either side… is something that the vice president opposes and would oppose as president."[44] He added that ideally Israel would not pursue annexation so that the Biden administration could "rebuild an environment in which it is possible for [Israel and the Palestinians] to reengage in the direction of two states." He maintained this position after being sworn in.

Some tools got specific scrutiny in the context of the internal Democratic debate. For instance, progressives criticize what they describe as an excessive use of economic sanctions in foreign policy. Representative Ilhan Omar (D-MN) introduced a bill requiring Congressional approval for approving or renewing sanctions. The executive vice president at the Quincy Institute, Trita Parsi, called sanctions "not an alternative to war, but an alternative form of war."[45] These calls have been heightened by the pandemic, with thirty-four progressive lawmakers, including Senator Sanders, calling for the lifting of all sanctions on Iran during the pandemic.[46]

Biden's Team and Allies and Their Ideas on the Middle East

Though Joe Biden won both the Democratic nomination and the presidency, the policy positions of the other Democratic candidates and the strains of opinion they represented have not ended with their campaigns. In turn, they have influenced the relationship between the Biden administration and congressional Democrats.

The presence of progressives in the race has influenced the foreign policy agenda of the party overall. Aside from the presidential candidates, other players such as Sen. Chris Murphy (D-CT) are advocating a more progressive foreign policy. Murphy favors pivoting away from traditional foreign policy toward a "more nimble and diverse foreign policy toolkit."[47] The victory of some progressives in Democratic congressional primaries, like Jamaal Bowman in New York over longtime pro-Israel incumbent Eliot Engel, suggests that the Biden administration might also come under more pressure from a more progressive Democratic caucus in Congress.

Biden himself consults with Congress more systematically than did the Trump administration, and thus enables the involvement of different wings of the Democratic caucus. As a member of Biden's foreign policy team explained, "You cannot overemphasize how Biden is going to give primacy to bipartisanship. The way the White House runs its diplomacy will incorporate a huge premium on consultation with Congress."[48] This affects the speed and process of foreign policy making and presents a challenge to U.S. partners to understand American governance and politics.

Beyond the question of the influence of progressives on the Biden administration, significant uncertainties remain regarding how Biden is going to react to a very new international environment. The president has indeed surrounded himself with many Obama-era officials, including Antony Blinken, William Burns, Jake Sullivan,[49] and Avril Haines.[50] Biden has a very long foreign policy record, but his campaign made clear that they understood "that he inherits a world both in disarray and a fractured country," as Antony Blinken put it at a public event.

The thinking of Biden advisors has also evolved. Several have acknowledged shortcomings in the Obama years, and are said to be in search of rebuilding a U.S. leadership inspired more by the Clinton years than by the ambiguous restraint of the Obama presidency.[51] The key uncertainty is, therefore, how Biden will react to the change in U.S. standing in the world since the Clinton years, as well as to the weakening of its alliances around the world, the rise of China and Russia in the Middle East, and the emergence and intensification of new categories of threats (e.g., from cyberattacks, cyberwarfare, and cyberterrorism; climate change; and aggression by nonstate actors). James Traub assumes, therefore, that Biden will seek to normalize U.S. relations with the Middle East: he will not ask as much as Obama did, but he also will not tolerate as much as Trump has.[52]

Beyond the Obama legacy, some have also identified a new line of thinking within the Biden team and labeled it as characterizing the "2021 Democrats."[53] Several members of the Biden team are said to think that the world has shifted significantly since 2012, and in particular with the Covid-19 pandemic. They believe that sustaining democracy takes serious effort, and they view the world as more geopolitically competitive than traditional Democrats, especially vis-à-vis China. For example, Ely Ratner, the deputy national security adviser to Biden in Obama's second term and now special assistant to the secretary of defense, wrote that the assumption that engaging China commercially would lead to China liberalizing economically proved untrue.[54] Democrats in 2021 prioritize standing up to authoritarian governments and understanding the role of technology in this competition. They support reforming the military to deal with new technologies and scaling back goals for the Middle East.

It is difficult to know what this soul-searching will produce in terms of a new foreign policy consensus or new options, especially regarding the Middle East, where it is not clear how more military restraint and more diplomatic engagement would be implemented and with what results. The lengthy review process pursued by the Biden administration in its first months gives a sense of the strategic doubt that still shapes his foreign policy team. For instance, Daniel Benaim writes that "the aim of a progressive policy should be to reform a partnership that still holds value."[55] He also argues that "a progressive course correction would enlist Saudi Arabia in a regional dialogue that, alongside renewed nuclear diplomacy with Iran, aims to pave the path for a less militarized U.S. policy and presence in a more peaceful, stable Middle East." This idea was also supposed to inspire the JCPOA, but it was never operationalized.[56]

The first steps taken by the Biden administration have made clear that the Middle East is not its main foreign policy priority. The pace and method with respect to Middle East issues have been consistent with what Antony Blinken had said publicly when asked if the United States should disengage from the Middle East: "Yes, we need to refocus our priorities and limit engagement in the Middle East."[57] Referencing the pivot to Asia under the Obama administration, he said it was important to once again understand that the United States is under-resourced in some areas, such as Asia, while allotting too many resources to places like the Middle East.

The Biden administration is more focused on the Indo-Pacific and on Latin America, and as a budget priority, the Middle East will likely decline. One senior advisor anonymously observed that the Middle East would be a "distant fourth" in terms of regional priorities, after Europe, the Indo-Pacific, and Latin America.[58] He did reemphasize the U.S. commitment to Israeli security, but noted that in the Middle East, it will be important to "allocate our resources where it matters most."

Jake Sullivan and Daniel Benaim have called for reducing military ambitions and efforts to remake nations while using diplomacy to de-escalate regional tensions. They call for leveraging low oil prices and the Covid-19 pandemic to thaw Gulf-Iran tensions, for example—perhaps by starting with a joint plan to resume Hajj travel and pilgrimages for Saudi Shia to build confidence toward a larger regional dialogue.[59] They argue for abandoning unrealistic goals, such as Secretary Pompeo's call for expelling "every last Iranian boot" from Syria. They suggest that even with a lighter footprint, the United States would still maintain a credible deterrent. They do not call for leaving the region outright, but for reassessing current strategy and setting conditions for increased diplomacy—beyond just a nuclear agreement with Iran—and a reduced military presence. Both the emphasis on working with Congress and the desire to not rush into Middle East crises have been evident in the administration's first steps toward renegotiating the nuclear deal with Iran.

The American Pursuit of Middle East Minimalism

Speculation about the foreign policy of the Biden administration goes beyond the traditional uncertainty at the start of any new administration. It also has broader significance: these debates reflect a larger consensus in the foreign policy community in Washington as well as important trends in public opinion. Experts like Mira Rapp-Hooper explain that the U.S. alliance system has become a victim of its own success: so many of its benefits are not readily apparent—including that it has made the world safer—that Americans (incorrectly) think it is not worth investing in anymore.[60] This global perception plays out in a particular way in the Middle East as a large number of experts seem to be looking to move beyond the post-9/11 phase of American foreign policy.[61] The general trend bends toward using existing or reduced military assets in the region to undergird an expanded campaign of diplomatic engagement. The debate within the Democratic Party is both a microcosm of and a reaction to a larger debate about Middle East foreign policy.

There is a growing bipartisan consensus that the Middle East is no longer the region of greatest importance to the country's interests. "Both parties are chasing their Middle East minimalism," in the words of a Senior State Department official who joined the White House when Biden was sworn in.[62] Although Presidents Trump and Obama diverged on rhetoric, both seemed to believe that the United States was overly involved in the Middle East. Obama overtly (and unsuccessfully) tried to rebalance militarily to Asia; Trump reduced troop levels in Syria.[63] And an increasing number of respected figures within the foreign policy community consider the Middle East less vital to American interests than in previous decades.

That conversation started in 2015 with articles by NSC veterans Steven Simon and Jonathan Stevenson and by Boston University professor Andrew Bacevich, who called for an end to "endless wars."[64] Then, Martin Indyk, a former diplomat and longtime advocate of American engagement in the Middle East, argued in early 2020 that "the Middle East isn't worth it anymore." He noted that America's two priorities in the past were "to keep Gulf oil flowing at reasonable prices and to ensure Israel's survival."[65] Now, he argues, those interests are less relevant: the United States no longer relies on imported petroleum, thanks to the domestic natural-gas revolution, and Israel is able to defend itself without American help. Others have made the same case. Aaron David Miller, also a peace process veteran, and Richard Sokolsky, a former State Department official, have written, "The United States now has the capacity to respond rapidly to price swings through market mechanisms; Middle East crises don't have the impact on oil prices that is generally assumed; and all the oil producing states, including a disruptive Iran, have an interest in getting their product to market."[66] Foreign policy experts Mara Karlin (appointed assistant secretary for strategy in the Biden Defense Department) and Tamara Cofman Wittes (appointed assistant administrator for the Middle East at USAID) had put forward a similar argument: they argue that American interests in the Middle East have diminished, but "U.S. strategy toward the Middle East...has yet to catch up with these changes." This combination, say Karlin and Wittes, leaves America "in a kind of Middle Eastern purgatory."[67] Simon and Stevenson observe that it is not only U.S. interests that call for a Middle East pullback, but also facts on the ground. They argue that the main drivers of the changing calculus are political and economic developments that "have reduced the opportunities for effective American intervention to a vanishing point."[68] Miller and Sokolsky summarize the prevailing view: "The U.S. is no longer the top dog in the Middle East neighborhood. And it doesn't need to be."[69]

Foreign policy expert Steven Cook offers a different view: he believes that Washington still has critical interests in the region, even if technological, political, and social changes have made them less vital. Cook agrees that Washington should abandon grand ambitions in the Middle East and focus instead on establishing and preserving regional stability. He believes, however, that a full U.S. withdrawal would lead to chaos, and to regional actors taking matters into their own hands—with Saudi Arabia, for example, potentially trying to acquire a nuclear weapon. He makes the case that a realistic Middle East policy would be centered on "containing Iran, retooling the fight against terrorism to reduce its counterproductive side effects, reorganizing military deployments to emphasize the protection of sea-lanes, and downscaling the U.S.-Israel relationship to reflect Israel's relative strength."[70]

Politicians on both sides of the aisle talk about winding down in the Middle East, but a meaningful foreign policy divergence persists between Democrats and Republicans. According to the 2020 Chicago Council on Global Affairs survey, there is no overlap between the top five leading threats to the United States, as identified by Democrats versus Republicans. On average, Republicans ranked international terrorism and Iran's nuclear program among their top five concerns, whereas none of the top five concerns for Democrats are inherently tied to the Middle East. Respondents from both parties viewed the transatlantic alliance positively, with 85 percent of Democrats and 65 percent of Republicans supporting it.[71]

It is all the more unlikely that Joe Biden will reject this structural transformation of American involvement in the Arab world because it reflects a domestic consensus. Nor will he challenge the medium-term dynamics of U.S. domestic politics spilling over into foreign policy in the absence of a big, unifying foreign threat. Though there is a debate both within and between both parties about the relative importance of pressure and diplomacy in Middle East foreign policy, Biden agrees with his predecessor on perhaps one issue alone: the need to end the "forever wars" undertaken by the United States in Afghanistan and Iraq. Biden's approach to restart negotiations with Iran on the nuclear deal as well as his decision to withdraw from Afghanistan have been consistent with this dynamic.

A new strategy for American influence in the Middle East, however, has not yet been elaborated. Moreover, for the time being, America will be wholly focused on domestic recovery in the wake of the coronavirus pandemic; insofar as the Biden administration attends to the Middle East, it may find itself at once too focused on the region to pivot to other priorities, but not invested enough to commit to making grand changes.[72] Certainly, neither Republicans nor Democrats have presented a clear vision of a future U.S. military posture in the region. Much of the discussion of Middle East foreign policy is shaped by a broader debate on U.S. priorities globally, as well as on the role America should play regarding them.

Ultimately, the system of U.S. deterrence in place since 1973 in the Middle East is being called into question,[73] while specific policies such as the four-decade-old Carter Doctrine, providing a security shield for Persian Gulf oil and the countries that produce it, have been unceremoniously abrogated. Washington and its regional allies must therefore renew their partnerships and clarify the terms of those partnerships. This transition of American policy toward a potentially less military-heavy model is delicate, however, because Washington and the region at the same time face pressure from actors seeking to take advantage of this new geopolitical environment. Both sides of the American political aisle will have to figure out how to navigate this new system.

Notes

1 Michel Duclos, interview by author, August 2020

2 "Strengthening European Autonomy Across MENA," in *Mapping European Leverage in the MENA Region*, European Council on Foreign Relations, November 2019, https://www.ecfr.eu/special/mapping_eu_leverage_mena/.

3 Presidency of the Republic of France, "Initiative for Europe: Speech by M. Emmanuel Macron, President of the French Republic," September 26, 2017, https://www.diplomatie.gouv.fr/IMG/pdf/english_version_transcript_-_initiative_for_europe_-_speech_by_the_president_of_the_french_republic_cle8de628.pdf.

4 German Federal Government, "Speech by Federal Chancellor Dr. Angela Merkel at the Ceremony Awarding the International Charlemagne Prize to French President Emmanuel Macron in Aachen," May 10, 2018, https://www.bundesregierung.de/breg-en/chancellor/speech-by-federal-chancellor-dr-angela-merkel-at-the-ceremony-awarding-the-international-charlemagne-prize-to-french-president-emmanuel-macron-in-aachen-on-10-may-2018-1008554.

5 Federal Foreign Office of Germany, "Opening Address by Foreign Minister Heiko Maas at the Virtual Annual Council Meeting of the European Council for Foreign Relations," June 29, 2020, https://www.auswaertiges-amt.de/en/newsroom/news/maas-ecfr/2358716.

6 Ayhan Simsek, "Merkel's Government Divided over Syria Safe Zone," Anadolu Agency, October 22, 2019, https://www.aa.com.tr/en/europe/merkel-s-government-divided-over-syria-safe-zone/1622751.

7 Josep Borrell, "Embracing Europe's Power," Project Syndicate, February 8, 2020, https://www.project-syndicate.org/commentary/embracing-europe-s-power-by-josep-borrell-2020-02?barrier=accesspaylog.

8 European Parliament, "Commitments Made at the Hearing of Josep Borrell Fontelles," October 2019, https://www.europarl.europa.eu/RegData/etudes/BRIE/2019/639311/EXPO_BRI(2019)639311_EN.pdf.

9 David Fernández, "Josep Borrell: A Realist European Foreign Policy?" *The New Federalist*, October 9, 2019, https://www.thenewfederalist.eu/josep-borrell-a-realist-european-foreign-policy.

10   Eduard Soler i Lecha and Pol Morillas, *Middle Power with Maghreb Focus: A Spanish Perspective on Security Policy in the Southern Neighbourhood* (Berlin: Friedrich Ebert Stiftung, June 2020), 12, available at http://library.fes.de/pdf-files/id/ipa/16307-20200722.pdf.

11   Eduard Soler i Lecha, interview by author, August 10, 2020.

12   Nathalie Tocci, interview by author, July 2020.

13   Robert Czulda, "What's Behind the Middle East Summit in Poland?" Atlantic Council, January 18, 2019, https://www.atlanticcouncil.org/blogs/iransource/what-s-behind-the-middle-east-summit-in-poland/.

14   Senior Northern European diplomat, interview by author, August 2020.

15   A framework for a small number of member states to launch a joint military project to which they can "willingly" and "capably" commit.

16   A specific funding mechanism to support European defense projects.

17   A mechanism to increase preparedness and coordination among European armies for potential quick military reactions to crises.

18   Alessandro Marrone, *Security Policy in the Southern Neighbourhood: A View from Rome* (Rome: Friedrich Ebert Stiftung, 2020), 7, available at http://library.fes.de/pdf-files/bueros/rom/16768-20200421.pdf.

19   Senior Northern European diplomat, interview by author, August 2020.

20   Nathalie Tocci, interview by author, July 2020.

21   Ibid.

22   Senior Northern European diplomat, interview by author, August 2020.

23   Emmanuel Macron (@Emmanuel Macron), "La situation en Méditerranée orientale est préoccupante. Les décisions unilatérales de la Turquie en matière d'exploration pétrolière provoquent des tensions. Celles-ci doivent cesser pour permettre un dialogue apaisé entre pays voisins et alliés au sein de l'OTAN," post on Twitter, August 12, 2020, 4:04 p.m., https://twitter.com/EmmanuelMacron/status/1293639394218385417.

24   Joseph de Weck, "Pariscope: Hegelian Diplomacy in the Eastern Mediterranean," *Internationale Politik*, September 2, 2020, available at https://ip-quarterly.com/en/hegelian-diplomacy-eastern-mediterranean.

25   Constantinos Filis, *Troubled Waters in the Eastern Mediterranean? A Greek Perspective on Security Policy in the Southern Neighbourhood*

(Berlin: Friedrich Ebert Stiftung, 2020), 4, available at http://library.fes. de/pdf-files/id/ipa/16306.pdf.

26　Senior Northern European diplomat, interview by author, August 2020.

27　"Strengthening European Autonomy," https://www.ecfr.eu/specials/ mapping_eu_leverage_mena/.

28　For the EU Civil Protection Mechanism, see https://bit.ly/3DyNhfU.

29　Erik Brattberg, "The E3, the EU, and the Post-Brexit Diplomatic Landscape," Carnegie Endowment for International Peace, June 18, 2020, https://carnegieendowment.org/2020/06/18/e3-eu-and-post-brexit-diplomatic-landscape-pub-82095.

30　Soler i Lecha and Morillas, *Middle Power with Maghreb Focus*, 12, available at http://library.fes.de/pdf-files/id/ipa/16307-20200722.pdf.

31　Senior Northern European diplomat, interview by author, August 2020.

32　Luke Baker, "Gaps Emerge Between Britain and EU over Trump Middle East Plan," Reuters, January 29, 2020, https://www.reuters. com/article/us-israel-palestinians-plan-europe/gaps-emerge-between-britain-and-eu-over-trump-middle-east-plan-idUSKBN1ZS26J.

33　Thomas Wright, "The Problem at the Core of Progressive Foreign Policy," *Atlantic*, September 12, 2019, https://www.theatlantic.com/ ideas/archive/2019/09/progressives-foreign-policy-dilemma/597823/.

34　Trevor Hunnicutt, "Biden Campaign Attacks Trump Policy on Saudi Arabia, North Korea," Reuters, December 8, 2019, https://www.reuters. com/article/us-usa-election-biden-trump/biden-campaign-attacks-trump-policy-on-saudi-arabia-north-korea-idUSKBN1YD087.

35　Alex Emmons, Aida Chavez, and Akela Lacy, "Joe Biden, in Departure from Obama Policy, Says He Would Make Saudi Arabia a 'Pariah,'" *Intercept*, November 21, 2019, https://theintercept.com/2019/11/21/ democratic-debate-joe-biden-saudi-arabia/.

36　Bryant Harris, "Election 2020: Where the Candidates Stand on the Middle East," Al-Monitor, October 21, 2019.

37　Daniel Benaim, "A Progressive Course Correction for U.S.-Saudi Relations," The Century Foundation, June 25, 2020, https://tcf.org/content/ report/progressive-course-correction-u-s-saudi-relations/?session=1.

38　Ibid.

39   Franco Ordoñez, "In Democratic Debate, a Fiery Clash over U.S. Role in Syria," National Public Radio, October 16, 2019, https://www.npr.org/2019/10/16/770502802/in-democratic-debate-a-fiery-clash-over-u-s-role-in-syria.

40   Jack Detsch, "Biden Gets Push from Left-Leaning Groups to Slash Pentagon Budget," *Foreign Policy*, May 11, 2020, https://foreignpolicy.com/2020/05/11/biden-left-leaning-groups-slash-pentagon-budget/.

41   Joseph R. Biden, "Why America Must Lead Again: Rescuing U.S. Foreign Policy After Trump," *Foreign Affairs*, March/April 2020, https://www.foreignaffairs.com/articles/united-states/2020-01-23/why-america-must-lead-again.

42   "Read the Full Transcript of Tuesday Night's CNN/*Des Moines Register* Debate," *Des Moines Register*, January 14, 2020, https://www.desmoinesregister.com/story/news/elections/presidential/caucus/2020/01/14/democratic-debate-transcript-what-the-candidates-said-quotes/4460789002/.

43   "Biden: 'Outrageous' to Leverage Aid to Israel Against Settlement Expansion," *Times of Israel*, November 1, 2019, https://www.timesofisrael.com/biden-conditioning-aid-to-israel-would-be-absolutely-outrageous/.

44   "A Conversation with Former Deputy Secretary of State Antony Blinken," transcript, Hudson Institute, July 9, 2020, https://www.hudson.org/research/16210-transcript-dialogues-on-american-foreign-policy-and-world-affairs-a-conversation-with-former-deputy-secretary-of-state-antony-blinken.

45   Matthew Petti, "Economic Sanctions: An Alternative to War or War by Alternative Means?" *National Interest*, April 28, 2020, https://nationalinterest.org/blog/2020-election/economic-sanctions-alternative-war-or-war-alternative-means-148996.

46   Bryant Harris, "Meet Joe Biden's Foreign Policy Advisers," Al-Monitor, April 20, 2020, https://www.al-monitor.com/pulse/originals/2020/04/joe-biden-foreign-policy-advisers-iran-saudi-arabia-trump.html?utm_campaign=20200420.

47   "Building Back Better: A Post-Trump Foreign Policy," video Quincy Institute for Responsible Statecraft, August 18, 2020, https://quincyinst.org/2020/08/18/building-back-better-a-post-trump-foreign-policy/.

48 Member of Biden's Middle East team, interview by author, September 2020.

49 Harris, "Meet Biden's Foreign Policy Advisers," https://www.al-monitor. com/pulse/originals/2020/04/joe-biden-foreign-policy-advisers-iran-saudi-arabia-trump.html?utm_campaign=20200420.

50 Robbie Gramer, Colum Lynch, and Darcy Palder, "Inside the Massive Foreign-Policy Team Advising Biden's Campaign," *Foreign Policy*, July 31, 2020, https://foreignpolicy.com/2020/07/31/ inside-biden-campaign-foreign-policy-team/?s=09.

51 Former senior U.S. official, interview by author, August 14, 2020.

52 James Traub, "Under Biden, the Middle East Would Be Just Another Region," *Foreign Policy*, September 9, 2020, https://foreignpolicy. com/2020/09/09/biden-is-planning-change-not-hope-for-the-middle-east/; also see Gramer, Lynch, and Palder, "Inside the Massive Foreign-Policy Team," https://foreignpolicy.com/2020/07/31/ inside-biden-campaign-foreign-policy-team/?s=09.

53 Thomas Wright, "The Quiet Reformation of Biden's Foreign Policy," *Atlantic*, March 19, 2020, https://www.theatlantic.com/ideas/ archive/2020/03/foreign-policy-2021-democrats/608293/.

54 Ibid.

55 Benaim, "A Progressive Course Correction," https://tcf.org/content/ report/progressive-course-correction-u-s-saudi-relations/?session=1.

56 See Ibid.; also former senior U.S. official, interview by author, August 2020.

57 "Conversation with Antony Blinken," https://www.hudson.org/ research/16210-transcript-dialogues-on-american-foreign-policy-and-world-affairs-a-conversation-with-former-deputy-secretary-of-state-antony-blinken.

58 Traub, "Under Biden, the Middle East," *Foreign Policy*, https:// foreignpolicy.com/2020/09/09/biden-is-planning-change-not-hope-for-the-middle-east/.

59 Daniel Benaim and Jake Sullivan, "America's Opportunity in the Middle East," *Foreign Affairs*, June 4, 2020, https://www.foreignaffairs. com/articles/middle-east/2020-05-22/americas-opportunity-middle-east.

60   Mira Rapp-Hooper, *Shields of the Republic: The Triumph and Peril of America's Alliances* (Cambridge, MA: Harvard University Press, 2020).

61   Ben Rhodes, "The 9/11 Era Is Over," *Atlantic*, April 6, 2020, https://www.theatlantic.com/ideas/archive/2020/04/its-not-september-12-anymore/609502/.

62   Former State Department senior official, interview by author, August 2020.

63   Martin Indyk, "The Middle East Isn't Worth It Anymore," *Wall Street Journal*, January 17, 2020, https://www.wsj.com/articles/the-middle-east-isnt-worth-it-anymore-11579277317. Indyk is a founder of The Washington Institute, publisher of this study.

64   Andrew J. Bacevich, "Ending Endless War," *Foreign Affairs*, September/October 2016, https://www.foreignaffairs.com/articles/united-states/2016-08-03/ending-endless-war.

65   Indyk, "Middle East Isn't Worth It," https://www.wsj.com/articles/the-middle-east-isnt-worth-it-anymore-11579277317

66   Aaron David Miller and Richard Sokolsky, "The Middle East Just Doesn't Matter As Much Any Longer," *Politico*, September 3, 2020, https://www.politico.com/news/magazine/2020/09/03/the-middle-east-just-doesnt-matter-as-much-any-longer-407820.

67   Mara Karlin and Tamara Cofman Wittes, "America's Middle East Purgatory: The Case for Doing Less," *Foreign Affairs*, January/February 2019, https://www.foreignaffairs.com/articles/middle-east/2018-12-11/americas-middle-east-purgatory.

68   Steven Simon and Jonathan Stevenson, "The End of Pax Americana: Why Washington's Middle East Pullback Makes Sense," *Foreign Affairs*, November/December 2015, https://www.foreignaffairs.com/articles/middle-east/end-pax-americana.

69   Miller and Sokolsky, "The Middle East Just Doesn't Matter As Much," https://www.politico.com/news/magazine/2020/09/03/the-middle-east-just-doesnt-matter-as-much-any-longer-407820.

70   Steven A. Cook, "No Exit: Why the Middle East Still Matters to America," *Foreign Affairs*, November/December 2020, https://www.foreignaffairs.com/articles/united-states/2020-10-13/no-exit.

71 Dan Balz and Scott Clement, "Poll: Sharp Partisan Differences Now Exist on Foreign Policy, Views of American Exceptionalism," *Washington Post*, September 17, 2020, https://www.washingtonpost.com/politics/poll-foreign-policy-trump-democrats/2020/09/16/8e2d903e-f836-11ea-be57-d00bb9bc632d_story.html. For the study itself, see Dina Smeltz et al., *Divided We Stand: Democrats and Republicans Diverge on Foreign Policy* (Chicago: Chicago Council on Global Affairs, 2020), https://www.thechicagocouncil.org/research/public-opinion-survey/2020-chicago-council-survey.

72 Karlin and Wittes, "America's Purgatory," https://www.foreignaffairs.com/articles/middle-east/2018-12-11/americas-middle-east-purgatory.

73 Senior U.S. diplomat, interview by author, October 2019.

5

Toward Western Humility
in the Middle East

Given their diverging trajectories in the Middle East, the United States and Europe might be at a crossroads in their cooperation as conducted over the past few decades. This provides an opportunity to reset the way America and Europe discuss problems in the Middle East and work together to address them. The reset of transatlantic dialogue and cooperation in the Middle East will be difficult, however, as crises are likely to limit decisionmakers' ability on both continents to commit to such a process. Global ambitions and the bilateral relationships European countries and the United States have with Middle East countries are likely to frame the possibilities of transatlantic relations more than any other factor.

A Division of Labor in Great Power Politics

U.S. foreign policy is shifting to a focus on Great Power competition. The United States wants to withdraw from "endless wars" in the Middle East and, in turn, focus on pressing domestic issues. As Russian and Chinese influence increases, so does the American focus on combating their strength. But the United States will need to consider a strategy, along with more practical steps, if it is to win this competition.

Europeans have no choice but to acknowledge this factor in their Middle East policy, while recalling that an American strength in its world posture comes from its strong alliances. Different administrations have emphasized these alliances to different degrees, but Europeans should demonstrate that they are an indispensable resource in Great Power competition. Some of America's strongest allies are in Europe, so working with these allies could result in a favorable outcome.

If they want Washington to pay attention, however, Europeans must first provide an answer to how Middle East foreign policy fits into the American understanding of the rivalry with China and Russia. The challenge is to go beyond affirming that the United States must work with its European allies—and to share specific ideas about Great Power competition, and about the tradeoffs Washington will have to make if it invests more to compete with China.

A transatlantic reset would not be only about the Middle East, but it should include a clear Middle East component. And when it comes to the region, Europeans and Americans need to prioritize the issues they would like to include in the transatlantic agenda. Otherwise, the United States and Europe risk, as in 2011, being dragged into events they have not prepared for. An overambitious agenda would also trigger legitimate criticism about Western pretensions to rule over the region, and in any case is unlikely to be successful given the limited resources Europe and the United States will have in the post-Covid context. A number of regional crises necessarily involve Europe and America, however, financially, geographically, and militarily. And a key issue for Europeans will be to select priorities that could serve as tests of a transatlantic reset. Fundamental to everything will be what the Europeans can bring to the relationship, and what they need to ask of the United States.

The Iranian issue is at the top of the transatlantic agenda, because the JCPOA provided both a framework and precedent to work with. Regional conflicts like Syria and Libya must also remain key issues of the transatlantic dialogue and should lead to a better division of labor based on shared strategic goals. The United States should acknowledge the ramifications for Europe of these conflicts, from the issue of refugees to the impact they have on relations with Turkey. U.S. leaders might not want to get involved, but need to consider the strategic impact of these conflicts on Europe and not just look at them through the lens of the U.S. rivalry with Russia. In the long term, the U.S. interest might be to support the development of the EU's ability to deal with its neighborhood more autonomously, in coordination with NATO. But Europeans would have to be more united first, and, according to one U.S. diplomat, will have to be clear about what they propose.[1]

Regarding all these priorities, a key issue will be how the United States engages in a dialogue with Europe while it pursues its bilateral relations in the region. Will Washington be interested in shaping a regional architecture, or rather focus only on rebuilding bilateral relationships? The end of "endless wars" requires an architecture of nonintervention, and that requires allies. In Obama's case, the only allies were the regional players. But the Democratic primaries have revealed a desire among many to reassess partnerships in the region, and the Biden administration might therefore pay more attention to a possible European role. For the United States as well as for Europe, the past decade has shown how difficult it can be to influence bilateral partners—and this could create a renewed interest in Western coordination.

Europe's Moment to Act

The ball is in the EU's court, then: to organize itself, and to agree on a coherent way to engage Washington on the Middle East, among other issues. And the best way for Europe to avoid the U.S. divide-and-conquer approach toward the continent would be to create small contact groups of "willing and capable" countries that can contribute meaningfully to resolving particular Middle East issues, and to present these contact groups as effective interlocutors vis-à-vis the United States.

The paradox is that Western engagement in the Middle East is likely to be less and less militarized, yet Europe must still show the United States that it can step in quickly militarily if necessary. Though neither the United States nor Europe wants to be heavily engaged militarily in the Middle East anymore, military capabilities and their leveraging to support diplomatic solutions will likely remain central to Middle East diplomacy. The Syrian and Libyan conflicts have demonstrated how political outcomes are ultimately shaped by the ability to resort to limited but effective use of force at critical moments. The EU's credibility in the eyes of local and regional actors also demands the capability to display military power.[2]

As Dennis Ross has remarked, "It is important to delineate what Europeans can bring to the table." Europeans have to make clear what kind of capabilities they can make available for operations in the Middle East. Ross continues: "We don't have to replicate each other; we need to complement each other. Where the Americans have invested more, this is not where Europeans should invest."[3]

It will be pivotal to the transatlantic discussion, therefore, to focus on the right indicators: actual deployable military capabilities, for example, rather than vague targets with respect to the portion of each country's GDP dedicated to military spending. A key source of much of the tension surrounding burden sharing has been a lack of clarity with respect to what exactly is expected of different countries. This can be seen, to take one example, in the case of the 2 percent threshold for defense spending, which does not include other key metrics, such as those relating to crisis prevention or diplomatic action. European allies have contributed greatly in ways other than defense spending—involving, for example, cyberattacks, hybrid warfare, crisis prevention, and diplomatic deterrence.

A robust metric of burden sharing must go beyond defense spending, therefore, to take into account allocations for development, intelligence, and diplomacy. The lack of clarity in expectations has been one of the key barriers to improving Western effectiveness in the Middle East. When the Trump administration called for more burden sharing within NATO, it was unclear whether greater spending on the part of member countries would deliver more capabilities soon enough, or whether these capabilities should involve more training missions, more troops deployable on the ground, more intelligence spending, or something else.

NATO remains an effective framework for these discussions, and could play an important but not leading role, in close cooperation with the EU.[4] NATO does not need to be the primary operational framework for operations, however, if such are too far from NATO's traditional geographic scope. A key issue for the transatlantic relationship is actually for the United States to actively support the strengthening of European defense as the European pillar of NATO, especially when it comes to capabilities that can be relevant for military deployment in the Middle East (peacekeeping missions, training missions, special forces). A number of European member states have been reluctant to support a more unified European defense, based on the assumption that it would harm NATO. The U.S. role in clarifying this matter is critical. This might also require France, say, to reiterate the intent behind proposals like the European intervention initiative—though French officials have systematically emphasized the complementarity of this idea with existing security frameworks.

Ultimately, this is not about restoring a one-size-fits-all standard of cooperation, but rather about designing a process through which allies better understand what they can do together, and what capabilities they should each develop in light of the political goals and threat assessment they share. Europeans will have to increase burden sharing capacity as well as their decisionmaking speed in order to support such a positive new dynamic. But a reduced U.S. footprint in the Middle East will also have an impact on the *American* political space. The U.S. tendency to lead without listening to contradictory opinions from allies might have been justified when the United States was providing 95 percent of the effort. But in a world where the United States does not so often intervene militarily, or does so within more balanced frameworks, creating space for better policymaking with allies is essential. As Dennis Ross put it: "Hopefully the U.S. will do a better job at listening and do a better job of defining what burden sharing is."[5]

The transatlantic relationship has enough institutional channels for communication, but some informal ad hoc formats with a selected number of European countries might be helpful in launching the process, before opening it up to regional stakeholders. The two parties will have to design concentric circles together based on what European member states can offer in terms of resources and political will. Such a process might create some pushback from member states rejecting a two-track Europe, but this could also be seen as a way to push member states to stop free riding and design a more effective division of labor: for a division of labor to be effective at the transatlantic level, it first must be effective at the European level. Europeans may therefore have to organize themselves and agree on their own division of labor before engaging with the United States.

A key priority for Washington should therefore be to support a renewed multilateral engagement. The multilateralization of U.S. foreign policy constitutes a major challenge, because American diplomats themselves tend to acknowledge that they have not been trained to consider multilateral forums as anything more than an echo chamber for their national initiatives. One such diplomat explained it this way: "The U.S. system has a bias for bilateral framework. There is a European bias in favor of multilateralism because Europe is well represented and knows the rules well."[6] This disharmony has been damaging for transatlantic dialogue, and for designing small coalitions with Arab countries. Thus, the United States did not really engage in the Small Group on Syria to gather like-minded countries (France, Germany, Britain, Saudi Arabia, Jordan, Egypt), preferring instead to invest in a bilateral track with Russia that has not proven very successful.

Toward a Healthier Engagement

Because military interventions in the Middle East have been a major aspect of Western engagement in the region, the policy debate tends to be excessively framed in military terms: engagement is often assessed on the basis of how many troops are involved. The combination of likely American restraint, however, and European reluctance and lack of capability to intervene alone militarily suggests that the probability of extensive new Western military operations is limited. So thinking about the renewal of Western engagement and cooperation in the Middle East has to be based on a different metric.

The emphasis of the Biden campaign on "more realistic" goals refers to another novelty in Western policies regarding the Middle East: humility. In both Europe and the United States, many experts and decisionmakers simply acknowledge that grand strategies and ambitions have not worked. In response, some advocate for "withdrawal," often without specifying what that means. But the human connections, business relationships, and educational linkages between the Middle East, Europe, and the United States indicate that the West cannot really be "unplugged" from the Middle East. The only way to make Middle East policies acceptable to Americans and Europeans is to make them less ambitious but more thoroughly carried out—and more responsive to the needs of communities in the region.

In this context, a practical consequence of the region's fragmentation and the collapse of state structures in several countries is that external actors lack traditional diplomatic partners. Conventional cooperation between governments is still the best option when possible, but it is also less relevant when state structures are dysfunctional and the real drivers of growth and jobs are within very different layers of the private sector, from warlord to well-intentioned businessperson. At the same time, not to invest in traditional state structures through cooperation weakens them even more. This paradox in the search for local partners is a limiting factor faced by both the United States and Europe, and requires reassessment of a wide range of policy tools, such as how money for humanitarian assistance can be best provided. In many cases, direct cash transfers to local communities through contacts in their respective diasporas are far more impactful than expensive multilateral programs. And the process of vetting possible partners or engaging with nonstate actors on the ground is a challenge that Western diplomats will face more and more acutely in the future.

The key issue in the region, therefore, is less about military engagement and more about addressing the governance crisis at the heart of most regional challenges. The EU has experience and legitimacy in this field, without the same toxic American legacy in Iraq. In addition, given the likelihood of Western countries' reducing their external assistance funding in the post-pandemic period, a dialogue on joint priorities to support economic opportunities in Middle East countries would help support multilateral institutions with programs in the region and also foster relations between civil societies.

As for cuts in external assistance, Britain has already announced a reduction of its overseas aid budget from 0.7 percent of gross national income to 0.5 percent for 2021.[7] The U.S. contribution in the region has traditionally been focused on security assistance: the last Trump administration budget included $5.46 billion for such, accounting for 83.4 percent of the total request to Congress for the Middle East and North Africa, while democracy assistance represented a mere 2.9 percent.[8] This priority indicates the sort of transatlantic discussion that the United States and Europe might need to have to make sure that they also invest in soft power and economic development.

A key part of resetting transatlantic cooperation will be to rebalance the dialogue on tools of soft power possessed—sometimes to a greater degree than they realize—by both the EU and the United States. The U.S. fatigue with regard to military action and the EU priority of avoiding another migration wave should bring transatlantic partners together to reassess their tools of humanitarian assistance, stabilization, and socioeconomic support. A renewed transatlantic consensus and road map on these issues would have a powerful effect on the NGOs and international institutions that both Europe and the United States fund. Joint priorities and advocacy to support economic opportunities in MENA countries could also be a valuable item driving multilateral institutions with programs in the region.

In the end, the overarching challenge Western soft power faces is the necessity of adapting to a Middle East that is more fragmented internally, but at the same time more connected internationally. Old issues like corruption or social protests will remain, but Western cooperation in the region will have to address them in a new environment, with more state and nonstate players involved and with technological changes that will be very unequally distributed in the region. In that respect, the best resources Western countries can use to drive their cooperation with Middle East countries and societies are those that have worked at home to tackle global issues, including EU regulations on climate change, American entrepreneurial culture, and safety nets for social cohesion. Innovation, consistency, and transparency may be currencies as valuable as military power and funding in this new geopolitical landscape.

Conclusion: A New Triangle

Since the end of the Cold War, the United States has led its foreign policy in the Middle East rather unilaterally, expecting European allies to follow its lead without challenging America's dominant position in the dynamic. This imbalance was largely explained by the disparity in military capabilities and contributions, along with the limited willingness of most European countries to make risky decisions. A key feature of this unbalanced cooperation has been the broad satisfaction held by most European countries regarding the American tendency to control both the political strategy and the conduct of military operations attached to it. With few exceptions, the European contribution to U.S. efforts was more a function of bilateral relations with Washington than of a specific assessment of the European interest in the Middle East.

U.S. foreign policy, however, has changed. The Iraq and Afghan military legacies have reduced U.S. soft power and political leverage in the Middle East, and profoundly changed policy discussions in the United States. Washington's steady intention to reduce its military footprint in the Middle East, along with its focus on competing with China, has already changed U.S. engagement in the region.

At the same time, the Middle East has also changed, especially since the invasion of Iraq and even more after the Arab uprisings of 2011. In several countries, the political fragmentation and the collapse of state structures are making it more difficult for societies to address their structural, social, economic, and environmental challenges, and for external actors to find solid local partners with whom to cooperate on responding to these challenges. Regional actors, whether or not allied with the United States, also conduct increasingly autonomous foreign policies and fill the vacuum left by Washington, often in accordance with zero-sum strategies.

Finally, Europe is also changing. For one thing, Europe's own borders are questioned, as evidenced by Russia's 2014 invasion of Crimea and tensions in the eastern Mediterranean. In addition, rising populism and Brexit show that European stability is not necessarily a given, especially since these trends are fed by migration influxes, among other things. America's sway internationally has weakened, owing to Trump's policies as well as the rise of China.[9] In reaction, Europeans are experiencing a slow, messy, but steady process of increasing the EU foreign policy profile. Each crisis in the continent's southern neighborhood demonstrates European weaknesses and divisions, but also

European progress. Washington remains the central element of most Europeans' security thinking, but Europeans are less and less central in Washington's security thinking. This evolution has forced even the most transatlanticist Europeans to invest more in European strategic assets.

The paradox has been, then, that European geopolitical empowerment in its southern neighborhood requires U.S. support. Even if a number of countries in the European Union have come to realize that the EU needs to strengthen its own preparedness in order to protect itself, as well as to maintain its relevance to the United States, the dynamics of transatlantic relationships have been such that some member states use Washington and its tradition of dividing and conquering Europe in order to limit the possibilities of EU foreign policy integration.

The United States will need to support the EU as a bloc, despite tactical differences on some issues, if it wants to help build up an effective partner with respect to the Middle East. Resetting the transatlantic dialogue in the Middle East is therefore not only about finding common ground on a specific set of priorities, but about changing the mindset underlying the transatlantic relationship.

Beyond the intricacies of the transatlantic relationship, the United States and Europe have lost influence in the Middle East in the past decade. In a region that suffered under European colonization and American hegemony, this is not inherently problematic. It is healthier and timely for Arab politics to no longer be seen as driven from abroad, whether from London, Paris, or Washington. Ultimately, it will be up to Middle Eastern and North African populations to design their own futures.

The United States and Europe nevertheless still have legitimate interests in the region. And by rethinking their cooperation, they can make a multilateral contribution to helping address social crises and tensions between regional actors. De-escalation and reform in the Middle East are vital for Europe and essential to the United States if the Biden administration really wants to end the "endless wars" and reformulate a relationship with the region.

By designing more effective and also more modest possibilities of action and cooperation in the region, Western countries can not only better achieve their policy goals (on counterterrorism, migration, or trade) but also redefine their role in the region, distancing themselves from colonial and imperial legacies that still undermine their standing. With a West more distant from daily political life in the Middle East, the three-way relationship between the region, Europe, and the United States can be reestablished on a more equal footing.

The key question in this context will be whether the United States and Europe can settle on a new approach to the Middle East quickly enough for Washington to pivot, and for the EU to gain sufficient strategic relevance and efficiency before shocks from its southern neighborhood upend its institutions irreversibly. Transforming the triangle linking the Middle East to Europe and the United States would further extinguish the very notion of the West in the Middle East. This is a good thing that all stakeholders should welcome, and that will enable new avenues of cooperation and connection in a globalized, multilateral world in which each region is likely to be more focused on preserving its own stability, at the same time as it is forced into more confrontational and competitive international relations.

Notes

1   U.S. diplomat, interview by author, August 2020.
2   Asli Aydintasbas, "Turkey," in *Mapping European Leverage in the MENA Region*, European Council on Foreign Relations, November 2019, https://www.ecfr.eu/special/mapping_eu_leverage_mena/turkey.
3   Dennis Ross, interview by author, June 10, 2020.
4   Alessandro Marrone and Karolina Muti, "Policies and Tools for Dealing with Nonstate Actors," in *New Perspectives on Shared Security: NATO's Next 70 Years*, ed. Tomáš Valášek (Washington DC: Carnegie Endowment for International Peace, 2019), https://carnegieendowment.org/files/NATO_int_final1.pdf.
5   Dennis Ross, interview by author, June 10, 2020.
6   U.S. diplomat, interview by author, August 2020.
7   Patrick Wintour, "UK Aid Budget Facing Billions in Cuts," *Guardian*, November 17, 2020, https://www.theguardian.com/global-development/2020/nov/17/uk-aid-budget-facing-billions-in-cuts.
8   Andrew Miller, Seth Binder, and Louisa Keeler, "President Trump's FY21 Budget: Examining U.S. Assistance to the Middle East and North Africa in the Shadow of COVID-19," Project on Middle East Democracy, June 10, 2020, https://pomed.org/fy21-budget-report/.
9   Max Bergmann, "Is Europe Ready for America's Embrace?" Friends of Europe, June 8, 2020, https://www.friendsofeurope.org/insights/is-europe-ready-for-americas-embrace/.

Index

The Author

Charles Thépaut is a French career diplomat who was a resident visiting fellow at The Washington Institute from 2019 to 2021. An expert on Middle East and North African affairs, he has worked for European institutions in Syria, Algeria, Iraq, Belgium, and Germany. Fluent in French, English, Arabic, and German, Thépaut graduated from the College of Europe in Bruges and the Institut d'Etudes Politiques de Lille. He has taught Middle East politics at Sciences Po Lille as well as at Paris Dauphine University. He is a frequent contributor to French think tanks and international relations journals. His previous book, *Le monde Arabe en morceaux: Des Printemps Arabes au recul Américain* (Anatomy of the Arab world: From the Arab Spring to the American pullback), was published by Armand Colin in March 2020.

www.ingramcontent.com/pod-product-compliance
Lightning Source LLC
Chambersburg PA
CBHW061721270326
41928CB00011B/2064